Look Smarter Than You Are with Hyperion Essbase

Edward Roske
Tracy McMullen

1st Edition

interRel Press, Arlington, Texas

Look Smarter Than You Are with Hyperion Essbase

Edward Roske
Tracy McMullen

Published by:

> interRel Press
> A Division of interRel Consulting Partners
> Suite 304
> 1000 Ballpark Way
> Arlington, TX 76011

Library of Congress Cataloging-in-Publication Data
Roske, Edward, McMullen, Tracy
> Look Smarter Than You Are with Hyperion Essbase

Edward Roske, Tracy McMullen 1st ed.
> p. 450 cm.
> Includes index.
> ISBN 978-1-4357-0530-2

Trademarks
Various trademarked names appear throughout this book. Rather than list all the names and the companies/individuals that own those trademarks or try to insert a trademark symbol every time a trademarked name is mentioned, the author and publisher state that they are using the names only for editorial purposes and to the benefit of the trademark owner with no intention of trademark infringement.

To

Paulet Howard

who taught me that

"the strong take it from the weak,
but the wise take it from the strong."

Edward Roske

ABOUT THE AUTHORS

Edward Roske fell in love with Hyperion at first sight. In 1995, Edward was working for the Moore Business Forms printing facility in Mundelein, Illinois. While his official title was "Coordinator of Finance", his role focused on coordinating the linking of many, many Microsoft Excel sheets. When someone in his area would delete a row in a supporting workbook and #REF errors would show up in the summary workbook, Edward personally tracked them down cell-by-cell. When he saw his first demonstration of Arbor Essbase (as it was known at the time), he quit his job to become a full-time Essbase consultant (becoming in the process one of those rare individuals who quit a stable job to consult on a product for which he had absolutely no experience).

Edward is a pioneer. He was one of the first Essbase Certified consultants in the world. He was also one of the first people in the world to become Certified in Hyperion Planning. While at Moore, he also obtained his first patent proving that there are still new ideas waiting to be discovered and exploited for financial gain.

In May of 1997, Edward left his senior consulting position with a Chicago-based firm to co-found interRel Consulting. Proving that being humble will get you nowhere, Edward helped write interRel's original motto: "Reaching for perfection, we deliver the impossible in record time." He has been the CEO of interRel Consulting since its inception growing them to be a multi-million dollar firm with offices from coast-to-coast.

Edward still keeps his Essbase skills sharp. He has overseen successful Hyperion implementations at over 100 companies. His optimizations have resulted in Essbase calculation improvements of more than 99.99%.

Continuing his quest to become the world's foremost Essbase-evangelist, Edward has been a regular speaker at annual Hyperion user conferences since 1995 and he is noted for his humorous slant to technically boring information.

Though not especially relevant, he also likes puppies.

ABOUT THE AUTHORS

Tracy McMullen has been leading the development of Business Performance Management and Data Warehousing applications for over 9 years. Roles on projects have ranged from developer, to architect and project manager on technologies from Hyperion and Business Objects to Cognos and Oracle. She's seen all of the business intelligence tools and Hyperion is her favorite.

Tracy started her career at Arthur Andersen Business Consulting on a project programming in RPG (fun stuff!). Thankfully, her next project introduced her to the world of multi-dimensional databases with a Cognos PowerPlay implementation for an oil and gas client (many years ago Tracy was certified in Cognos PowerPlay and Impromptu). Next, she helped clients from various industries revolutionize their information delivery with Hyperion and other technologies. After years of successful business intelligence implementations, a few shredded documents changed her career path from future Partner to eliminating cancer.

Tracy next joined The University of Texas M.D. Anderson Cancer Center where she lead the charge in implementing budget and planning solutions utilizing Hyperion Planning. Fate stepped in once again with a relocation to the Texas Coast and Tracy found her new home with interRel Consulting as Director of Special Projects (which really means she does a million different things from consulting to training to project management to sales).

Tracy is a Hyperion Certified Consultant for Hyperion Essbase, Hyperion Certified Solutions Architect for Hyperion Planning and a Certified Project Management Professional (PMP). Tracy has been a regular instructor at interRel, Hyperion's user conferences and other professional seminars since 2000 on topics including information delivery, business intelligence, data warehousing, and Hyperion implementations. Her strong technical background is complimented by comprehensive practical experience in project management, a skill important not only on the job but at home as well where she manages her three year old and one year old on a daily basis (ok, she attempts to manage with moderate success).

ACKNOWLEDGEMENTS

If we were to thank all of those who assisted us in the creation of this book, we would have to not only personally mention hundreds of people but also several companies and one or two federal agencies (though we will give a special shout-out to those wacky guys over at the Internal Revenue Service: keep it real, yo!). Suffice to say, if this book stands tall, it is only by balancing on the heads of giants.

Those contributing significant content to this book include Eduardo Quiroz, Ricardo Caso, John Scott, and Jim Webb at interRel. We want to send a "thank you" to our Editing Dictator, Graham Hunter. His attention to detail was invaluable to this book, so we love him even though he removed the best jokes.

A special thank you is extended to John Kopcke for agreeing to write our foreword.

Edward also wants to say "thank you" to Melissa Vorhies Roske, Vanessa Roske, and Eliot Roske for giving up their time with him on evenings and weekends, so he could make his publishing deadline. On a related note, Edward would also like to thank in advance anyone who can figure out a way to get rid of publishing deadlines.

Tracy McMullen would like to thank Edward for the chance to join him in writing this book. She would like to thank all of her current and previous mentors and coworkers as they are the ones who helped her learn everything so far. Thanks to Blanche and Randy McMullen Sr. for babysitting so that she could write a large portion of this book. Most importantly, she sends a "thank you" to her mom and dad, Dot and Bob Collins, for their never-ending support and Randy, Taylor and Reese McMullen for their patience and understanding.

We give our sincerest gratitude to all the people above, and we hope that they feel that this book is partly theirs as well (just without the royalties).

DISCLAIMER

This book is designed to provide supporting information about the related subject matter. It is being sold to you and/or your company with the understanding that the author and the publisher are not engaged by you to provide legal, accounting, or any other professional services of any kind. If assistance is required (legal, expert, or otherwise), seek out the services of a competent professional such as a consultant.

It is not the purpose of this book to reprint all of the information that is already available on the subject at hand. The purpose of this book is to complement and supplement other texts already available to you. For more information (especially including technical reference information), please contact the software vendor directly or use your on-line help.

Great effort has been made to make this book as complete and accurate as possible. That said, there may be errors both typographic and in content. As such, use this book only as a general guide and not as the ultimate source for specific information on the software product. Further, this book contains information on the software that was generally available as of the publishing date.

The purpose of this book is to entertain while educating. The author and interRel Press shall have neither liability nor responsibility to any person living or dead or entity currently or previously in existence with respect to any loss or damage caused or alleged to be caused directly, indirectly, or otherwise by the information contained in this book.

If you do not wish to abide by all parts of the above disclaimer, please stop reading now and return this book to the publisher for a full refund.

TABLE OF CONTENTS

FOREWORD

When I was told that someone outside of Hyperion was finally going to write a book on Hyperion Essbase, I was neither surprised nor impressed. Not surprised because, with over three million Essbase users worldwide, it was actually an anomaly that there was no independent book on learning the leading multidimensional database analytics platform. Sure, there are plenty of training classes out there and Hyperion had always included the Database Administrator's Guide and the Essbase Excel Add-In manuals with the software, but you couldn't go out to Amazon.com and find a book on Essbase.

And so why I wasn't impressed? Over the years, I've heard at least a hundred people say, "As soon as I get the time, I'm going to write the first Essbase book." This is generally followed by a mighty rough estimate of the tens of thousands of copies that will be sold in just the first year, as well as the proposed title. I must have heard "Essbase for Fun and Profit" proposed at least ten times. Purely for my own amusement, I often ask those people months later how the Essbase book is going. The reply is something along the lines of, "Well, things have gotten really busy, what with the economy and all."

Now, I am impressed. Edward Roske and Tracy McMullen have finally written the Essbase book. While I don't expect that it will ever be a *New York Times* bestseller, it may well be remembered in the Hyperion world as our *Da Vinci Code*. End users will pick up a copy to help figure out better ways to use the Essbase Add-In. Administrators will buy it to help build a better application. Companies may one day give out copies to new Essbase users instead of leaving them to figure it out on their own.

I've been architecting decision support systems for over 25 years, and I've been involved with Essbase virtually since its inception. I'm proud that yet another avenue has been opened to bring this great product to even more people. Use the information in it to become the Essbase expert at your company.

John Kopcke
Chief Technology Officer
Hyperion Solutions
March 30, 2007

Become an Essbase End User

Chapter 1:
Worst Mistake Ever

It was a dark and stormy night on the streets of New Orleans. Actually, it was mid-afternoon and I was in an office building, but that's a lousy way to start a story. Outside, it was very stormy, though, and that did make it much darker than it should have been. The year was 1998, and Entergy Corporation, the largest power company in Louisiana and the primary provider of electricity to New Orleans sent out a summons for Edward Roske to report to their corporate headquarters in the Big Easy. The server room was more than twenty stories up in a building overlooking downtown.

Entergy had been trying to get Crystal Reports to talk to Essbase (version 3.2, if I recall correctly). That was back in the days when Crystal was its own company and Essbase was the primary product of a Sunnyvale, California startup named Arbor. I had a reputation at the time for being a troubleshooter and Entergy needed some trouble shot. While we hadn't gotten into the details yet, I did know that Essbase was shutting down whenever someone tried to connect to it with Crystal. Arbor tech support and Crystal tech support were blaming each other when they weren't trying to blame the hardware. Since I was one of the few consultants in the world with both a Crystal and an Essbase background, I was truly their last option. The pressure to solve the problem was intense and you could feel the electricity in the room. Of course, being in a server room of a power company, this made perfect sense.

There must have been twenty people crowded around the server to watch me begin by recreating the problem. Even with the windows looking out on to the city, my claustrophobia was kicking into high gear. I diligently followed the instructions of Entergy's Essbase administrator. I hesitated before clicking the button that would execute the query and, presumably, crash the Essbase server. I wanted to make sure that I observed precisely what happened in order to quickly solve the problem, save the day, and get on a Southwest flight back to Dallas where it wasn't nearly as stormy. "When I click here, everything will shut down, right?" Their administrator assured me that it would, so I pressed the button, and the monitor shut off.

For that matter, all the lights in the server room shut off... and the servers themselves shut off. We went over to the window since server rooms are quite spooky with the lights off. We looked down twenty-plus stories to the street below and were shocked to realize that power was off to the entire city. My heart stopped and everyone turned to me.

We stood speechless in the dark until the back-up generators kicked in. Power was eventually restored. That was the only day of consulting I've ever done at Entergy and considering what happened, I don't even think we billed them for my time. It turns out that the storm had knocked power out to greater New Orleans and my Essbase actions were nothing but proof that God has a very dry sense of humor. For a time, though, I *knew* that I had committed the worst Essbase blunder ever.

I'm writing this book so that *you* will not repeat my mistakes.

Edward Roske

Chapter 2:
The Beverage Company

A traditional computer book would begin at the beginning, giving you the complete history of the topic at hand from when the product was a twinkle in the eye of its creator through all the various versions up to the current, cutting edge product. This book will do no such thing. While we will cover the history of Essbase, let's first grab a beverage and actually learn to do something.

Imagine a company that sells soft drinks. The Beverage Company sells products across the United States and they want to find out which products and markets are profitable and which are losing money faster than their poorly named drink from 2001, "Diet Enron with Lemon."

To help with their analysis, they bought a product from Hyperion Solutions called Essbase. They followed the more than 400 pages of instructions to get Essbase installed. During installation, they chose to install the sample applications and were pleasantly surprised to find that one of those applications was dedicated to analyzing The Beverage Company proving that Carson Daly and Earl were right about Karma.

To follow along as a temporary employee of TBC (**T**he **B**everage **C**ompany, *do* try to keep up), make sure that whoever installed Essbase at your company installed the sample applications. If she hasn't installed them, please ask her to do so. While she's at it, ask her to populate the database with sample data (see chapter 10) and grant you access (see chapter 12). Until she's prepared the sample applications, you can either stop reading or follow along in your own mind instead of on the computer.

CONNECTING TO ESSBASE

Go ahead and launch Microsoft Excel. You should see the *Essbase* menu appear on your menu bar. If not, head over to Appendix A to install the Essbase Add-In.

At this point, temporary TBC employee, you're probably faced with a blank Excel workbook and you have no idea where to begin. Luckily, you have a book, so go up to the *Essbase* menu (up there between Window and Help) and near the very bottom of the menu, you're going to find *Connect*.

Essbase	Help

Retrieve

Keep Only

Remove Only

Zoom In

Zoom Out

Pivot

Navigate Without Data

Sample Data (Zoom In)

Linked Objects...

Query Designer...

Visualize & Explore...

FlashBack

Options...

Member Selection...

Currency Report...

Cascade...

Retrieve & Lock

Lock

Unlock

Send

Calculation...

Connect...

Disconnect...

Before you click *Connect*, though, notice some of the items in the *Essbase* menu that we'll be using later. For instance, the first menu option is *Retrieve*. Presumably, we'll be using this to retrieve data later on. When we want to drill-down to detailed information, we'll be using *Zoom In*. When we need to send data back into Essbase (for budgeting, say), we'll use the *Send* option. Before you begin to question whether or not you need this book if Essbase is going to be so darned easy to use, click *Connect*.

Essbase System Login ✕

Server: ▾   OK

Username: Cancel

Password: Help

Change Password...

Application/Database:

Update

Note...

If this is the first time you've used the Essbase add-in, the Server, Username, and Password boxes will be empty. Let's begin with Server. Somewhere off in the basement of your company (or more likely these days, in a server farm in Malaysia) is a really powerful machine that holds the Essbase software and all of the data for the Essbase databases we'll be using. The sample applications mentioned earlier are stored on this server.

Your computer (which in computer terms is called the "client") talks to this server (through a networking protocol called TCP/IP, but you probably could care less about that). While all the data is stored on the server, all of the analysis happens on your client. Once we connect to the server, we can pull data back to the client and look at it in Excel. If we change the data, we should send it back to the server so that everyone else in the company can look at the same set of numbers. In Hyperion terms, they say that everyone is looking at "a single version of the truth."

Before you continue, you need to know the name of your server as well as your Username and Password. Your login information controls access to various parts of the Essbase server. Depending on your Username, you might have access to the entire Essbase server, specific databases on the server, or you might have no access at all (in which case, this book will be somewhat unhelpful to you).

For instance, at my company, I am an Essbase supervisor. In this God-like state, I am master of all Essbase databases. For the servers that I supervise, there is not a database that I cannot see, not a setting that I cannot change, and not a user that I cannot delete. While this does make me feel really special, it also means that whenever anything goes wrong, I am probably going to get blamed.

Only get Essbase access to what you need to do your regular job and avoid getting blamed for everything!

Tip!

The Username and Password given to you by your Essbase Administrator (see "God-like supervisor" above) will grant you access to only some of the databases. Put in the Server, Username, and Password you were given into the boxes and then click OK.

Essbase System Login	
Server: localhost	OK
Username: Username	Cancel
Password: **********	Help
Change Password...	
Application/Database:	
ASOsamp Sample	Update
Demo Basic	
DMDemo Basic	Note...
Sampeast East	
Sample Basic	
Sample Interntl	
Sample Xchgrate	
Sample_U Basic	

You will see a series of Application/Database combinations appear in a list at the bottom of this window. The application name is on the left and the database name is on the right. An Essbase application is a collection of one or more Essbase databases, but usually an application will contain only one database. In the image above, the Demo application has one database, Basic. The Sample application has three databases within it: Basic, Interntl, and Xchgrate.

Note!   If your company uses Hyperion Planning, the Essbase applications that support Planning often have more than one database and can have as many as five.

We'll be using the Basic database in the Sample application. We'll call it Sample.Basic, for short. Select *Sample Basic* and then click *OK*. In general, nothing interesting will happen and you'll be returned to a blank Excel spreadsheet. If something interesting does happen, that's usually bad, because it usually is an error of some sort. We'll be tackling some of those errors later.

The current spreadsheet tab in the current Excel workbook is the only one that's connected to Essbase. If you went from Sheet1 to Sheet2, Sheet2 wouldn't be connected. It is possible to click over to Sheet2 and connect it to Essbase, but at the moment, it's not.

This does bring up the interesting point that each sheet can be connected to a different Essbase database or no database at all. Sheet2 could be connected to Demo.Basic while Sheet1 is connected to Sample.Basic. All this can get a bit confusing, so there is an easy way to tell which sheets are connected to which databases. Conveniently, it's also where we go to disconnect the sheets from the databases. Go up to the *Essbase* menu and click *Disconnect*.

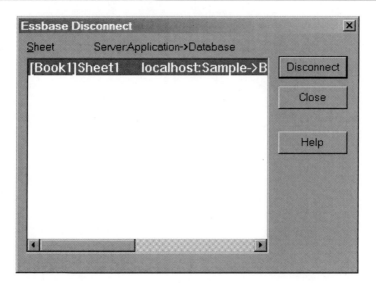

You'll see that the only current connection from Excel to Essbase is from Book1.Sheet1 (in Excel) to Sample.Basic (on the Essbase server).

Try It!

Switch to a different sheet in the same workbook, connect to an Essbase database, and then go to *Essbase >> Disconnect* to disconnect it.

DIMENSIONALITY

Now it's time to see some data. If you're still connected, go up to the *Essbase* menu and choose *Retrieve*. Hopefully, you will see something similar to the following:

	A	B	C	D	E	F
1		Measures	Product	Market	Scenario	
2	Year	105,522				
3						
4						
5						
6						

There are a couple of problems that might show up. The first one is that you might not see a number in cell B2. Instead of a number, there might be a dash or the word "#Missing" (more on that later). You also might see an error message:

Essbase Error

❌ No data was generated. Suppress Missing = [TRUE]. Zeros = [FALSE]. Sheet not overwritten.

OK

The clue to solving both problems is in the first part of the error message: "No data was generated." Quite simply, the Sample.Basic database doesn't have any data. Nicely ask your Essbase Administrator to load the Sample.Basic database, click *Essbase >> Retrieve* again, and you should see the spreadsheet shown above.

What is a Dimension?

Those five words at the top of the spreadsheet (Year, Measures, Product, Market, and Scenario) are the dimensions of Sample.Basic. To oversimplify, a *dimension* is something that can be put into the rows or columns of your report (or it applies to the whole page). Different databases have different dimensions, and Sample.Basic has the five just mentioned.

Let go of your mouse for a second, and have a look at this really simple Profit & Loss Statement:

	Actual	**Budget**
Sales	400,855	373,080
COGS	179,336	158,940
Margin	221,519	214,140
Total Expenses	115,997	84,760
Profit	**105,522**	**129,380**

It only has two dimensions. Down the rows, we have our "Measures" dimension (often called "Accounts"). Across the columns, we have our "Scenario" dimension. Some people like to call this dimension Category, Ledger, or Version. It's Essbase tradition to call the dimension that contains Actual, Budget, Forecast, and the like "Scenario," and we'll follow the tradition.

The only two dimensions so far are Scenario and Measures. The more detailed breakdowns of Measures (Sales, COGS, Margin, et al) are the members of the Measures dimension. Actual and Budget are members in the Scenario dimension. A *member* identifies a particular element within a dimension.

If we pivot the Measures up to the columns and the Scenario dimension over to the rows, our report will now look like this:

	Sales	COGS	Margin	Total Expenses	Profit
Actual	400,855	179,336	221,519	115,997	105,522
Budget	373,080	158,940	214,140	84,760	129,380

While it doesn't look very good, it does illustrate a couple of important points. First, a dimension can be placed into the rows, columns, or the page (as we'll see in a second). If it's really a dimension (as Scenario and Measures both are), there are no restrictions on which dimensions can be down the side or across the top. Second, notice that the values in the second report are the same as the values in the first report. Actual Sales are 400,855 in both reports. Likewise, Budgeted Profit is 129,380 in both reports. This is not magic.

Three Dimensions

A spreadsheet is inherently two dimensional (as are most printed reports). They have rows and columns. This is great if your company only produces a Profit & Loss Statement one time, but most companies will tend to have profit (be it positive or negative) in every month. To represent this in Excel, we use the spreadsheet tabs (one for each month):

All Products and Markets.xls

	Actual	Budget
Sales	31,538	29,480
COGS	14,160	12,630
Margin	17,378	16,850
Total Expenses	9,354	6,910
Profit	8,024	9,940

Jan / Feb / Mar / Apr / May / Jun / Jul / Aug / Sep / Oct / Nov / Dec /

We've now introduced a third dimension. Most people call it "Time" but Sample.Basic calls it "Year" just to be contrary. It could be across the columns (if you wanted to see a nice trend of twelve months of data) or down the rows, but we've put in the pages. That is, if you click on the "Jan" tab, the whole report will be for January.

If you're looking for Actual Sales of 400,855, you won't find it now because that was the value for the whole year. We could get it by totaling the values of all twelve tabs onto a summary tab.

Four Dimensions and More

Right now, this spreadsheet is not broken down by product or market. Within Excel, it's problematic to represent more than three dimensions (since we've used the rows, columns, and tabs). One way is to have a separate file for each combination of product and market:

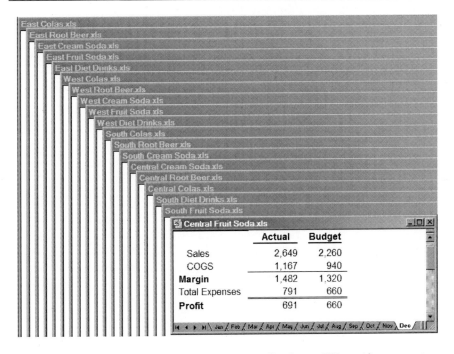

As you can see, this is getting ridiculous. What if we want to pivot our market dimension down to our columns so that we could compare profitability across different regions? To do this, we'd either have to have a series of linked spreadsheet formulas (which would break as soon as we added or deleted a new product or market) or we could hire a temporary employee to print out all the spreadsheets and type them in again with the markets now in the columns. While the latter method is obviously error-prone, the "rekeying" method is the one used by the majority of the companies in the world that do not own Essbase.

Since Market and Product are dimensions, it should be no more difficult to put them in the columns or rows than Scenario or Measures. As we'll learn about later, producing a report with markets down the side and products across the top is no more difficult than dragging-and-dropping:

		Actual	**Profit**	**Year**	
	Colas	Root Beer	Cream Soda	Fruit Soda	**Product**
East	12,656	2,534	2,627	6,344	**24,161**
West	3,549	9,727	10,731	5,854	**29,861**
South	4,773	6,115	2,350	-	**13,238**
Central	9,490	9,578	10,091	9,103	**38,262**
Market	**30,468**	**27,954**	**25,799**	**21,301**	**105,522**

In the bottom-right corner, you'll see our familiar actual profit for the year of 105,522. At the top of the report, you'll see that we have to specify the three dimensions in our application that are not in our rows or columns or Essbase wouldn't know which values to display. For instance, if we didn't specify "Profit", Essbase wouldn't know if we wanted Profit, Sales, Margin, or some random measure to be named later.

Always specify a member from each dimension for each intersection. If Essbase doesn't know which member of a dimension to use for an intersection, it will use the topmost member of that dimension.

Tip!

RETRIEVING DATA

Now that we understand that a dimension is anything that can be placed in the rows, columns, or the page, let's get back to retrieving data.

Go to a blank sheet in your workbook, connect to Essbase and then choose *Essbase >> Retrieve*.

Try It!

Click on the cell that shows 105,522 and look at the formula bar just above the spreadsheet grid:

B2	▾	*ƒx*	105522		
	A	B	C	D	E	F
1		Measures	Product	Market	Scenario	
2	Year	105,522				
3						

105,522 represents the total of all the months, products, and markets in our application, but notice that the content of the cell is not an Excel formula summing up other values. The total is being calculated on the Essbase server and then returned back to us as a plain, old number. This is one of the main reasons that Essbase is far faster than, say, a pivot table: all of the detail stays on the Essbase server and only the value we care about is returned to us.

Tip!

Since there are no formulas linking this spreadsheet to Essbase (but only values), you can send this spreadsheet to people in your company who don't have access to the Essbase server.

Select the cell that says Scenario (cell E1 if you're following along). Scenario tells us nothing, so go ahead and type the word "Budget" into that cell instead and press Enter. The numbers will not change, because you haven't told Essbase to re-retrieve your data yet.

Tip!

Several Essbase actions have mouse shortcuts (so we don't have to use the menus). The shortcut for retrieving data is to double-click on a blank cell.

Go to the Measures cell and change it to the word "Profit." Budget and Profit are both members of dimensions in this application. Choose *Essbase >> Retrieve*:

	A	B	C	D	E	F
1		Profit	Product	Market	Budget	
2	Year	129,380				
3						
4						

If you spelled Profit or Budget wrong (for example, you typed in "Budgets" instead of "Budget"), Essbase will kindly put the dimension it thinks you didn't specify into the first row for you:

	A	B	C	D	E	F	G
1		Profit	Product	Market	Budgets	Scenario	
2	Year	105,522					
3							

Notice that cell E1 says "Budgets" so when we retrieved, Essbase put "Scenario" in cell F1 (thinking that we had forgotten a dimension). Essbase is very particular about spelling. It has no idea that "Budgets" and "Budget" means the same thing to you, so watch your spelling if you're going to be typing in the names of members.

Tip! While spelling is important, members are not case-sensitive (unless the person setting up an Essbase application specified that it should be case-sensitive). Type in "BuDgEt" and Essbase will retrieve the data and replace your funky capitalization with "Budget".

Unless you've turned off the warning messages, Essbase will tell you when it thinks you've spelled something wrong. When we retrieved the report above, we got this warning:

Essbase Message

? The sheet contains an unknown member: Budgets.
This item will be ignored when you retrieve data from the server.

There may be additional cells that contain unknown database members.
Do you want to display additional unknown members in this retrieval?

[Yes]   [No]

The first two sentences are telling you that "Budgets" isn't a valid member for this application. The last two sentences are asking you if you want to continue to be pestered about spelling errors during this retrieve. If you want to be reminded of why you failed 7th grade English, click *Yes*. If your remaining spelling errors in this report are intentional, click *No* and Essbase won't warn you about any further unknown members until the next time you choose *Retrieve*.

Zooming In and Out

Assuming that your spreadsheet looks something like the one on page 15, select the cell that says Year (cell A2) and choose *Essbase >> Zoom In*. Though your report might not look exactly like this (depending on your current Essbase Options and Excel formatting), you should see the quarters that make up the total year:

	A	B	C	D	E	
1		Profit	Product	Market	Budget	
2	Qtr1	30,580				
3	Qtr2	32,870				
4	Qtr3	33,980				
5	Qtr4	31,950				
6	Year	129,380				
7						

Select the Qtr1 cell (cell A2) and again choose *Essbase >> Zoom In*. This will show you the three months that comprise Qtr1.

Tip! There are also mouse shortcuts for zooming in and zooming out. To Zoom In using the mouse, double-click with the *left* mouse button on a member name. To Zoom Out, double-click with the *right* mouse button on a member name.

To get back to where we were, we can either *Zoom Out* (highlight any of those three months and choose *Zoom Out* from the *Essbase* menu) or we can use Essbase's version of Undo.

Essbase Undo

To undo your last Essbase action, don't look under the *Edit* menu for Undo (and don't click the 🔄 button on the toolbar). Essbase's undo function dates back to the days of Lotus when it didn't have undo and no one could agree on what to call it. Essbase went for a catchy marketing name, and it's still there: go to the *Essbase* menu and choose *Flashback*.

While *Flashback* is similar to Excel's undo, its major limitation is that it will only go back one action. Before you get huffy and write a letter to your Essbase congressman to complain, realize that there's actually a reason for this. To maintain its

Flashback information, Essbase takes a snapshot of your entire worksheet right before it does any Essbase action. If your report has 100 columns and 2,000 rows, that snapshot contains 200,000 cells of data. That takes up a lot of RAM, so Essbase only keeps one snapshot at a time and thus, only one level of undo.

Try It!

Assuming that your report is back to looking like the one above with only the quarters and the year showing, click on Qtr1 and choose *Zoom Out*. This should return your spreadsheet to what it was on page 15. Either *Flashback* or *Zoom In* to display the quarters again.

Let's say that you want to remove Year from the report. There are two ways to accomplish this. The first is by using the power of Excel: highlight row six and choose *Delete* from Excel's *Edit* menu. You can also use the power of Essbase by highlighting the Year cell and choosing *Remove Only* from the *Essbase* menu.

Remove Only works on multiple cells as well. Select the Qtr2 cell, hold down the control key, and then click the Qtr4 cell. Now select *Essbase >> Remove Only*. Your report should be reduced to two quarters:

	A	B	C	D	E	F
1		Profit	Product	Market	Budget	
2	Qtr1	30,580				
3	Qtr3	33,980				
4						

Since this report is putrid, click on Qtr1 and choose *Zoom Out* to return to the report on page 15. *Zoom In* to again display the quarters above the year. Let's drill down a second dimension: highlight the Profit cell and choose *Zoom In*:

	A	B	C	D	E
1			Product	Market	Budget
2	Margin	Qtr1	51,540		
3		Qtr2	54,780		
4		Qtr3	56,410		
5		Qtr4	51,410		
6		Year	214,140		
7	Total Expenses	Qtr1	20,960		
8		Qtr2	21,910		
9		Qtr3	22,430		
10		Qtr4	19,460		
11		Year	84,760		
12	Profit	Qtr1	30,580		
13		Qtr2	32,870		
14		Qtr3	33,980		
15		Qtr4	31,950		
16		Year	129,380		
17					

Not only does this show the two members that make up Profit (Margin and Total Expenses, in this case), it also shows how two dimensions can both be on the row or column axis at the same time. To get the quarters and years up to the columns, we could do that "hiring the temp to rekey method" we mentioned above, or we can do it the Essbase way. Highlight any of the member names in column B (Qtr1, say), and choose *Essbase >> Pivot*:

	A	B	C	D	E	F
1		Product	Market	Budget		
2		Qtr1	Qtr2	Qtr3	Qtr4	Year
3	Margin	51,540	54,780	56,410	51,410	214,140
4	Total Expenses	20,960	21,910	22,430	19,460	84,760
5	Profit	30,580	32,870	33,980	31,950	129,380
6						

Admit it: you're impressed. There is also a mouse shortcut for pivoting dimensions: it's called a "right drag-and-drop." Select the Qtr1 cell using your left mouse button. Now, with the mouse cursor over that cell, hold down the right mouse button. After a little while, a row of gray member names should appear showing you what you're about to pivot. Don't let go of the right mouse button yet:

	A	B	C	D	E	F	G
1		Product	Market	Budget			
2		Qtr1	Qtr2	Qtr3	Qtr4	Year	
3	Margin	Qtr1 Qtr2 Qtr3 Qtr4 Year 0	56,410	51,410	214,140		
4	Total Expenses	20,960	21,910	22,430	19,460	84,760	
5	Profit	30,580	32,870	33,980	31,950	129,380	
6							

Move the grey cells over to the cell where you want to pivot the dimension. In our case, drag the members over to cell A3. Okay, now let go of the right mouse button:

	A	B	C	D	E	
1			Product	Market	Budget	
2	Qtr1	Margin	51,540			
3		Total Expenses	20,960			
4		Profit	30,580			
5	Qtr2	Margin	54,780			
6		Total Expenses	21,910			
7		Profit	32,870			
8	Qtr3	Margin	56,410			
9		Total Expenses	22,430			
10		Profit	33,980			
11	Qtr4	Margin	51,410			
12		Total Expenses	19,460			
13		Profit	31,950			
14	Year	Margin	214,140			
15		Total Expenses	84,760			
16		Profit	129,380			
17						

While you're back to having two dimensions on the rows, you've changed the orientation of the two dimensions to show each measure by each time period. If all we wanted to show for each time period was Profit, we can use the Essbase *Keep Only* function. Select one of the Profit cells (cell B4, say), and choose *Essbase >> Keep Only*. This will remove all the instances of Margin and Total Expenses (yes, we could also have used *Remove Only* on the other two members).

	A	B	C	D	E	
1			Product	Market	Budget	
2	Qtr1	Profit	30,580			
3	Qtr2	Profit	32,870			
4	Qtr3	Profit	33,980			
5	Qtr4	Profit	31,950			
6	Year	Profit	129,380			
7						

This method is much more efficient than simply adding and deleting rows in Excel.

To clean up the report (since it looks a bit silly showing the same member repeatedly in the rows), again select one of the Profit cells and choose *Pivot*. Since there is only one member to be pivoted, Essbase will assume that you want the member to be pivoted up to the page instead of the columns. You should now be looking at the same spreadsheet as we had on page 17.

Tip! When a dimension is at the top of the page (like Market in the picture above), if you hold down the Alt key while you left double-click the member, it will zoom across the columns instead of the rows.

Try It! Try zooming in, zooming out, and pivoting the five dimensions of Sample.Basic. While you can make a very ugly report (no offense, but you *can*), you can't harm the data in any way: it's safely stored on the Essbase server.

ESSBASE OPTIONS

As mentioned before, your report might not be looking identical to the pictures in this book. The most common reason for this is that your Essbase Options have been changed. Essbase Options are tab-specific settings (well, for the most part, tab-specific) that control how Essbase operates. All of these settings are found under *Options* on the *Essbase* menu.

Adjust Columns

One of the problems that you may be encountering is that as you drill-down through a dimension (Year and Measures, so far), your columns may not be wide enough to show all the information. You probably know how to do an Excel auto-fit to make the columns wide enough, so it's not that big of a problem. That said, there is a way to make Essbase automatically widen the columns after each retrieve. Choose *Options* from the *Essbase* menu, go to the *Display* tab and check the box for *Adjust Columns*:

All of your retrieves on this tab will now automatically fit the column widths to the data in the column.

If you save your workbook, your settings are saved with it. If you go to a new tab or new workbook (one that's never had the Essbase Options set) and retrieve, Essbase will use the Essbase Options from the last tab that had them set. For instance, if we went to a brand-new workbook and immediately did a Retrieve, the columns would be adjusted and that setting would now be associated with the new tab. All setting are tab-specific except for the ones set on the *Global* tab.

Indentation

Notice that in our retrieves to this point, the detail beneath each member (for example, the quarters underneath the Year member) is indented. For those who went to accounting school prior to 1990, it might seem better to indent the totals. On the "Indentation" section on the Display tab, you can switch the indentation from *Subitems* to *Totals*. The next time you retrieve your data, each summary-level of totals will be further indented:

	A	B	C	D	E	F
1		Profit	Product	Market	Budget	
2	Jan	9,940				
3	Feb	10,350				
4	Mar	10,290				
5	Qtr1	30,580				
6	Qtr2	32,870				
7	Qtr3	33,980				
8	Qtr4	31,950				
9	Year	129,380				
10						

To turn off indentation entirely, choose *None* under Indentation.

Zoom In Level

One of the other things that might have been changed under your options is the "Zoom In level." When you zoom in, you tend to want to see the members that comprise the current member. When you *Zoom In* on Year, you most likely want to see the quarters. Likewise, a *Zoom In* on Qtr1 should show the first three months of the year. Some impatient people don't like passing through the levels in the middle on the way to the bottom-level of a dimension. To control how far Essbase drills with each zoom, go to the *Zoom* tab under *Options*:

Display | Zoom | Mode | Style | Global |

Zoom In
- ⦿ Next Level
- ○ All Levels
- ○ Bottom Level
- ○ Sibling Level
- ○ Same Level
- ○ Same Generation
- ○ Formulas

Member Retention
- ☑ Include Selection
- ☐ Within Selected Group
- ☐ Remove Unselected Groups

Hybrid Analysis
- ☐ Enable Hybrid Analysis

Sampling

Sampling Percentage: `100`

Right now, Zoom In is set to *Next Level*. This means that when you drill into Year, you see the quarters. If when you drill into Year, you want to see every single member in the Year dimension, set your Zoom In to *All Levels*. If you then drill on Year, you'd see every month and every quarter.

If you want to jump from the Year down to showing all the months without showing any of the quarters, select *Bottom Level*.

Try It!

Change your Zoom In level and then try zooming in and out on several dimensions. You can make a very large spreadsheet very quickly, and Essbase still remains extremely fast.

Tip!

Before you drill into a dimension that has thousands of members, make sure that your Zoom level is not set to *All Levels* or *Bottom Level*. Sample.Basic has no dimension with more than 25 members, so you're safe for the moment.

Aliases

Get back to our familiar spreadsheet from page 15. Set your Zoom In level to *Next Level* and zoom in on Product. Pivot the Year dimension up to the pages and you should see:

	A	B	C	D	E	F
1		Year	Profit	Market	Budget	
2	100	41,940				
3	200	35,950				
4	300	29,360				
5	400	22,130				
6	Diet	36,720				
7	Product	129,380				
8						

Note! Product does not equal the sum of the products underneath this, but it does equal the sum of products 100, 200, 300, and 400. Diet Drinks is a custom total that includes select products from the other product groupings. This is called an alternate hierarchy and is discussed in detail on page 190.

Product 100 is doing very well this year especially compared to product 400. "100" is the member name of a specific Product member. Member names are the short "computer-like" way of referencing things that is completely unintuitive to the average user. Essbase allows member names to have longer, more user-friendly descriptions for members called "Aliases." For instance, the alias for "100" is "Cola," To show these aliases, go to the *Display* tab for your Essbase options and check the *Use Aliases* box.

```
┌─ Aliases ──────────────────────────────────────┐
│  ☑ Use Aliases                                 │
│                                                │
│  ☐ Use Both Member Names and Aliases           │
│      for Row Dimensions                        │
│                                                │
│  Alias:                                        │
│  ┌──────────────────────────────────────┬───┐ │
│  │ Default                              │ ▼ │ │
│  └──────────────────────────────────────┴───┘ │
└────────────────────────────────────────────────┘
```

Go back to your report and re-retrieve to see the far more helpful product names. If you type in a member, you can type in either the member name or the alias, and Essbase will be able to find it. For instance, below the cell with Product, type in the word "100-20" (without the quotes). "100-20" is the actual product member name. Re-retrieve your data and you'll see that Essbase replaced "100-20" with "Diet Cola". "Diet Cola" is the alias name.

	A	B	C	D	E
1		Year	Profit	Market	Budget
2	Colas	41,940			
3	Root Beer	35,950			
4	Cream Soda	29,360			
5	Fruit Soda	22,130			
6	Diet Drinks	36,720			
7	Product	129,380			
8	Diet Cola	9,530			
9					

Tip! To type in a member name that Essbase could confuse with a number (like "100"), type in a single apostrophe before the member name. For "100", you would type in: '100. This tells Essbase (and Excel) that this is text and not a number.

Since some companies have multiple ways of referring to the same items (for instance, product 100 might be called "Cola" in the Northeast and "pop" in the Northwest), Essbase allows up to nine different aliases for each member. Right now, you're using the "Default" alias, but if your application has other descriptions for members beyond the defaults (called "alternate alias tables"), you can choose to use those in the drop-down box under Alias in the *Display* options.

Note! Sample.Basic comes with another alias table called Long Names in addition to Default.

Missing Data

On your Display options, uncheck the box for *Missing Row* and make sure that the box next to *#Missing Label* is blank. Before you click *OK*, make sure that your Display options look like this:

Click *OK* and go back to your report. *Keep Only* on Fruit Soda so that you only have one row of data. Now, *Zoom In* on Market:

	A	B	C	D	E	F
1			Year	Profit	Budget	
2	East	Fruit Soda	7,910			
3	West	Fruit Soda	5,670			
4	South	Fruit Soda	#Missing			
5	Central	Fruit Soda	8,550			
6	Market	Fruit Soda	22,130			
7						

Notice that the South is not a big fan of Fruit Soda. Budget Profit for the year is missing (denoted by Essbase with the term "#Missing"). A missing value to Essbase is very different from a value of zero. A profit of zero means that your sales were cancelled out exactly by your expenses. A profit of #Missing means that we have neither sales nor expenses at this particular combination.

Data for Budgeted, South, Fruit Soda Profit for the year simply does not exist.

If you don't want to see #Missing on your reports, you can replace it with a label that makes more sense to you. Go to your Display options and in the box next to "#Missing Label", fill in something that makes sense to you.

Tip!

The most common #Missing labels are: N/A, 0, -, and a space.

In general, there will be lots of intersections of data in your applications that don't exist, and retrieving them into a report takes unnecessary time. If you have 100,000 products and 5,000 stores, as few as 2,000 products might be sold each day at each store. Do you really want to see a report that's 98% empty? If you don't, check the box next to suppress *#Missing Rows*. This will suppress any rows where the data all the way across the row is #Missing. If a single column has a real number, the row will not be suppressed.

If you also don't want see intersections where all the values in the row are zero, check the box to suppress *Zero Rows* as well.

Turn off Essbase

While those who use Essbase regularly love the mouse shortcuts, some people don't like Essbase turning off traditional Excel shortcuts. With Essbase mouse actions turned on, right-clicking on a cell does not bring up a context menu (with things like cut, copy, paste) and double-clicking on a cell does not allow in-cell editing.

To enable Excel actions, select *Essbase >> Options* and choose the Global tab:

Uncheck *Enable Secondary Button* and *Enable Double-Clicking* and you'll be back to the Excel mousing you're used to. If you're curious why it says "Secondary" button instead of "Right" mouse button, it's so as not to offend left-handed people who have switched their mouse buttons. While it's nice not to offend the lefties, it confuses the heck out of the righties. For our purposes, secondary generally means "right."

There are some cases where you want to use the Essbase shortcuts but only when you're ready to retrieve data from Essbase. To enable Essbase shortcuts on sheets that are currently connected to Essbase (i.e., sheets on which you've already chosen *Essbase >> Connect*), check the box for *Limit to Connected Sheets*.

While you're on the *Global* tab, make sure that your Display Messages are set to show *Warnings*. If they're set to *Errors* or worse, *None*, when things go wrong, it will be very hard to tell why. Unless you're one of those people who only writes things in pen, show your "*Warnings*".

We'll cover a number of the other Essbase options throughout the rest of the book.

CHANGING DATA

So far, all of your work with the add-in has been for reporting and analysis. One of the major uses of Essbase is for budgeting (or planning or forecasting or whatever you call putting information back into Essbase instead of just taking it out).

Using the techniques you've learned to this point, make a report that looks like the following:

	A	B	C	D	
1		Jan	Sales	Cola	
2		Actual	Budget		
3	New York	678	640		
4	Massachusetts	494	460		
5	Florida	210	190		
6	Connecticut	310	290		
7	New Hampshire	120	110		
8	East	1,812	1,690		
9					

Tip! To make a quick report, you can always just type the member names into a blank spreadsheet. Put a zero where you want the numbers to appear, and retrieve. Make sure that each intersection is represented by all dimensions.

Locking Data

If we're going to be changing the numbers in Essbase, we need to prevent other users from trying to update the same intersections at the same time we're trying to update them. "Locking" the data prevents any other user from sending data to these same data points. They will be told that you have the data locked and prevent the accidental overwriting of numbers. To Lock the data, choose *Essbase >> Lock*.

Tip! You can also choose *Retrieve and Lock* which will refresh your data and lock it at the same time. Most people choose *Retrieve* and then choose *Lock* just to be precise.

If another user already has the data locked, you'll see this error:

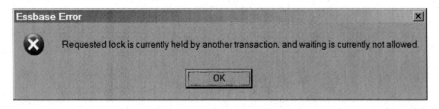

There are four ways for locked data to be released: a user can unlock it manually, a user can send data to that intersection (which unlocks the intersection), an administrator can unlock it manually, or the lock will automatically time out after a specified number of minutes (usually 60, but this can be altered by an Administrator).

If you choose *Essbase >> Lock* and you don't have security rights to lock the data (because you don't have the rights to edit the data), you'll see this error:

This is a tricky error, because you'll only see it if you don't have the rights to lock *any* of the intersections in your current retrieve. For instance, in the report above, you might have write access to Budget but only read access to Actual. As long as you can write to the budget cells, you'll be able to perform a Lock on this worksheet. You won't even get an error when you try to send newly changed Actual data: your changes just won't stick. In this example, you would only see the error above if you didn't have the Budget column in your report at all.

> If you decide that you don't want to update the data, it's polite to choose *Unlock* from the *Essbase* menu to unlock it for the next person.

Tip!

Sending Data

Let's assume that you've been able to lock the data (if not, talk to your Essbase Administrator about getting access to send data into Sample.Basic). The budget for cola sales in New York is looking a little light, so let's up it to 700. Type 700 into cell C3 (or wherever your report has the intersection of New York and Budget) and choose *Essbase >> Send*.

One of the most common errors is that you haven't locked the data. The cure, of course, is to choose *Lock* before you choose *Send*:

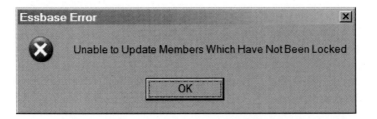

The other error that occurs fairly frequently is when Essbase appears to accept your changes but they didn't actually go back into Essbase. The most common causes are due to insufficient rights to edit those numbers and due to sending numbers into summary members (also called upper-level members).

To make sure that your changes were sent to and stored by Essbase, blank out all your numbers (change them to zero or just highlight the cells and press delete) and then double-click cell A1 (remember that double-clicking on a blank cell is a mouse shortcut for *Essbase >> Retrieve*). You should see:

	A	B	C	D
1		Jan	Sales	Cola
2		Actual	Budget	
3	New York	678	700	
4	Massachusetts	494	460	
5	Florida	210	190	
6	Connecticut	310	290	
7	New Hampshire	120	110	
8	East	1,812	1,690	
9				

Running Calculations

Math wizards in the audience will immediately note that 700+460+190+290+110 does not equal 1,690. It's actually 60 short, because we haven't told the Essbase server to recalculate the totals. For the most part, this is not done automatically. The majority of the summary members in an Essbase application are "stored" meaning that Essbase stores the pre-calculated totals to speed retrieval. This follows the common Essbase belief that analysis tends to start at the top of the hierarchy and then drill down.

Note!

One of the major differences between Essbase and a relational database is that relational databases assume that you want to look at detail (so displaying totals is much slower) and Essbase assumes that you want to look at summaries (though detailed data is not any slower).

Other members are "dynamically calculated" (though the cool kids say "dynamic calc") meaning that Essbase calculates those members at the time the user requests them. While some members in Sample.Basic are dynamically calculated (the upper-level Measures, for instance), it's always best to assume that you should recalculate the database after submitting data. We'll learn more about dynamic calcs on page 188.

Assuming that you have access to recalculate the database, choose Essbase >> *Calculation*. In the case of Sample.Basic, you'll only see one calculation. It is the default calculation that basically means "calculate everything in the database that needs to be recalculated."

Essbase Calculation   ☒

Connection Information
Localhost:Sample->Basic

Select Calc Script:

[Default]	Calculate
	Cancel
	Help
	Stop Calc

Database State

Data values have been modified since the last calculation.

In our case, running the default calculation will adjust the value for East (and total Market since it's affected by the New York change and total Product since it's affected by the Cola change and so on). At the bottom, notice that it says that your "data values have been modified since the last calculation." You already knew that, but it's good when the Essbase server is watching over you. Click on *Calculate,* and after less than five seconds, you'll see a message saying that your calculation has finished:

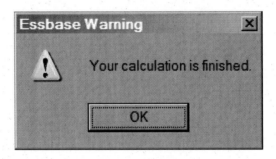

The Essbase Add-In will check with the Essbase server every few seconds to see if the calculation has completed yet. You can always continue to work in Excel in the meantime, just don't work with this Essbase database unless you're okay with potentially erroneous results.

While the default calculation for Sample.Basic will always take just a few seconds, complex calculations against large databases can take several minutes or even hours. For instance, if your company had a multi-step allocation process that allocated corporate expenses by thousands of stores for thousands of products (to get a complete Income Statement by location by SKU), it would take a whole lot longer than five seconds. Be patient, and the Essbase Add-In will let you know when the calculation is finished.

Once you get the calculation message, re-retrieve your data and you should see the correct value for East with the additional 60 in it:

	A	B	C	D	E
1		Jan	Sales	Cola	
2		Actual	Budget		
3	New York	678	700		
4	Massachusetts	494	460		
5	Florida	210	190		
6	Connecticut	310	290		
7	New Hampshire	120	110		
8	East	1,812	1,750		
9					

Attaching Supporting Information

If you're going to go around changing numbers willy-nilly, it's generally a good idea to explain why with supporting documentation or at the very least, a bit of commentary on the finer points of revised budgets. Essbase calls these bits of supporting information "Linked Objects" (also called cell text in other Hyperion products). Click on the Budget New York cell with 700 in it (cell C3 if you're following along exactly) and choose *Essbase >> Linked Objects.*

At the top of the "Linked Objects Browser" box, you'll see that Essbase is telling us that we're seeing all the information attached to the intersection of Jan, Sales, Cola, New York, Budget. Linked Objects (sometimes called "Linked Reporting Objects" or

"LROs" for short) must be attached to a specific intersection in the database. There is no way to say that your comment applies to, say, all of the products in January's budget.

Go ahead and click on the *Attach* button, and you'll see that we can attach three different types of information to this intersection:

The first type of information is a cell note. This is for textual commentary. Go ahead and type something in the box. Be aware that if you type something profane and your manager spots it, this may be the first as well as last Linked Object you ever write. In general, type in something relevant to the intersection and then click *OK*:

You should now be able to see the cell note in the list. The second type of information you can attach is a file. This file could be a Word document, an Excel spreadsheet, a PowerPoint presentation, your favorite virus, or any other type of document that you could possibly imagine. Your name will be attached to the file (along with the date you uploaded the virus, Mr. Soon-To-Be-Unemployed), so play nice. If you attach a file, it's generally considered polite to give your file a description in addition to just the file name itself since file names are often cryptic.

Try It!

Go ahead and attach a file. Since Essbase copies the file to the Essbase server (to store it in a central place where everyone can find it), try to keep the files small.

The third type of information is a URL (a web address). It should include the "http://" part of the address (the link could also have a "ftp://" url or UNC like "\\ServerName.com\ShareName\FileName.doc"). Note that while there can be a limit imposed on the size of files stored as Linked Objects (the default is 50 megabytes), there is no limit to the number of Linked Objects that can be attached to a specific intersection. Here is the same intersection with a cell note, a file, and a URL:

Member Combination: Jan,Sales,Cola,New York,Budget

Linked Objects:

Object Type	Object Description	Linked Object and Object	Created	Last Modified
Cell Note	Sales budget for New		username	Sunday, February 12, 2006 2:
File	Example spreadsheet	Examples.xls	username	Sunday, February 12, 2006 2:
URL	interRel Home Page	http://www.interrel.com/	username	Sunday, February 12, 2006 2

Attach... | Edit. | View/Launch | Delete | Help | Close

To view a cell note, open a previously attached file, or launch a web browser showing a saved URL, click on the *View/Launch* button. The *Edit* button is used to edit an object (such as the description) and if you are really displeased with an object, use the *Delete* button to eradicate it from the server (just the copy, not the original file or URL).

Tip!

If you have several spreadsheets that you want to share with other users of a specific Essbase application, attach all of them as Linked Objects to the top intersection in the database. If a user wants a convenient starting point, she pulls up the Linked Objects Browser on that top intersection. In the case of Sample.Basic, that intersection is the cell containing 105,522 as shown on page 9.

Formatting with Essbase

Click on *Close* to go back to your spreadsheet, and you'll notice that it isn't obvious which cells have Linked Objects attached. There's no nice triangle in the corner of the cell like Excel provides. Excel can't put a cute triangle in the corner, because only the Essbase server knows which data has Linked Objects; however, there is a way to make Essbase change the look of data to provide a verbal cue that supporting information lies back on the server.

Note!

Essbase formatting is called "Styles" and it completely takes over your Excel formatting. For instance, if you bold some cells and then turn on Essbase Styles, your original bolding will be overwritten by Essbase's own formatting.

Enabling Essbase formatting (Styles) is a two-step process. First, go to the *Display* tab on your Essbase Options and check the box under Cells next to *Use Styles*:

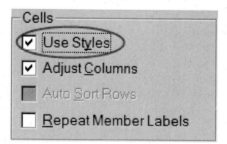

Before you click on *OK*, go to the *Style* tab.

Tip!

If you don't see the Style tab (it happens more often than you'd think), it's because Essbase will only display this if the Excel worksheet you're on is currently connected to

Essbase. If you're missing the tab, click on *Cancel*, connect to Essbase, and then go back into your Essbase Options.

While there are three types of information you can ask Essbase to format, for now we're only going to use the "Data Cells" section. The Members and Dimensions sections are used to color-code the rows and columns of your spreadsheet. They can be used to make the ugliest spreadsheets known to humanity, and should only be used by a trained artist. So as not to cause your eyes to bleed (last time that happened, we had a big lawsuit on our hands...), we'll leave Members and Dimensions for you to figure out on your own.

Under Data Cells, check the box next to *Linked Object* and click *OK*. Once you're back to your report, re-retrieve your data, and you should see our 700 in blue letting us know that it has one or more Linked Objects attached.

One of the other things that Styles is used for (okay, about the *only* other thing we use them for) is to show which numbers can be edited and which ones are read-only. Go back to the *Style* tab of your Essbase Options and notice the check box for *Read Only*. Check it and click *OK*. As you drill up and down through your data, you'll see that certain data cells are gray (for instance, Profit will always be gray) to let you know that you can not edit them.

Once you're finished playing with Styles (and before burning matching holes in your retinas due to horrendous color schemes), go to the *Display* tab on your Essbase Options and uncheck *Use Styles*. It's not necessary to uncheck all the boxes on the *Style* tab.

Note!

Turning off Styles does not set your spreadsheet back to its "pre-Essbase" formatting. You'll have to manually set your formatting back to what you want it to be.

Chapter 3:
What Does Essbase Stand For?

Essbase is currently produced by a company named Hyperion Solutions Corporation. Although Hyperion was founded in 1981, the Essbase product came along in the early 1990's compliments of a company whose only product was Essbase: Arbor Software. Up until 1998 when Hyperion and Arbor "merged", the two companies were fierce competitors who were just as likely to spit on each other in waiting rooms as work together. (we are kidding, but only slightly.)

Arbor Software was founded in 1991 by Jim Dorrian and Bob Earle. They noticed at the time that companies were beginning to use spreadsheets not just for presentation of information but as a place to store data and business logic. Often, multiple sources of data were being consolidated together in spreadsheets and they were even seeing companies begin to release analysis to the public based on data in spreadsheets.

Jim/Bob wanted to build a database for spreadsheets. Essbase actually stands for **E**xtended **S**pread**S**heet data**BASE**. Thanks to some creativity and some venture capital (of course) from Hummer Winblad, they released the first version of Essbase in 1992. This original release of the product garnered three whole paragraphs of press coverage in Software Magazine on May 15, 1992. Here it is in all its "babe in the woods waiting to be eaten by bears" naiveté:

DATA SERVER "FEEDS" 1-2-3 OR EXCEL
Arbor Software Corp.'s Essbase data server
Software Magazine; May 15, 1992

Following a three-year development effort, start-up Arbor Software Corp., Santa Clara, Calif., has built a data server that "feeds" popular desktop offerings, including 1-2-3 from Lotus Development Corp., and Excel from Microsoft Corp., on client machines.

"We conceded the front end to [widely installed] spreadsheets," said James Dorrian, president and co-founder. "We built the product with two assumptions: that people knew their spreadsheets and that people knew their jobs."

> According to Marketing Vice President Michael Florio, the OS/2-based $22,000 Essbase offers users in client/server environments simultaneous access to large volumes of multidimensional spreadsheet data.

Notice that it was originally developed to run on OS/2 and its claim to fame was that it fed spreadsheets. Also, notice that you could get a copy for only $22,000 which sort of goes to show you that technology doesn't always get cheaper over time.

The first version of the product wasn't nearly as user friendly as it is today. Ignoring the Herculean steps required to actually build an Essbase database, retrieving data into Excel (or Lotus, at the time) required writing requests to Essbase in a language known as "Essbase Report Scripting." If you want to kick it old school, go to the *Mode* tab under *Essbase >> Options* and check the box for *Free Form* (under Retrieval). Click on *OK*, go to a blank spreadsheet and type the following:

	A
1	<PAGE (Measures, Product, Market)
2	Profit
3	Product
4	Market
5	<COLUMN (Scenario)
6	<CHILD Scenario
7	<ROW (Year)
8	<ICHILD Year
9	!
10	

Now choose *Essbase >> Retrieve*. If all goes well (and it often didn't back in 1992), you'll see:

	A	B	C	D	E
1			Profit	Product	Market
2		Actual	Budget	Variance	Variance %
3	Qtr1	24703	30580	-5877	-19.21844343
4	Qtr2	27107	32870	-5763	-17.53270459
5	Qtr3	27912	33980	-6068	-17.85756327
6	Qtr4	25800	31950	-6150	-19.24882629
7	Year	105522	129380	-23858	-18.44025352
8					

Tip!

If you try to use "Free Form" retrieval mode, don't forget to turn it off by going back to the *Mode* tab under *Essbase >> Options* and checking *Advanced Interpretation*.

OLAP AND OTHER TERMS

When Essbase was first released, no one was quite sure what it was. Was it some sort of spreadsheet on steroids? Was it a temporary employee who was really good at typing? Was it a database? If so, why didn't it have records and fields and most importantly, how come it didn't let IT geeks write SQL to access it?

Everyone was pretty sure what it wasn't: a typical relational database. The creators originally called it a "data server." Shortly after Essbase was created, they commissioned a study by the late Dr. E.F. Codd (the same Ph.D. who came up with the original rules for what constituted a true relational database) to determine what the heck Essbase was.

Dr. Codd was definitely impressed. He felt that this wasn't a relational database yet it was definitely a database and a very important new type to boot. He called it an "OLAP" database to separate it from every other database up to that point.

To put it simply, all databases prior to Essbase were built for the purpose of storing transactions. The goal for these systems was to get individual records into the database as quickly as possible and to get those same records back out again as quickly as possible. A side goal was to store that data in as small a space as possible, because those were the days when hard drive space cost as much as a good mule. Summarization of these types of databases was possible, but definitely not what the databases were designed for. Dr. Codd classified traditional relational databases "OLTP" (On-Line Transaction Processing).

He knew that Essbase was the first database designed purely to support analysis. Knowing that this was going to be The Next Big Thing, he created a term to describe these databases: OLAP (On-Line Analytical Processing). There were several features that Essbase offered that no previous database could handle.

Multi-Dimensional Databases

First of all, Essbase was a multi-dimensional database (MDDB or MDB, for short). What did the good doctor mean when he said Essbase was multi-dimensional? Simply that any of the dimensions set up in a database could be put in the rows or the columns (or applied to the whole page/report).

All databases up to this point were two-dimensional: records and fields. Essbase had no theoretical dimension limit (though there was certainly a practical limit). The Sample.Basic database we were accessing above has five base dimensions: Year, Measures, Product, Market, and Scenario. (It actually has five more "attribute" dimensions that we haven't even seen yet: Caffeinated, Ounces, Pkg Type, Population, and Intro Date.) The ASOSamp.Basic database (a sample database that you get if you purchased an option known in Essbase 7x as "Aggregate Storage") has 14 dimensions. The largest database we've ever seen had over 100 dimensions, but we think they were just trying to show off. In general, Essbase databases have five to ten base dimensions. By base dimension, we mean dimensions that show up all the time (like the five mentioned above in Sample.Basic).

While any relational database can be set up to give the appearance of having multiple dimensions, it takes a lot of up front work by developers. Essbase and other OLAP databases have dimensionality built-in.

Optimized for Retrieval

Essbase databases were also optimized for retrieval at any level of the hierarchy, even the very topmost number that might represent every dollar the company has ever made in its history. OLTP databases (relational databases) were nicely optimized for retrieval of detailed records but definitely not hierarchical information. By pre-saving summarized information, Essbase allows analysis to happen from the top down with no decrease in performance.

For OLAP databases, the hierarchy is native to the database itself. This is far different from relational databases that store the data in one table and then have one or more other tables that can be joined in to view data in a rolled-up fashion. For Essbase, the hierarchy is the database. When you change the hierarchy logic in Essbase as to how a product is grouped or a market rolls-up, you actually change where the data is stored.

Because hierarchy is inherent to OLAP databases, drill-down (sometimes known as "slicing and dicing" but never known as "making julienne data") is inherent as well. Essbase is great at doing Ad hoc analysis (see Chapter 2) because it knows that when a user double-clicks on Qtr1, she wants to see Jan, Feb, and Mar. This is because the roll-up of months to quarters is pre-defined back on the server.

Dr. Codd came up with ten rules for defining OLAP databases. Some of them (such as the ability to write-back data) were more interesting than others. While some other databases at the time met one or more of the qualifications, the only OLAP database to meet all ten was Arbor Software's Essbase. (Remember that Arbor is the company that commissioned the study.)

DSS, EIS, BI, BPM...

For the first few years, everyone called Essbase (and its competitors like Cognos and Business Objects) either an MDDB or OLAP database. The problem was that this was very difficult to explain to a casual user. Since casual users (CEOs, COOs, CFOs, etc.) are the ones who tend to sign checks at most companies, this produced a marketing problem of the highest order. What do you actually use one of these OLAP databases for?

The overarching belief was that OLAP/MDDB databases "helped users make decisions and then provide them the information they needed to support those decisions." Since HUMDATPTTITNTSTD makes for a lousy acronym, the term DSS was created and thus the "Decision Support Systems" term was coined.

Since 1992 when Essbase was released, other terms have been bandied about at various times including EIS (either "Executive Information Systems" or "Enterprise Information Systems" depending on whom you ask) and BI (Business Intelligence). Business Intelligence is still used fairly frequently (thanks to a well funded marketing campaign by IBM in the late 90's), but its popularity is quickly being overtaken by BPM.

BPM (Business Performance Management) is meant to include BI and expand it to also include any information a user needs to manage the performance of her company. Nowadays, this goes well beyond just a database and includes applications such as scorecarding, planning, and financial consolidation. If there is a number that needs to be manipulated, rolled-up, sliced, or diced, BPM should be able to handle it whether the original number is in an OLAP or OLTP database.

Historically, Essbase (and pretty much every other product Hyperion makes) has been seen as a financial tool. The reason for this is two-fold. First, financial minds tend to understand Essbase really well. Financial analysis is inherently multi-dimensional. Income Statements tend to have accounts, time periods, scenarios, organizations, departments, companies and years on them. Since relational databases do a poor job at multi-dimensional data, finance types started using spreadsheets. Since Essbase was a database for spreadsheets, it made it really easy to explain the value to CFOs, Controllers, VPs of Planning, and the like.

The second reason for Essbase's traditional stereotyping as "something the bean counters use" has to do with sales and marketing. Since Essbase was so easy to explain to end users in accounting and finance, that's the group that the Essbase sales representatives tended to call on. The sad part about this is that the IT organization often felt left out and turned to inferior products from competing vendors because those vendors were seen as developing products that were more "IT-centric."

As for the current market, Hyperion is generally accepted to be the market leader in the BPM space. They should be since they created the term in the first place in the early 21st century. BPM is quite the hot software niche these days thanks in no small part to Sarbanes-Oxley bringing compliance and management of data to the forefront. Simply put, Sarbanes-Oxley can put you in jail, and BPM can help keep you out.

Putting Essbase, Hyperion, and BPM on your resume may very well get you a 10% boost in salary at your next job. Feel free to share half of that with the authors of this book.

Tip!

ESSBASE TERMINOLOGY

We managed to make it all the way through the last chapter without learning a lot of Essbase terminology, but to truly succeed in the world of Essbase, there are some handy terms to pick up. Some of them we've already learned.

A "dimension" defines different categories for your data. A dimension can be located on the rows, columns, or pages of your queries. A "member name" is the short, computery name for the member of an Essbase dimension (like "100-10"). An "alias" is the longer, more descriptive name for a member (like "Cola"). All of the dimensions in a database make up the "outline."

Here is a portion of Sample.Basic outline:

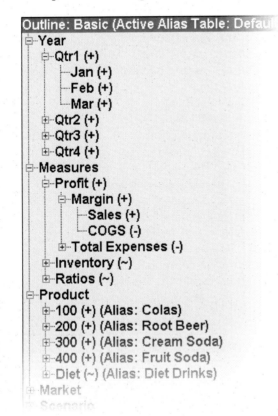

Family Tree Relationships

The most common way to refer to members in an outline relative to each other is by using "family tree" relationships. The members directly below a member are called its children. For instance, the Product dimension has five children: Colas, Root Beer, Cream Soda, Fruit Soda, and Diet Drinks. If we ever wanted to refer to those members on a report without hard coding them, we could say "give us all the children of Product."

The advantage to this aside from the saving in typing is that if a new product line was to be added (say, "Water"), we wouldn't have to modify our reports. Any report designed to display the children of Product would pick up the new "Water" product and add it to the list automatically.

If Colas, Root Beer, and the other rug rats are all the children of Product, what relation is Product to its children? Assuming you didn't fail "Birds and the Bees 101," you'll know that Product must be the *parent* of Colas, Root Beer, and the rest. In other words, the parent of any member is the one that the member rolls-up into. Qtr2 is the parent of May. Year is the parent of Qtr2.

Since Colas and Root Beer are both the children of Product, Colas and Root Beer are siblings. This is simple, but what relationship do January and May have? Well, their parents are siblings so that makes them... cousins. Correct, but "cousins" while technically correct isn't used that often. In general, people say that January and May are at the "same level."

What if you want to refer to all the members into which May rolls (not just the one right above)? Well, those are its ancestors which in this case would be Qtr2 and Year. Correspondingly, the descendants of Year would include all four quarters and all twelve months.

Note that there are members that don't have any children. In the picture above, May is childless. We refer to childless members as being "level-0". If you ever want all of the bottom, child-less members of a dimension, just ask for the level-0 members. For example, the level-0 members of the Year dimension are the months and the level-0 members of the Market dimension are the states.

Level-0 members are sometimes also referred to as "leaves," because they're at the edges of the family tree. Edward sometimes refers to level-0 members as "the ones who aren't allowed to sit at the main table on Thanksgiving," but we think he is the only one.

Try It!

Make up your own name for level-0 members and try to get it to catch on at your company!

All of the parents of the level-0 members are referred to as level-1. Since the level-0 members of the Year dimension are the months, then the level-1 members are the quarters. For the Market dimension, the level-1 members are the regions: East, West, South, and Central.

Just as the parents of the level-0 members are level-1 members, the parents of level-1 members are level-2 members. Their parents are level-3 members and so on up the hierarchy. There are many places in Essbase that you can specify, for example,

"All the level-2 members of the Product dimension," so remember that levels count up from the bottom of a dimension starting at 0.

If you want to count down the hierarchy, use generations instead of levels. The dimension itself is considered generation-1 (or "gen1," for short). Its children are gen2. For the Year dimension, the gen2 members are the quarters.

Yes, the quarters are both level-2 and generation-2. Why do we need both levels and generations? Well, in some dimensions with many, many levels in the hierarchy, you'll want to count up from the bottom or down from the top depending on which you're closer to. We've seen a dimension with 17 levels in the hierarchy, and it definitely was nice to have both options available to me. The children of gen2 members are gen3 and so on down the hierarchy.

Note! Why do generations start counting from 1 and levels from 0? It's because generation 0 is considered to be the outline itself making its children, the dimensions, generation 1.

While counting with generations is pretty straight-forward, levels can sometimes be a bit tricky. Look at this portion of the Measures dimension from Sample.Basic:

For this dimension, Gen1 is Measures. Gen2 is Profit and Inventory. Gen3 is Margin, Total Expenses, Opening Inventory, Additions, and Ending Inventory.

So far this is looking pretty easy, but let's switch our focus to the levels. The level-0 members are Sales, COGS, Marketing, Payroll, Misc, Opening Inventory, Additions, and Ending Inventory. The level-1 members are Margin, Total Expenses, and Inventory. What are the level-2 members? Profit (because it's the parent of level-1 members Margin and Total Expenses) and Measures (because it's the parent of level-1 member Inventory).

The trickiness is that Measures is *also* a level-3 member because it's the parent of Profit, a level-2 member. This means that if you ask Essbase for level-2 members, you'll get Measures, but you'll also get Measures if you ask for level-3 members. Notice that this counting oddity does not occur with generations.

Note!

This instance of a dimension is also known as a ragged hierarchy.

Chapter 4:
Become a Power User

Up to this point, we've primarily been navigating our way to data by either zooming in or out, using keep/remove only, or just typing members into our spreadsheet. What if we wanted to make a fairly large report with all of the states down the rows and all of the months across the top of the page:

	A	B	C	D	E	F
1		Measures	Product	Scenario		
2		Jan	Feb	Mar	Apr	May
3	New York	512	601	543	731	720
4	Massachusetts	519	498	515	534	548
5	Florida	336	361	373	408	440
6	Connecticut	321	309	290	272	253
7	New Hampshire	44	74	84	86	99
8	California	1,034	1,047	1,048	1,010	1,093
9	Oregon	444	417	416	416	400
10	Washington	405	412	395	368	378
11	Utah	237	251	256	277	262
12	Nevada	219	267	289	330	365
13	Texas	504	547	531	507	547
14	Oklahoma	241	234	243	277	27
15	Louisiana	259	263	251	228	23
16	New Mexico	(7)	2	9	29	

You create this sheet by opening up a blank spreadsheet, typing Measures into cell B1, Product into C1, Scenario into D1, all the months into B2:B13, and all the states into the cells starting at A3. This, however, is silly since we all know that the correct method is to hire a temp to type all this in for you.

Alternatively, you can use a previously ignored _Essbase_ menu item called _Member Selection_.

MEMBER SELECTION

Member Selection is like your own personalized temp typist. Let's see how handy he can be at generating spreadsheets like the one above. Start by opening a blank spreadsheet and connecting to Essbase. First, we'll make Member Selection (often shortened to Member Select) type in our months for us. On your blank sheet, select cell A2 and then choose *Essbase >> Member Selection*. The Member Selection window will display.

Notice that the dimension that comes up is Year. In general, Essbase will make a guess as to what dimension you want to use for picking members based on what's in the cell you currently have selected. In this case, you were on a blank cell, so it defaulted to the first dimension in the outline: Year. Go ahead and change the drop-down to the Market dimension since it contains the states we want.

The members in the left box should change to show the Market dimension. The numbers in parentheses to the right of each member show the number of children for that member. This can make for a rather handy warning when you're about to click the box next to a member that has 1,337 children.

Double-click the box next to East and it will expand to show you the states in the East. Click the first state, New York, and then hold down the shift key before you click the last East state, New Hampshire. If all goes well, you should have highlighted all the East states. Now click the big *Add* button:

You should now see five of the fifty most important states in the USA appear in the box to the right under Rules. Use this same method to add the states under West, South, and Central to the list on the right. You should now be looking at the following:

Essbase Member Selection

Dimension: Market

Members

- Oklahoma
- Louisiana
- New Mexico
- Central   (6)
- Illinois
- Ohio
- Wisconsin
- Missouri
- Iowa
- Colorado

Rules:

- New York
- Massachusetts
- Florida
- Connecticut
- New Hampshire
- California
- Oregon
- Washington
- Utah
- Nevada
- Texas
- Oklahoma
- Louisiana

Add ->

OK

Cancel

Help

Open...

Save...

Preview...

0 of 25 Selected.

Note: Use the right mouse button to apply advanced selection rules.

Find...   Expand To Descendants   Move Item Up   Remove Item

Clear   Member Information...   Move Item Down   Remove All

View Method
- ● By Member Name
- ○ By Generation Name
- ○ By Level Name
- ○ By Dynamic Time Series

Output Options
- ☐ Use Aliases   Default
- ☐ Suppress Shared Member
- ☑ Place Down the Sheet
- ☐ Insert List Before Active Cell

Tip!

To see an entire dimension without having to expand each parent member, click on the member at the top of the dimension (in the Members box) and choose the *Expand To Descendants* button.

If you're an obsessive-compulsive type and want to manually alphabetize your state names before entering them into the sheet, highlight the state you want to rearrange in the list and then click either the *Move Item Up* or *Move Item Down* buttons. If you accidentally add any member more than once, highlight the member to remove and choose the *Remove Item* button. To clear the whole list, click *Remove All*.

Assuming your list is complete (and alphabetized if that's how you roll), click *OK* and you'll be able to watch while Essbase enters the states down the left side of your spreadsheet.

Note!

After you use Member Selection to type in your members, you will need to choose *Essbase >> Retrieve* yourself. Member Selection does not do a retrieve on its own.

Let's use a slightly different method to type in the months. Select cell B1 and choose *Essbase >> Member Selection*. The Year dimension should appear. Under "View Method" in the bottom-left corner of the Member Selection window, choose *By Level Name*.

Remember that the months are level-0 since they don't have any children (through no lack of trying, mind you) so select *Lev0,Year* and click the *Add* button. Don't click *OK* yet, because if you do, it will type the months down the rows in column B. What you want is to see the months go across the columns, so this time uncheck the *Place Down the Sheet* box under "Output Options" in the bottom-right corner.

Essbase Member Selection

Dimension: Year

Members
Lev0,Year
Lev1,Year
Lev2,Year

Add =>

0 of 3 Selected.

Find... Expand To Descendants
Clear Member Information...

View Method
○ By Member Name
○ By Generation Name
◉ By Level Name
○ By Dynamic Time Series

Rules:
Lev0,Year

Note: Use the right mouse button to apply advanced selection rules.

Move Item Up Remove Item
Move Item Down Remove All

Output Options
☐ Use Aliases Default ▼
☐ Suppress Shared Members
☑ Place Down the Sheet
☐ Insert List Before Active Cell

OK
Cancel
Help
Open...
Save...
Preview...

If you want to see what members choosing "Lev0,Year" will actually enter into your spreadsheet, you can click on the *Preview* button. Once you've closed the Preview window, click *OK* and your spreadsheet should now look like this:

	A	B	C	D	E	F
1		Jan	Feb	Mar	Apr	May
2	New York					
3	Massachusetts					
4	Florida					
5	Connecticut					
6	New Hampshire					
7	California					
8	Oregon					
9	Washington					
10	Utah					
11	Nevada					
12	Texas					
13	Oklahoma					
14	Louisiana					
15	New Mexico					
16	Illinois					

Select *Essbase >> Retrieve* and you should see something very similar to the spreadsheet on page 51.

You can type a level or generation name (such as Lev0,Year) directly into a cell and select *Essbase >> Retrieve* (there's no space between Lev0, and Year). The Essbase server will automatically expand the level/generation name list for you.

Dynamic Time Series

What if the year wasn't complete and we only had data through May? Start by blanking out the cells in row 2 to the right of column F (leaving only the months from January to May). How do we get a year-to-date total column? We could add a total column to the right of column F to add January through May, but Essbase can do this work for us.

Select cell G2 (to the right of May) and open the Member Selection box. The Year dimension should appear in the drop-down. Most every Essbase database has a time dimension. In Sample.Basic, that dimension is called Year. When the time dimension for a given database is selected (Year, for us), an extra view method called *Dynamic Time Series* becomes available in the bottom-right. Go ahead and select it.

Essbase Member Selection

Dimension: Year

Members

H-T-D
Q-T-D

0 of 2 Selected.

Find... Expand To Descendants

Clear Member Information...

View Method
- By Member Name
- By Generation Name
- By Level Name
- By Dynamic Time Series

Dynamic Time Series means that Essbase will take and dynamically add up time periods up to whatever period you specify just as if that member was stored in the outline. For instance, if you ask for Q-T-D (Q-T-D is short for Quarter-To-Date) through May, Essbase will total the data for April and May (since those are the months in the quarter containing May) and put them into a Q-T-D member. This member can then be pivoted and for the most part treated just like a stored member.

Sample.Basic has two Dynamic Time Series members (often abbreviated as "DTS members"): Q-T-D and H-T-D. H-T-D stands for History-To-Date. Other common DTS members include Y-T-D (Year-To-Date), M-T-D (Month-To-Date), and W-T-D (Week-To-Date). Since we want January through May to be totaled for us, select H-T-D and add it to the right side.

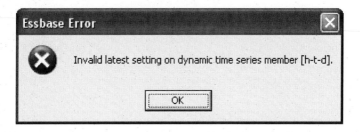

Notice that below H-T-D it says "using a to-date calculation of..." Since no month is specified, it will use whatever month you have specified as your "Latest time Period" on the Display tab of Essbase Options. If you don't specify a specific member here and you also haven't specified one in Essbase Options, you will see an error like this when you try to retrieve:

The easiest way to remedy this is to make sure that you always have a Time Period selected in Essbase Options (at the very bottom of the *Display* tab). From the Member Selection window, you can also specify a specific time period. Right-click on the H-T-D member under Rules and choose *Specify Latest*.

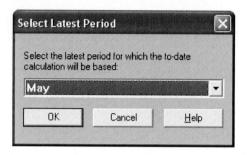

Choose *May*, click *OK*, and then click *OK* again. H-T-D(May) should now be typed into your spreadsheet. Retrieve data and you should see:

	A	B	C	D	E	F	G
1		Measures	Product	Scenario			
2		Jan	Feb	Mar	Apr	May	H-T-D(May)
3	New York	512	601	543	731	720	3,107
4	Massachusetts	519	498	515	534	548	2,614
5	Florida	336	361	373	408	440	1,918
6	Connecticut	321	309	290	272	253	1,445
7	New Hampshire	44	74	84	86	99	387
8	California	1,034	1,047	1,048	1,010	1,093	5,232
9	Oregon	444	417	416	416	400	2,093
10	Washington	405	412	395	368	378	1,958
11	Utah	237	251	256	277	262	1,283
12	Nevada	219	267	289	330	365	1,470
13	Texas	504	547	531	507	547	2,636
14	Oklahoma	241	234	243	277	279	1,274
15	Louisiana	259	263	251	228	231	1,232
16	New Mexico	271	2	9	28	39	

Note! You can also type in DTS members directly. To specify a specific month, put it in parentheses after the member. For instance to get Q-T-D through March, type in Q-T-D(Mar). There is no space between the member and the parenthesis.

Attribute Dimensions

All the analysis of Sample.Basic up to this point has been done using five dimensions. There are five other dimensions in Sample.Basic that we could be using but to this point, we've been ignoring them. These dimensions are known as "Attribute Dimensions" and they are alternate ways of summarizing our base (sometimes called "standard" or "stored") dimensions.

Note! Unlike base dimensions, the totals for attribute dimensions are not pre-calculated in Essbase. As such, retrieval of attribute dimensions will often be slower as Essbase dynamically calculates the results.

Sample.Basic has five attribute dimensions: Caffeinated, Ounces, Pkg Type, Intro Date, and Population. The first four of these are alternate ways of rolling up the Product dimension. Population is an alternate way of rolling up the Market dimension. As an example, let's limit the report we just made to only caffeinated drinks.

Select cell E1 (which should be blank) and select *Essbase >> Member Selection*. In the Dimension drop-down, scroll down in the list until you see the attribute dimensions. Click on the *Caffeinated* dimension (right after Scenario).

```
Essbase Member Selection

Dimension:  Caffeinated                ▼
Members
     ◹ Caffeinated   [2]
        Caffeinated_True
        Caffeinated_False
```

Since we haven't been getting much sleep lately, let's focus just on Caffeinated products. Highlight *Caffeinated_True* and click on the *Add* button.

Tip! Instead of highlighting a member and clicking the *Add* button, you can also double-click on a name in the Members box and it will automatically add to the Rules box.

Click *OK* and then select *Essbase >> Retrieve*. The numbers in your report should change to show the following:

	A	B	C	D	E	F
1		Measures	Product	Scenario	Caffeinated_T
2		Jan	Feb	Mar	Apr	May
3	New York	88	53	73	213	221
4	Massachusetts	361	354	378	398	430
5	Florida	280	289	299	331	356
6	Connecticut	239	240	225	211	194
7	New Hampshire	11	12	16	18	23
8	California	694	688	711	711	769
9	Oregon	264	253	246	220	199
10	Washington	244	267	260	261	271
11	Utah	156	171	167	190	185
12	Nevada	235	257	270	321	337
13	Texas	451	489	477	459	505
14	Oklahoma	175	164	169	179	178
15	Louisiana	251	261	250	227	22
16	New Mexico	1	9	12	37	

Notice that the numbers are reduced to show just the totals for caffeinated products. Of course, you could have just typed "Caffeinated_True" into cell E1 and selected *Essbase >> Retrieve*, but what are the odds that you can actually spell Caffeinated correctly? Let Member Selection do the hard work for you.

Try It! Using cell F1, add a member of another attribute dimension into your report and re-retrieve.

There is one more hidden dimension that is only accessible when you're displaying an attribute dimension on your spreadsheet. This dimension is called the "Attribute Calculations" dimension. Type the word sum into cell F1 and then select *Essbase >> Member Selection*:

The default member for this dimension is Sum. When you have Caffeinated_True on your spreadsheet, this means that Essbase grabs all the products that are caffeinated and Sums them up to get a total for each intersection. What if, instead, you wanted to know how many caffeinated products were sold in each month in each state? Double-click on *Count* (so it appears in the Rules box) and click *OK*. Back in your spreadsheet, select *Essbase >> Retrieve*.

	A	B	C	D	E	F
1		Measures	Product	Scenario	Caffeinated_True	Coun
2		Jan	Feb	Mar	Apr	May
3	New York	4	4	4	4	
4	Massachusetts	3	3	3	3	
5	Florida	7	7	7	7	
6	Connecticut	5	5	5	5	
7	New Hampshire	3	3	3	3	
8	California	7	7	7	7	
9	Oregon	6	6	6	6	
10	Washington	6	6	6	6	
11	Utah	7	7	7	7	
12	Nevada	7	7	7	7	
13	Texas	6	6	6	6	
14	Oklahoma	6	6	6	6	
15	Louisiana	6	6	6	6	
	New Mexico	6	6	6		

Try using the other members of the Attribute Calculations dimension: Avg (average), Min (minimum), and Max (maximum).

Try It!

Notice that in Massachusetts (another member you'd be very likely to misspell if not for Member Selection), out of seven caffeinated products that TBC sells, only three are actually sold there.

There's a quick way to figure out which products those are. Select the cell containing Massachusetts and choose *Essbase >> Keep Only*. Highlight the Caffeinated_True member and choose *Essbase >> Zoom In* or just double click on Caffeinated_True.

	A	B	C	D	E	F
1				Measures	Scenario	Count
2				Jan	Feb	Mar	Apr
3	Caffeinated_True	Cola	Massachusetts	1	1	1
4		Old Fashioned	Massachusetts	1	1	1
5		Dark Cream	Massachusetts	1	1	1
6		Product	Massachusetts	3	3	3

Your spreadsheet might look slightly different depending on what you have set in your Essbase Options, but we can now easily tell that the only caffeinated products sold in Massachusetts are Cola, Old Fashioned, and Dark Cream.

Saved Selections

In some cases, you might come up with specific selections you want to use repeatedly. For instance, you might have a set of products that you want to keep a closer eye on. Select *Essbase >> Member Selection* and select a few products to watch. If you see member names (like 100-20) instead of aliases, check the Use Aliases box. Once you have a list of products in the Rules box, click the *Save* button.

Essbase Member Selection

Dimension: Product

Members
- Old Fashioned
- Diet Root Beer
- Sasparilla
- Birch Beer
- Cream Soda [3]
- Dark Cream
- Vanilla Cream
- Diet Cream
- Fruit Soda [3]
- Diet Drinks [3]

0 of 22 Selected.

Rules:
- Diet Cola
- Old Fashioned
- Sasparilla
- Vanilla Cream

Note: Use the right mouse button to apply advanced selection rules.

OK
Cancel
Help
Open...
Save...
Preview...

Add...

Find... | Expand To Descendants | Move Item Up | Remove Item
Clear | Member Information | Move Item Down | Remove All

View Method
- By Member Name
- By Generation Name
- By Level Name
- By Dynamic Time Series

Output Options
- Use Aliases | Default
- Suppress Shared Members
- Place Down the Sheet
- Insert List Before Active Cell

A window will appear asking you where you want to save your selection object (in our case, our list of products to watch):

Save Selection Object

Location
- Server
- Client

Connection Information:
Server: Localhost
Application: Sample
Database: Basic

Selection Object:

Available Selection Objects:

Application:
Sample

Database:
Basic

OK
Cancel
Help
File System...

The default location to save your selection is the server. While this is handy for sharing your selection with others, it is very unlikely (unless you're, say, a God-like supervisor) that you will have the security rights to save your selection to the server. In our case, select *Client*.

The *File System* button becomes available once you select *Client* giving you the option to save your selection to a specific place on your local hard drive .

Note!

In the box under "Selection Object" type in the name you want to call your list. We've called ours "ProdList" to prove to the world that we are not all that creative. Select *OK* to close the "Save Selection Object" window and then *Cancel* to close Member Selection.

Now let's say that you want to make a new report using your previously saved list. Go to a blank spreadsheet and choose *Essbase >> Member Selection*. From the Member Selection box, select the Product dimension from the drop-down and then choose the *Open* button (right above the *Save* button). Select *Client* as your location and you should see your saved selection:

Open Selection Object

Location
- ○ Server
- ● Client

Connection Information:
- Server: Localhost
- Application: Sample
- Database: Basic

Selection Object:
ProdList

Available Selection Objects:
ProdList

Application:
sample ▼

Database:
[all dbs] ▼

☑ Lock Object
☐ Merge with Existing Selection Rules

[OK] [Cancel] [Help] [File System...]

If you already had other products selected in your rules box and you wanted to keep them, check the box for *Merge with Existing Selection Rules*. Highlight your selection object and click *OK* to see your list in the Member Selection box.

Advanced Selection Rules

What if we want a list of everything in the entire Product dimension? Is there a faster way in Member Selection than highlighting every member in the dimension, moving them all to the right, and then having Essbase type them all in?

Actually, there are two faster ways. The first method doesn't use Member Selection. You could change your Zoom Level to *All Levels* in your Essbase Options and then *Zoom In* on Product.

While there's nothing wrong with doing it this way (it's actually rather fast), this section is about Member Selection.

Click on the cell where you want all the products to appear. Select *Essbase* >> *Member Selection* and select the *Product* dimension. Add the Product member to the Rules box and then right-click on *Product*. A list of "advanced selection rules" will appear.

Essbase Member Selection

Dimension: Product

Members
Product [5]
☑ Colas [3]
☑ Root Beer [4]
☑ Cream Soda [3]
☑ Fruit Soda [3]
☑ Diet Drinks [3]

Rules:
Product

All Children
All Children and Member
All Descendants
All Descendants and Member
Subset...

OK
Cancel
Help
Open...
Save...
Preview...

0 of 22 Selected.

Note: Use the right mouse button to apply advanced selection rules.

Find.. | Expand To Descendants | Move Item Up | Remove Item
Clear | Member Information... | Move Item Down | Remove All

View Method
● By Member Name
○ By Generation Name
○ By Level Name
○ By Dynamic Time Series

Output Options
☑ Use Aliases   Default
☐ Suppress Shared Members
☑ Place Down the Sheet
☐ Insert List Before Active Cell

Choose *All Descendants and Member* which will give us the entire product dimension (i.e., all of the descendants of Product and the member Product itself). Click *OK* and the list will appear in the spreadsheet.

Now let's say we wanted to get a list of all the states that start with the letter "C". While we could wander through the list of states looking for ones that start with "C", there's a faster way using Member Selection

Go back into Member Selection and choose the *Market* dimension. Add the Market member to the right side, right-click and choose *Subset*. The "Subset Dialog" will appear:

Subset Dialog ☒

Select member Market and its descendants where:

| User-defined Attribute ▼ | is ▼ | Major Market ▼ |

[Add as OR Condition]   [Add as AND Condition]

OK

Cancel

Help

Conditions:

[Remove Item]

[Add [ ]   [Add]]

[Remove ( )]

[Remove All ( )]

[Preview...]

The first option to appear in the top-left drop-down box is for *User-defined Attribute*. A User-Defined Attribute (often referred to as a "UDA") is basically a text property of a member. A given member can have one or more UDAs applied to it. In the Sample.Basic outline, several states have UDAs of Major Market, Small Market, or New Market.

Before we go on to our "C-state" list, let's find out which states are both Major Markets and New Markets. Go ahead and click the *Add as AND condition* box to add "Major Market" as a condition. Change Major Market to New Market and click *Add as AND condition* again.

You can add a maximum of fifty conditions. We have no idea why you would ever need this many, but fifty is the limit.

Note!

Click on the *Preview* button and you'll see that the only state that's both Major and New is Colorado.

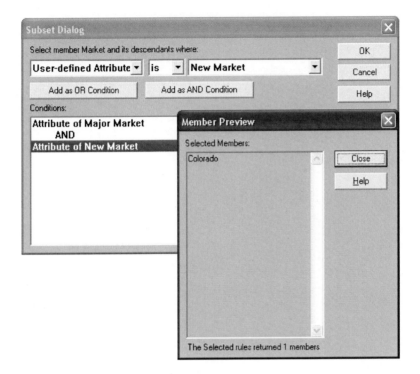

Click *Close* to close the Preview window. In the Subset window, click on "Remove Item" twice to clear the conditions list. Now change the top-left drop-down from "User-Defined Attribute" to Pattern.

The pattern that we want to look for is "C*" where the asterisk is a wildcard that tells Essbase that it needs to start with C but we don't much care what it ends with. Note that an asterisk can only be at the end of a string. The only other wildcard you can use is a question mark which tells Essbase that that specific character can be any character. For instance, "Ju?" as a pattern on the Year dimension would return both Jun and Jul since both start with Ju and then have one last character. The pattern "J?" would not return any members as there are no two-letter months in the hierarchy. Enter C* in the far-right box and choose the *Add* button. Click *Preview*.

Subset Dialog ☒

Select member Market and its descendants where:

| Pattern | ▼ | is | ▼ | C* |

OK

Cancel

Help

Add as OR Condition   Add as AND Condition

Conditions:

Pattern Matching C*

Member Preview ☒

Selected Members:

Connecticut
California
Colorado
Central

Close

Help

The Selected rules returned 4 members

You'll immediately notice that our four states starting with "C" are Connecticut, California, Colorado, and Central. Those of you who passed U.S. History will immediately notice that while "Central" is a time zone (one in which everyone tends to go to bed an hour early), it is not a state. To limit our list to just states, click on *Close* to go back to the Subset window. Change the *Pattern* drop-down to say *Level Name*. The top-right box will change to *Lev0,Market* which is perfect for our needs since we want the states. Click on the *Add as AND Condition* button and then click *Preview* to see our list reduced by one.

Try It!

Experiment with other conditions in the top-left drop-down like *Generation Name* and the various attribute dimensions.

FORMATTED REPORTS

Everything we've done up to this point has been fairly Ad hoc and formatting has been kept to a minimum. One of the reasons we're using Excel to display our data is that it's a great place to pretty up boring numbers (or as we used to say back on the farm:

"making 'em look fancy"). Essbase will still be used as the source of the data, but Excel will provide all of our formatting.

Seven Steps to Creating a Formatted Report

The secret to creating a formatted report (sometimes called a "template") is to use Essbase to get all of your data before you add any formatting. In general, there are seven steps to creating a formatted report:

1. Retrieve your data from Essbase.
2. Move your row, column, and page members around to where you want them.
3. Add any text descriptions.
4. Insert Excel formulas.
5. Turn on Essbase Formula Preservation.
6. Apply formatting.
7. Save.

Step 1: Retrieve Data

Let's say we want to make a fairly simple Profit and Loss Statement. (Considering we'll be using Sample.Basic, it's going to have to be pretty darned simple.) Go to a blank spreadsheet and enter Year into cell B1 and Profit into cell A2:

	A	B	C
1		**Year**	
2	**Profit**		
3			

Retrieve from Essbase and you should see:

	A	B	C	D
1		**Product**	**Market**	**Scenario**
2		**Year**		
3	**Profit**	**105,522**		
4				

Zoom In on Year to show the quarters and Profit to show its children. Zoom In on both of the children of Profit (Margin and Total Expenses) too and you should see something like this:

	A	B	C	D	E	F
1		Product	Market	Scenario		
2		Qtr1	Qtr2	Qtr3	Qtr4	Year
3	Sales	95,820	101,679	105,215	98,141	400,855
4	COGS	42,877	45,362	47,343	43,754	179,336
5	Margin	52,943	56,317	57,872	54,387	221,519
6	Marketing	15,839	16,716	17,522	16,160	66,237
7	Payroll	12,168	12,243	12,168	12,168	48,747
8	Misc	233	251	270	259	1,013
9	Total Expenses	28,240	29,210	29,960	28,587	115,997
10	Profit	24,703	27,107	27,912	25,800	105,522
11						

If your spreadsheet doesn't look quite like this one, try the following:

- Make sure your Essbase display Options are set to indent sub-items and automatically adjust columns.
- Highlight all your cells and using Excel formatting, change the number format to display only whole numbers with commas separating the thousands place.
- We also bolded our numbers and set the font to a 12 point Arial, but this is mostly so they are easier to read in print.

Step 2: Move Members

Since this is the data we want to see on our final report, we can proceed on to step two: moving our row, column, and page members around. Our data is a bit cramped at the moment, so let's space it out by inserting some blank rows. Highlight the following rows (by clicking the row number) and select *Insert >> Rows* from the Excel menu:

- Row 10: Profit
- Row 6: Marketing
- Row 2: the quarters
- Insert a total of 3 blank lines above the quarters. We'll move some members to these blank lines in a bit.

	A	B	C	D	E	F	
1		Product	Market	Scenario			
2							
3							
4							
5		Qtr1	Qtr2	Qtr3	Qtr4	Year	
6	Sales	95,820	101,679	105,215	98,141	400,855	
7	COGS	42,877	45,362	47,343	43,754	179,336	
8	Margin	52,943	56,317	57,872	54,387	221,519	
9							
10	Marketing	15,839	16,716	17,522	16,160	66,237	
11	Payroll	12,168	12,243	12,168	12,168	48,747	
12	Misc	233	251	270	259	1,013	
13	Total Expenses	28,240	29,210	29,960	28,587	115,997	
14							
15	Profit	24,703	27,107	27,912	25,800	105,522	
16							

Even though we've inserted a bunch of extra lines, this is still a valid Essbase retrieval.

Try It! Type a zero into cell B6 (Qtr1 Sales) and then select *Essbase>>Retrieve*. It should replace the zero with 95,820.

Essbase is quite content to have you move the member names around. Its only requirement is that it needs to encounter a member from every dimension before it sees the first number. Essbase scans a spreadsheet from the left-to-right (cell A1, B1, C1... IV1) and then from top-to-bottom (row 1, row 2, row 3, ... row 65536). As it is reading the first line, the first name it encounters is Product. At this point, it doesn't know if Product applies to the whole page or it's a column member (because theoretically, column C could contain another Product member such as Cola).

Essbase proceeds on to the next cell and sees Market. Since this is from a different dimension, it now knows that this row must contain page members. Essbase calls this a title row. At this point, it's expecting that the next member over will either be blank or a member from another dimension. If the next member over was a different member from either the Product or Market dimension, it would get very confused since it already decided that this was a row of page. An error would appear:

If you ever see this error, look for a row that has multiple dimensions on it that also has multiple members from the same dimension. Since everything is positioned properly in our current example, Essbase will continue scanning to the right and sees the member Scenario. Essbase now has three of the five dimensions specified.

Essbase continues scanning through the rest of row 1 but it encounters nothing but blank cells (and the same occurs with all of rows two, three, and four). In cell B5 it sees the member Qtr1. It recognizes this as being a member of the Year dimension, but like before, it doesn't know yet if row five is a title row or a column row. Looking to the next cell, it sees Qtr2 so it makes the determination that row five is a column row (specifically a row of Year members). Essbase goes on to see Year members in the remaining cells in row five and Essbase becomes very happy.

Moving on to row six, it sees the member Sales in the first column. Essbase has now identified all five of the base dimensions in Sample.Basic. It now knows that the value that should be entered into cell B6 is the intersection of the three page dimensions (Product, Market, Scenario), Qtr1, and Sales.

The general requirement that Essbase must encounter every dimension before the first number is called "the natural order for Essbase." Whenever your retrievals aren't working, look to see if you've violated the natural order rule. For instance, if we typed a zero into cell A5 and chose *Essbase >> Retrieve*, we'd see this error:

The error appears because Essbase thinks you want it to put the first number at cell A5 and it hasn't identified two of the dimensions at that point. The solution is to delete the zero in A5.

Being practically perfect in every way, our retrieve has none of these problems. Before we conclude step 2, let's move Product to cell C2 and Scenario to cell C3. Before you continue to step 3, make sure your retrieve looks like this:

	A	B	C	D	E	F	G
1			Market				
2			Product				
3			Scenario				
4							
5			Qtr1	Qtr2	Qtr3	Qtr4	Year
6		Sales	95,820	101,679	105,215	98,141	400,855
7		COGS	42,877	45,362	47,343	43,754	179,336
8		Margin	52,943	56,317	57,872	54,387	221,519
9							
10		Marketing	15,839	16,716	17,522	16,160	66,237
11		Payroll	12,168	12,243	12,168	12,168	48,747
12		Misc	233	251	270	259	1,013
13		Total Expenses	28,240	29,210	29,960	28,587	115,997
14							
15	Profit		24,703	27,107	27,912	25,800	105,522
16							

Step 3: Add Text

As Essbase is scanning the sheet, it will often run into names it doesn't recognize. As we learned back on page 16, if it runs into an unknown name, it will display a spelling error and then continue on its merry way with really no harm done. The retrieve will still function even though unknown names are present.

We can use this to our advantage by adding extraneous text to our retrieve knowing that the retrieve will continue to work just fine. Extra text can include header information such as the company or the name of the report. In our case, we're going to add some descriptions to let people know what should be selected in cells C1:C3. Type in the following:

- In cell B1, "Market:"
- In cell B2, "Product:"
- In cell B3, "Scenario:"

The top of your retrieve should now look like this:

	A	B	C
1		**Market:**	**Market**
2		**Product:**	**Product**
3		**Scenario:**	**Scenario**
4			
5		**Qtr1**	**Qtr2**	Qtr
6	**Sales**	**95,820**	**101,679**	10
7	COGS	42,877	45,362	

When we retrieve data, we'll get a number of unknown member errors. Since we know full well that the three things we just typed are not going to be in Essbase, we can disable the unknown member warning. Go to *Essbase >> Options* and click on the *Global* tab. Uncheck the box next to *Display Unknown Members*.

Note! Display Unknown Members is a global setting and will apply to all of your spreadsheets. You might want to turn it back on when you're finished with this spreadsheet.

Step 4: Insert formulas

At times, you may want to add formulas to your report to calculate things that aren't in Essbase. We are of the belief that whenever possible, you should try to add these types of calculations to the Essbase database itself. The main reason is that if you add the calculation to Essbase, anyone else will be guaranteed to calculate that value the exact same way you do. This prevents the embarrassing situation of two people walking into a meeting with different ideas of what Profit as a percent of Sales was last month.

This is likely to get one or both people fired (usually, they'll fire the one who has the lower Profit number). If both people were getting their Profit % from Essbase, then they'd at least have the same number. While this doesn't guarantee that Essbase was calculating it correctly, at least everyone was using the same incorrect number.

The other nice benefit of performing the calculation in Essbase is that the next time you need the calculation; you don't have to remember how you calculated it last time. There's a member waiting for you to use with the calculation already defined. Sample.Basic, for instance, has members called "Profit %" and "Margin %" in the Measures dimension. Go ahead and type Profit % into cell A17 and Retrieve. You'll see that Profit as a percent of Sales is about 26% for the year.

While adding all of your calculations to Essbase may be great in theory, there are plenty of times when a calculation will occur to you on the spot and you don't want to bother your Essbase admin, asking her to add the calculation to the database. For instance, say we want to add a line to our report that calculates Total Expenses as a percent of Sales. "Expense %" is not a member in the database. Type in the following:

- In cell A17, "Expense %"
- In cell B17, "=B13/B6*100"

Copy the formula in cell B17 to cells C17:F17. Your report should now look like this:

	A	B	C	D	E	F
1		Market:	Market			
2		Product:	Product			
3		Scenario:	Scenario			
4						
5		Qtr1	Qtr2	Qtr3	Qtr4	Year
6	Sales	95,820	101,679	105,215	98,141	400,855
7	COGS	42,877	45,362	47,343	43,754	179,336
8	Margin	52,943	56,317	57,872	54,387	221,519
9						
10	Marketing	15,839	16,716	17,522	16,160	66,237
11	Payroll	12,168	12,243	12,168	12,168	48,747
12	Misc	233	251	270	259	1,013
13	Total Expenses	28,240	29,210	29,960	28,587	115,997
14						
15	Profit	24,703	27,107	27,912	25,800	105,522
16						
17	Expense %	29	29	28	29	29
18						

Formulas can be in the rows or the columns just like a normal Excel spreadsheet. Retrieve your data and something really annoying will most likely happen: your Expense % formulas will all disappear.

Step 5: Formula Preservation

If you retrieved your data (and got annoyed at the formula disappearance), please reenter the formulas now. Unless we specifically tell Essbase to keep our formulas, it will tend to remove them. To the best of my knowledge, the developers of the add-in didn't do this out of spite. The primary reason seems to be that when you're doing Ad hoc analysis, it's difficult to figure out what to do with the formulas as you drill down, pivot dimensions, and so forth. For instance, if we pivot the quarters down to the rows, what should the Expense % formula be changed to? While we could probably figure it out from a business perspective, there's no hard and fast rule that Essbase could apply in all cases.

The solution that the developers picked was to delete the formulas unless you insist that they be left. To insist, go to the *Mode* tab under *Essbase >> Options* and look under the section for Formula Preservation. Don't be surprised if the checkboxes are all grayed out:

Formula Preservation (on the *Mode* tab) and Suppression (on the *Display* tab) are mutually exclusive. If you're suppressing #Missing rows (as we are, at the moment) or zero rows, you can't turn on Formula Preservation. Again, this is because Essbase wouldn't know what to do with your formulas if rows were suddenly eliminated because they have no data. Imagine what would happen if you had no sales for a month and this row was suppressed: what should the Expense % formula do?

To enable Formula Preservation, go back to the *Display* tab and uncheck the boxes next to *#Missing Rows* and *Zero Rows*. Come back to the *Mode* tab, and you should now be able to check the box for *Retain on Retrieval*. Click *OK*, and now when you retrieve your data, your formulas will not disappear.

In earlier versions of Essbase, you couldn't do things like Keep/Remove Only or Zoom In/Out without losing your formulas. Essbase has gotten smarter over the years. If you want to keep your formulas while doing functions like Keep Only or Zoom Out, check those boxes under Formula Preservation. Essbase has even gotten smart enough these days that if you have formulas in a column and you zoom on a member in the row, it will copy the formula to the new members you zoomed to. To enable this, check both *Retain on Zooms* and *Formula Fill*.

You should leave formula preservation turned off until after you've got your rows and columns set. If you turn it on and then try to do something wacky like pivot, you'll see an error like this one:

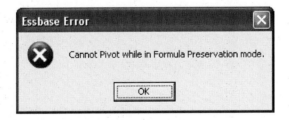

Step 6: Apply Formatting

Once you get to step 6, Essbase's work is done and it's up to you, Excel Jockey. Format to your heart's content.

Take your existing report and apply whatever Excel formatting you want.

Try It!

Here's our early report with some centering, borders, underlining, bolding, and number formatting (and the gridlines turned off):

	A	B	C	D	E	F
1		**Market:**	Market			
2		**Product:**	Product			
3		**Scenario:**	Scenario			
4						
5		**Qtr1**	**Qtr2**	**Qtr3**	**Qtr4**	**Year**
6	Sales	95,820	101,679	105,215	98,141	**400,855**
7	COGS	42,877	45,362	47,343	43,754	**179,336**
8	**Margin**	52,943	56,317	57,872	54,387	**221,519**
9						
10	Marketing	15,839	16,716	17,522	16,160	**66,237**
11	Payroll	12,168	12,243	12,168	12,168	**48,747**
12	Misc	233	251	270	259	**1,013**
13	**Total Expenses**	28,240	29,210	29,960	28,587	**115,997**
14						
15	**Profit**	**24,703**	**27,107**	**27,912**	**25,800**	**105,522**
16						
17	Expense %	29.47 %	28.73 %	28.48 %	29.13 %	**28.94 %**
18						

It's also a good idea once you've started adding formatting to go up to your Essbase Options and turn off *Adjust Columns*. This is because when you print your report, you don't want what was a one page report to spill over onto two pages due to some automatic Essbase column widening.

Step 7: Save

Before you save the workbook, blank out all your numbers (keep your formulas, though). This makes the file size that much smaller thereby making the file that much faster to open next time.

The next time you want to use this report, open it up, use Member Select to select your Market, Product, and Scenario members (or just type them in), and finally choose *Essbase >> Retrieve*.

Save your spreadsheet where you'll be able to find it later. We'll be using it in future exercises.

Try It!

Cascade

Once you start building reports, the time will come when you want to run the same report for multiple selections. On the report you just built, you might want to run it for every region. While you could use Member Select to pick each region (East, Central...) and choose *Essbase >> Retrieve* after each one, there is an *Essbase* menu item that will speed the process for us: *Cascade*.

On the report we just created, select the cell that has Market in it (cell C1, if you've been following along exactly). Select *Essbase >> Cascade*. You'll notice that the "Essbase Cascade Options" window comes up with the second tab, *Destination Options*, selected. We have no idea why the default isn't the first tab, so ponder that for a while and then click on the *Cascade Information* tab.

This tab shows what members are going to be drilled on (and to what level) as Essbase creates several worksheets for us. The default is always the next level below the member(s) you highlighted before launching Cascade. In our case, we want the regions, which are indeed the next level below Market, so click back to the *Destination Options* tab:

The destination directory is where Essbase will put all of the worksheets and workbooks it creates. For right now, leave it blank. Leaving it blank causes Essbase to put the worksheets in whatever Windows considered to be the current directory at the time Cascade runs. Check the box next to *Open Created Files* since the odds of you locating that directory are roughly equivalent to your odds of developing X-ray vision by lunch next Tuesday. Let Essbase find it and open it for you.

Under "Destination Types," you'll notice three options:

- *Separate Workbooks*. This option will put each worksheet in its own workbook. This is handy if you'll be e-mailing each worksheet to a different person.
- *One Workbook, Separate Sheets*. This option will put each generated worksheet on a separate tab in the same workbook. Though this choice seems a bit segregationist, in general, this is the option you'll want (so of course it defaults to the one above).
- *Printer*. This option sends each generated sheet to the printer specified by the *Printer* button. This is handy if you have something against trees and want to kill as many of them as possible. In all seriousness, unless you're sending out spreadsheets to someone without computer access, you probably should be using one of the above options. It's the 21st century, people.

For our purposes, check the box next to *One Workbook, Separate Sheets*. Go ahead and leave the "Naming Information" boxes empty. As you'll soon find out, all the tabs will be numbered sequentially (from 1 to however many sheets you have) and putting something in the Prefix box just puts that name before the number.

Note! The *Workbook* box will be grayed out unless you specify *One Workbook, Separate Sheets*. If it's not grayed out and you leave this box blank, your workbook will probably be named 0.XLS.

Click on the *Format Options* tab:

Check the box next to *Copy Formatting*. If you don't, all of the sheets that Essbase creates will have the correct Essbase members and data but none of your Excel formatting. Checking this box will copy *most* of your formatting but not all. Some of the formatting that doesn't get copied includes your Page Setup information, any graphs or shapes on each worksheet, your page breaks, and any column widths.

Tip! If you're looking for a better Cascade function that does things like copy all of your formatting and has intelligent tab naming, visit http://dev.hyperion.com/. Their Downloads section has several replacements for Cascade.

Since your headers and footers will not be copied when Cascade makes your new spreadsheets, you can enter it in the boxes next to Header and Footer. Since we have a formatted report, do not check the box next to *Suppress Missing Rows* or our formatting will get messed up as rows get suppressed. Don't check the box next to *Include Table of Contents*. Click *OK* and watch as sheets are generated in front of your very eyes:

	A	B	C	D	E	F
1		**Market:**	Central			
2		**Product:**	Product			
3		**Scenario:**	Scenario			
4						
5		**Qtr1**	**Qtr2**	**Qtr3**	**Qtr4**	**Year**
6	Sales	31,412	33,056	33,754	31,458	**129,680**
7	COGS	13,724	14,413	14,736	13,681	**56,554**
8	**Margin**	17,688	18,643	19,018	17,777	**73,126**
9						
10	Marketing	4,801	5,013	5,115	4,777	**19,706**
11	Payroll	3,705	3,723	3,705	3,705	**14,838**
12	Misc	73	81	86	80	**320**
13	**Total Expenses**	8,579	8,817	8,906	8,562	**34,864**
14						
15	**Profit**	**9,109**	**9,826**	**10,112**	**9,215**	**38,262**
16						
17	Expense %	27.31 %	26.67 %	26.39 %	27.22 %	**26.88 %**
18						

Notice that there is a tab for each of the four regions. Also notice that the tabs are annoyingly (as previously mentioned) numbered sequentially with no hint as to what's in each one. Feel free to rename the tabs at this point if that's your thing.

If we had checked the box on the *Format Options* tab next to *Include Table of Contents*, Essbase would have created a text file for us telling us what each tab number corresponded to. The file is placed in the same directory as the workbook is stored and it ends in a .LST extension. Here's what it looks like:

```
0.lst - Notepad
File  Edit  Format  View  Help
/****************************************************/
/*  File name:        c:\temp\0.lst */
/*  Creation date:    wednesday, October 25, 2006 9:27:42 PM */
/****************************************************/
1                       /* East    */
2                       /* west    */
3                       /* south   */
4                       /* Central */
```

We have no idea why it seems to have a fondness for slashes and asterisks, but as you can see, tab 4 is Central just as we see in the image above.

While it has many shortcomings, one of the neat things about Cascade is that it can cascade on multiple dimensions at the same time. Let's say that we wanted to generate a budget template for each state for each product that we'll then e-mail to the people in charge of entering the budgets. Generating all these sheets manually would take quite a while, but thankfully, we have Cascade.

Close the cascaded workbook with the four tabs, and go back to your original workbook. In the cell that says "Scenario" (cell C3, probably), type in the word Budget. This time, highlight *both* Market and Product (presumably, cells C1:C2) and choose *Essbase >> Cascade*. Go to the *Cascade Information* tab.

Notice that this time we see multiple dimensions. Highlight each one and change the zoom level from *Next Level* to *Bottom Level*. Click on *Destination Options*:

Since we're going to want to e-mail the cascaded workbooks to different people, leave the "Destination Types" set to *Separate Workbooks*. Go ahead and select a destination directory by clicking on the *Browse* button. We've chosen C:\Temp\, but feel free to put the files wherever you'll remember to delete them later. Don't check the box for *Open Created Files*, because we're going to be generating a lot of files. Finally, type the letter "B" in the Prefix box to let the users know that the file they're receiving is brought to them by the letter *B* (actually, it's so they'll know it's *B*udget-related, but we always did like Sesame Street). Click on the *Format Options* tab:

Check *Copy Formatting* and *Include Table of Contents*. With all the spreadsheets we're going to be making, we're going to need a table of contents to tell everything apart. Before you click on *OK*, we want to give you a fair bit of warning: you're about to generate over 300 spreadsheets of information. If you have a slow desktop, a slow network, a slow Essbase server, a lack of patience, or are prone to seizures brought on by flashing lights, you do not want to click *OK*. Just trust me that it will work and move on to the next paragraph.

If you clicked OK (you foolish, foolish child), your screen flashed for a few minutes as it generated 320 spreadsheets of data:

B0.LST | B132.xls | B167.xls | B200.xls | B235.xls | B27.xls | B303.xls | B5.xls | B84.xls
B1.xls | B133.xls | B168.xls | B201.xls | B236.xls | B270.xls | B304.xls | B50.xls | B85.xls
B10.xls | B134.xls | B169.xls | B202.xls | B237.xls | B271.xls | B305.xls | B51.xls | B86.xls
B100.xls | B135.xls | B17.xls | B203.xls | B238.xls | B272.xls | B306.xls | B52.xls | B87.xls
B101.xls | B136.xls | B170.xls | B204.xls | B239.xls | B273.xls | B307.xls | B53.xls | B88.xls
B102.xls | B137.xls | B171.xls | B205.xls | B24.xls | B274.xls | B308.xls | B54.xls | B89.xls
B103.xls | B138.xls | B172.xls | B206.xls | B240.xls | B275.xls | B309.xls | B55.xls | B9.xls
B104.xls | B139.xls | B173.xls | B207.xls | B241.xls | B276.xls | B31.xls | B56.xls | B90.xls
B105.xls | B14.xls | B174.xls | B208.xls | B242.xls | B277.xls | B310.xls | B57.xls | B91.xls
B106.xls | B140.xls | B175.xls | B209.xls | B243.xls | B278.xls | B311.xls | B58.xls | B92.xls
B107.xls | B141.xls | B176.xls | B21.xls | B244.xls | B279.xls | B312.xls | B59.xls | B93.xls
B108.xls | B142.xls | B177.xls | B210.xls | B245.xls | B28.xls | B313.xls | B6.xls | B94.xls
B109.xls | B143.xls | B178.xls | B211.xls | B246.xls | B280.xls | B314.xls | B60.xls | B95.xls
B11.xls | B144.xls | B179.xls | B212.xls | B247.xls | B281.xls | B315.xls | B61.xls | B96.xls
B110.xls | B145.xls | B18.xls | B213.xls | B248.xls | B282.xls | B316.xls | B62.xls | B97.xls
B111.xls | B146.xls | B180.xls | B214.xls | B249.xls | B283.xls | B317.xls | B63.xls | B98.xls
B112.xls | B147.xls | B181.xls | B215.xls | B25.xls | B284.xls | B318.xls | B64.xls | B99.xls
B113.xls | B148.xls | B182.xls | B216.xls | B250.xls | B285.xls | B319.xls | B65.xls |
B114.xls | B149.xls | B183.xls | B217.xls | B251.xls | B286.xls | B32.xls | B66.xls |
B115.xls | B15.xls | B184.xls | B218.xls | B252.xls | B287.xls | B320.xls | B67.xls |
B116.xls | B150.xls | B185.xls | B219.xls | B253.xls | B288.xls | B33.xls | B68.xls |
B117.xls | B151.xls | B186.xls | B22.xls | B254.xls | B289.xls | B34.xls | B69.xls |
B118.xls | B152.xls | B187.xls | B220.xls | B255.xls | B29.xls | B35.xls | B7.xls |
B119.xls | B153.xls | B188.xls | B221.xls | B256.xls | B290.xls | B36.xls | B70.xls |
B12.xls | B154.xls | B189.xls | B222.xls | B257.xls | B291.xls | B37.xls | B71.xls |
B120.xls | B155.xls | B19.xls | B223.xls | B258.xls | B292.xls | B38.xls | B72.xls |
B121.xls | B156.xls | B190.xls | B224.xls | B259.xls | B293.xls | B39.xls | B73.xls |
B122.xls | B157.xls | B191.xls | B225.xls | B26.xls | B294.xls | B4.xls | B74.xls |
B123.xls | B158.xls | B192.xls | B226.xls | B260.xls | B295.xls | B40.xls | B75.xls |
B124.xls | B159.xls | B193.xls | B227.xls | B261.xls | B296.xls | B41.xls | B76.xls |
B125.xls | B16.xls | B194.xls | B228.xls | B262.xls | B297.xls | B42.xls | B77.xls |
B126.xls | B160.xls | B195.xls | B229.xls | B263.xls | B298.xls | B43.xls | B78.xls |
B127.xls | B161.xls | B196.xls | B23.xls | B264.xls | B299.xls | B44.xls | B79.xls |
B128.xls | B162.xls | B197.xls | B230.xls | B265.xls | B3.xls | B45.xls | B8.xls |
B129.xls | B163.xls | B198.xls | B231.xls | B266.xls | B30.xls | B46.xls | B80.xls |
B13.xls | B164.xls | B199.xls | B232.xls | B267.xls | B300.xls | B47.xls | B81.xls |
B130.xls | B165.xls | B2.xls | B233.xls | B268.xls | B301.xls | B48.xls | B82.xls |
B131.xls | B166.xls | B20.xls | B234.xls | B269.xls | B302.xls | B49.xls | B83.xls |

Our saving grace in this morass of files is the little file in the top-left corner: B0.LST. This file contains the table of contents detailing what's in every spreadsheet. If you clicked *OK* (sucker), go ahead and open B0.LST in Notepad:

```
B0.lst - Notepad                                                      _ □ X

File  Edit  Format  View  Help
/************************************************************/
/*  File name:      c:\Temp\Cascade\B0.lst */
/*  Creation date:  Wednesday, October 25, 2006 9:55:22 PM */
/************************************************************/
c:\Temp\Cascade\B1.xls         /*  New York, Cola  */
c:\Temp\Cascade\B2.xls         /*  New York, Diet Cola  */
c:\Temp\Cascade\B3.xls         /*  New York, Caffeine Free Cola  */
c:\Temp\Cascade\B4.xls         /*  New York, Old Fashioned  */
c:\Temp\Cascade\B5.xls         /*  New York, Diet Root Beer  */
c:\Temp\Cascade\B6.xls         /*  New York, Sasparilla  */
c:\Temp\Cascade\B7.xls         /*  New York, Birch Beer  */
c:\Temp\Cascade\B8.xls         /*  New York, Dark Cream  */
c:\Temp\Cascade\B9.xls         /*  New York, Vanilla Cream  */
c:\Temp\Cascade\B10.xls        /*  New York, Diet Cream  */
c:\Temp\Cascade\B11.xls        /*  New York, Grape  */
c:\Temp\Cascade\B12.xls        /*  New York, Orange  */
c:\Temp\Cascade\B13.xls        /*  New York, Strawberry  */
c:\Temp\Cascade\B14.xls        /*  New York, Diet Cola  */
c:\Temp\Cascade\B15.xls        /*  New York, Diet Root Beer  */
c:\Temp\Cascade\B16.xls        /*  New York, Diet Cream  */
c:\Temp\Cascade\B17.xls        /*  Massachusetts, Cola  */
c:\Temp\Cascade\B18.xls        /*  Massachusetts, Diet Cola  */
c:\Temp\Cascade\B19.xls        /*  Massachusetts, Caffeine Free Cola  */
c:\Temp\Cascade\B20.xls        /*  Massachusetts, Old Fashioned  */
c:\Temp\Cascade\B21.xls        /*  Massachusetts, Diet Root Beer  */
c:\Temp\Cascade\B22.xls        /*  Massachusetts, Sasparilla  */
c:\Temp\Cascade\B23.xls        /*  Massachusetts, Birch Beer  */
c:\Temp\Cascade\B24.xls        /*  Massachusetts, Dark Cream  */
c:\Temp\Cascade\B25.xls        /*  Massachusetts, Vanilla Cream  */
c:\Temp\Cascade\B26.xls        /*  Massachusetts, Diet Cream  */
c:\Temp\Cascade\B27.xls        /*  Massachusetts, Grape  */
c:\Temp\Cascade\B28.xls        /*  Massachusetts, Orange  */
c:\Temp\Cascade\B29.xls        /*  Massachusetts, Strawberry  */
c:\Temp\Cascade\B30.xls        /*  Massachusetts, Diet Cola  */
```

While not terribly pretty, it is easy to tell that the person responsible for New York's budget should get sheets B1 through B16.

Selection Retrievals

There are certain times when you'll want to have two sets of Essbase data on one sheet. Say we wanted to create a report that had Actual on the top half of the page and Budget on the bottom half:

	B	C	D	E	F	G
2			**Market**	**Product**	**Actual**	
3		**Qtr1**	**Qtr2**	**Qtr3**	**Qtr4**	**Year**
4	Sales	95,820	101,679	105,215	98,141	**400,855**
5	COGS	42,877	45,362	47,343	43,754	**179,336**
6	**Margin**	52,943	56,317	57,872	54,387	**221,519**
7						
8	Marketing	15,839	16,716	17,522	16,160	**66,237**
9	Payroll	12,168	12,243	12,168	12,168	**48,747**
10	Misc	233	251	270	259	**1,013**
11	**Total Expenses**	28,240	29,210	29,960	28,587	**115,997**
12						
13	**Profit**	**24,703**	**27,107**	**27,912**	**25,800**	**105,522**
14						
15			**Market**	**Product**	**Budget**	
16		**Qtr1**	**Qtr2**	**Qtr3**	**Qtr4**	**Year**
17	Sales	89,680	95,240	98,690	89,470	**373,080**
18	COGS	38,140	40,460	42,280	38,060	**158,940**
19	**Margin**	51,540	54,780	56,410	51,410	**214,140**
20						
21	Marketing	11,900	12,700	13,370	11,550	**49,520**
22	Payroll	9,060	9,210	9,060	7,910	**35,240**
23	Misc	-	-	-	-	**-**
24	**Total Expenses**	20,960	21,910	22,430	19,460	**84,760**
25						
26	**Profit**	**30,580**	**32,870**	**33,980**	**31,950**	**129,380**
27						

If you created this spreadsheet and chose *Essbase >> Retrieve*, you'd receive the following error:

This is actually my favorite Essbase Add-In error, because it almost comes across as a poorly worded marketing message. The presence of the word "Currently" gives you hope that if you just wait until the next release, Essbase will support multiple reports per retrieval! Not to dash your hopes, but this error message has been there for over ten years and they still haven't added it. Give up and stop waiting, because there is a workaround.

If you highlight a section of cells before you choose *Essbase >> Retrieve*, Essbase will ignore everything outside of those highlighted cells. The secret in this case is to highlight the top range (in the above example, cells B2:G13) and then retrieve:

	B	C	D	E	F	G
2			Market	Product	Actual	
3		Qtr1	Qtr2	Qtr3	Qtr4	Year
4	Sales	95,820	101,679	105,215	98,141	400,855
5	COGS	42,877	45,362	47,343	43,754	179,336
6	**Margin**	52,943	56,317	57,872	54,387	221,519
7						
8	Marketing	15,839	16,716	17,522	16,160	66,237
9	Payroll	12,168	12,243	12,168	12,168	48,747
10	Misc	233	251	270	259	1,013
11	**Total Expenses**	28,240	29,210	29,960	28,587	115,997
12						
13	**Profit**	24,703	27,107	27,912	25,800	105,522
14						
15			Market	Product	Budget	
16		Qtr1	Qtr2	Qtr3	Qtr4	Year
17	Sales	89,620	95,240	98,690	89,470	373,080
18	COGS					

Voila, no error. Now choose the cells below and choose *Essbase >> Retrieve* to get your second range of data. The Selection Retrieve method (as it's commonly known) is also valuable if you have extra text around your retrieve that you want Essbase to ignore during your retrieval.

Selection Retrieval can be used even if you have multiple ranges on your spreadsheet and each one needs to retrieve from a *different* database. In this case, here's what you do:

1. Connect to the first database.
2. Highlight the first range of cells and retrieve.
3. Connect to the second database.
4. Highlight the second range of cells and retrieve.

Tip! Make sure you highlight all your member names and the cells where you want the data to appear. If you just highlight the data cells, Essbase will return a "Data item found before member" error.

EssCell

There will undoubtedly come a day when you want to retrieve one or two values from Essbase into a much larger spreadsheet. Say you're creating a report and you need to retrieve Actual Profit for the year into a single cell. Essbase provides a function called *EssCell()* that will retrieve a single value from an Essbase database.

Go to a blank spreadsheet and connect to Sample.Basic. If you do not connect to Essbase, the *EssCell()* function will return #N/A. Go into a cell and enter the following formula:

```
=EssCell("Profit","Actual")
```

	A
1	Dear Boss,
2	
3	I would really like you to reconsider your decision to fire me and replace me with a large, potted plant. I'm sure that your decision was made before you saw that our profit for the year has increased to:
4	=EssCell("Profit", "Actual")
5	
6	
7	Sincerely,
8	Your Humble Servant
9	

For any dimensions we haven't included (in this case, Market, Product, and Year), Essbase will conclude that we want the top members of those dimensions. After you press Enter on the formula above, the cell should return the familiar value of 105,522:

	A
1	Dear Boss,
2	
3	I would really like you to reconsider your decision to fire me and replace me with a large, potted plant. I'm sure that your decision was made before you saw that our profit for the year has increased to:
4	105,522
5	
6	
7	Sincerely,
8	Your Humble Servant
9	

In addition to the #N/A error (which means that your spreadsheet is not connected to Essbase), *EssCell()* might return two other errors. #VALUE! means that one or more of the member names in your list is invalid. #NAME? will generally be shown when you forgot to surround one of more of your member names in double quotes.

Never use more than one or two *EssCell()* functions on a single spreadsheet. Each *EssCell()* on a sheet does a separate retrieve to Essbase, so they can be very time consuming. If you need multiple values, use a standard Essbase retrieve.

Tip!

If you are going to send someone a spreadsheet containing EssCell() formulas, replace the formulas first with their actual values (*Edit >> Copy, Edit >> Paste Values*). Otherwise, they will get #N/A errors when they open the spreadsheet unless they connect to Essbase too.

Chapter 5:
Become a Master User

Now that you've mastered the majority of the Essbase Add-In menu items, it's time to take your skills to the next level of mastery. It is not enough to simply understand how to retrieve data. Grasshopper, you must understand *why* data retrieves the way it does. One of the questions you must have been asking yourself at this point is "why do some retrieves take longer than others?"

SPEEDY RETRIEVES

Essbase retrieves are normally measured in seconds or sub-seconds. If your retrieves ever take more than thirty seconds, there are some things to check:
- Hardware performance.
- Retrieval size.
- Use of attribute dimensions.
- Use of dynamically calculated members.
- Use of dynamic time series.
- Dense vs. sparse retrievals.
- Essbase database settings.

Let's begin by assuming that your desktop, network, and Essbase server aren't older than dirt. If your hardware is more than a few years old, replace it, because doing so will definitely make things faster. Computers are easier to upgrade than people.

If your hardware is fairly recent, begin by looking at how much data you're retrieving. While 500 rows by 20 columns doesn't seem like much, that's over 10,000 cells of data you're asking Essbase to return. While you can't exactly eliminate every other row on your report to save space ("Sorry about the missing numbers, boss, but Edward Roske told me that deleting even numbered rows on my reports would cut my retrieval time in half!"), you'll at least be aware of why your report is taking a long time.

The next thing to look at is your use of members from attribute dimensions, dynamically calculated members, and dynamic time series members. As mentioned earlier, all of these members are not pre-calculated. A retrieve that is accessing stored members will almost always run more quickly than one that accesses dynamic members.

One of the most common mistakes people make is putting the top member from an attribute dimension on their report. Notice the "Caffeinated" member on this retrieve:

	A	B	C	D	E	F	
1			Market	Product	Actual	Caffeinated	
2		Qtr1	Qtr2	Qtr3	Qtr4	Year	
3	Sales	95,820	101,679	105,215	98,141	**400,855**	
4	COGS	42,877	45,362	47,343	43,754	**179,336**	
5	**Margin**	52,943	56,317	57,872	54,387	**221,519**	
6							
7	Marketing	15,839	16,716	17,522	16,160	**66,237**	
8	Payroll	12,168	12,243	12,168	12,168	**48,747**	
9	Misc	233	251	270	259	**1,013**	
10	**Total Expenses**	28,240	29,210	29,960	28,587	**115,997**	
11							
12	**Profit**	**24,703**	**27,107**	**27,912**	**25,800**	105,522	
13							

The presence of this member doesn't change the totals at all (we still have 105,522 in the bottom-right corner) but it takes a retrieve that would be against stored information and makes it entirely dynamic. Why? Because we are telling Essbase to go grab all the products that are Caffeinated_True and add them together, and then grab all the products that are Caffeinated_False and add them together, and finally, add Caffeinated_False to Caffeinated_True to get total Caffeinated. Well, this is the same value as if we'd never asked for Caffeinated at all!

The solution is obvious: delete the Caffeinated member and our retrieve will speed up by more than an order of magnitude. The more cynical among you might ask why Essbase isn't smart enough to notice that it's dynamically adding up every product when it could just take the stored Product total and be done with it. We don't have a good answer for that, so we'll pretend that we can't hear your question.

Dense vs. Sparse Retrievals

Density vs. Sparsity is a tricky subject, because it really gets in to how Essbase stores data behind the scenes and that's normally only of interest to an Essbase administrator, a developer, or a highly paid (but deservedly so) consultant. We're going to touch on the subject just enough so that you understand how it affects your retrieval times.

Our base dimensions (i.e., not the attribute dimensions) fall into one of two types: dense and sparse. Dense dimensions are dimensions for which most combinations are loaded with data. Sparse dimensions are often missing values.

In Sample.Basic, the dense dimensions are Year, Measures, and Scenario. This is because when there's a value for one month (say, Sales) there tends to be a value for every month. If there's a value for Sales, there tends to be a value for COGS, Marketing, and so on. If there's a number for Actual, there tends to be a value for Budget. As such, Year, Measures, and Scenario are said to be dense dimensions.

The sparse dimensions for Sample.Basic are Product and Market. This is because not every product tends to be sold in every state. As we saw earlier, out of seven possible caffeinated drinks, Massachusetts only sold three of them. As such, Product and Market are said to be sparse dimensions.

Why does this matter to you? Well, a retrieve consisting of dense dimensions (and only dense dimensions) in the rows and columns will tend to be much, much faster than a report with a sparse dimension in the rows or the columns.

When a report only has dense dimensions in the rows and columns, we refer to this as a dense retrieval. Here is an example of a dense retrieval against Sample.Basic:

	A	B	C	D	E	
1		Product	Market	Scenario		
2		Jan	Feb	Mar	Apr	Ma
3	Sales	31,538	32,069	32,213	32,917	33
4	COGS	14,160	14,307	14,410	14,675	15
5	Margin	17,378	17,762	17,803	18,242	18
6	Marketing	5,223	5,289	5,327	5,421	5
7	Payroll	4,056	4,056	4,056	4,081	4
8	Misc	75	71	87	96	
9	Total Expenses	9,354	9,416	9,470	9,598	9
10	Profit	8,024	8,346	8,333	8,644	8

It's a dense retrieval because Measures is in the rows, Year is in the columns, and both are dense dimensions. Notice that all the intersections tend to have values loaded to them. This is an example of a sparse retrieval against Sample.Basic:

	A	B	C	D	E	F
1		Jan	Sales	Actual		
2		New York	Massachusetts	Florida	Connecticut	New Hampshire	Cal
3	Cola	678	494	210	310	120
4	Diet Cola			200		
5	Caffeine Free Cola					93
6	Old Fashioned	61	126	190	180	90
7	Diet Root Beer			180	130	
8	Sasparilla					
9	Birch Beer	490	341			65
10	Dark Cream	483	130	120	190	76
11	Vanilla Cream	180		150	170	
12	Diet Cream			110		
13	Grape	234	80	80	123	45
14	Orange	219				
15	Strawberry	134	80	81	94	43

This is a sparse retrieval because Product is in the rows, Market is in the columns, and both are sparse dimensions. Notice that a number of the values are missing. Though it doesn't have many more cells to retrieve, this retrieval will take many times longer than the one above because of how Essbase retrieves data from sparse dimensions. Simply put, for sparse retrievals, Essbase retrieves a lot of data into memory on the server side that you'll never see or use.

While we can't change which dimensions are dense or sparse (that's a setting controlled for each database by the Essbase Administrator), we can be aware that sparse retrievals will take much longer than dense retrievals.

If you've tried all of the tips above and your retrieval is still taking a long time, it might be an issue with some of the database settings on the Essbase server. There are a number of settings such as density/sparsity (mentioned above), data caches, index caches, and so forth that someone qualified in Essbase can tune to improve retrieval performance. The bad news is that you can't tweak these yourself, but the good is that they can be tweaked by someone else.

QUERY DESIGNER

One of the hardest things about retrieving data into Excel is keeping track of where your data is located. Which dimension do we want in the rows? What Products do we currently have selected? Where in the name of all that's holy did my Measures dimension disappear to? The Essbase Query Designer (often called Query Designer or simply EQD) was created to give users a graphical means of building, saving, and running complex queries against Essbase.

Query Designer interacts with Excel but in a less direct manner than the rest of the Essbase Add-In. When you launch EQD, a window opens that floats above Excel in a big brother sort of way. Go to a blank spreadsheet and choose *Essbase >> Query Designer* to see the magical hovering window:

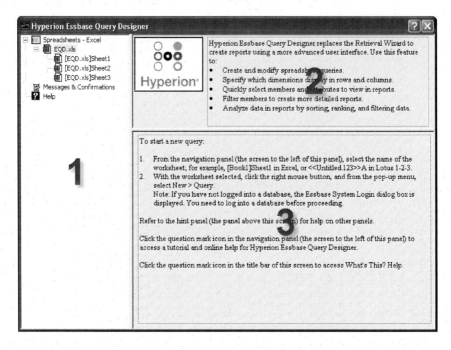

There are three main parts to the Query Designer:
1. Navigation Panel - This section (which is supposed to look kind of like Windows Explorer) lets you navigate to the various parts of a query. When in doubt about what actions are available to you, right-click on an item in this section.
2. Hint Panel - This section gives you a brief description of the item you have selected in the Navigation Panel. The hints aren't always helpful.
3. Properties Panel - This section shows you information about whatever you have selected in the Navigation Panel and lets you modify that information as well. This is where all the real work gets done.

Creating a Query

Let's say that we want to produce a report that lists states down the side and Actual, Budget, Variance, and Variance % across the columns. Further, let's make the report for Profit, Product, and Year.

Begin by right-clicking on the name of a blank sheet in the Navigation pane. A menu of actions should appear:

Some of these options are very similar to the choices under the *Essbase* menu. *Connect*, *Disconnect*, and *Retrieve* all perform exactly the same Essbase actions as the normal menu. Choose *Connect* to connect to Sample.Basic.

Right-click on your connected sheet and choose *New*. The *New* menu can be used to add a blank workbook or worksheet to Excel (in case you forgot to do that before opening EQD). In our case, we want to create a new query, so choose *Query* (strange, we know):

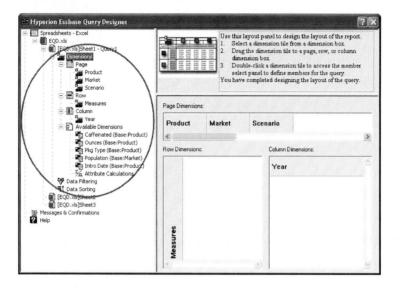

The Navigation panel will expand to show you the current orientation of all of your dimensions. The Properties panel will also show you your dimension layout but in a more graphical layout. Sharp-eyed readers paying attention to the Hint panel will notice that the Properties panel has temporarily been renamed the "Layout panel." This is designed to confused sharp-eyed readers. For our purposes, keep calling it the Properties panel.

In the Navigation panel, six new sub-items (each with its own sub-items) have been added:

- Page - This shows the dimensions that apply to the whole report.
- Row - This shows the dimensions that will be down the rows.
- Column - This shows the dimensions that will be across the columns.
- Available Dimensions - This shows the attribute dimensions (see page 60) that are not currently in use.
- Data Filtering - This is used for limiting the query to the top or bottom set of numbers (for instance, the Top 10 products based on sales). It can also be used to apply restrictions to the data (for instance, only show members that have sales greater than 500).
- Data Sorting - This is used to sort your data. It cannot be used to sort your members alphabetically, so don't even try it, Bub.

As you'll recall, our query wants to have Market in the rows and Scenario in the columns. Using the Properties panel, drag-and-drop the tile for *Market* to the rows, *Scenario* to the columns, and the other three dimensions (*Measures, Product, Year*) to the page. You can also drag-and-drop the dimensions around in the Navigation panel. When you're all done, your Properties panel should look like this:

To select specific members from each dimension, you can either double-click the appropriate tile or click the dimension in the Navigation panel. Let's start by clicking on the *Product* dimension in the Navigation panel.

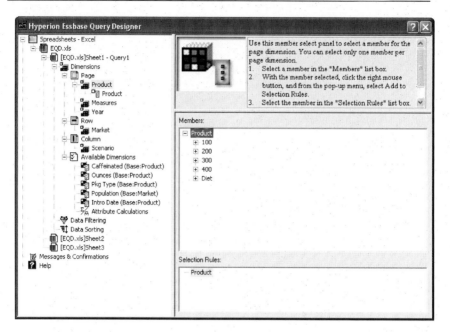

Highlight *Product* in the Properties panel (which the playful Hint panel has now taken to calling the "Member Select panel"). To add the Product member to the Selection Rules at the bottom, double-click on *Product* in the Properties panel. You can also right-click on *Product* and choose *Add to Selection Rules*:

Since Product is a page dimension, only one member is allowed in the Selection Rules section. Row and column dimension will allow multiple members. Use this same method to select *Profit* from the *Measures* dimension and *Year* from the *Year* dimension. Notice that the members you selected appear on the left in the Navigation panel:

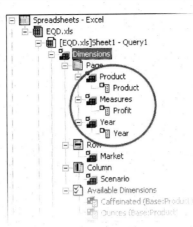

Click on the *Market* dimension in the Navigation panel. For the Market dimension, we don't want a specific member, but rather, we want all of the states (the level-0 members). Right-click on the *Market* member in the Properties panel and choose *View By >> Level*:

The three levels of the Market dimension will appear. Double-click on *Lev0,Market* so that it appears under Selection Rules.

Click on the *Scenario* dimension in the Navigation panel so that it appears in the Properties panel. For the Scenario dimension, we want the children of Scenario. While we could highlight the members from Actual to Variance % and add all of them at once to the Selection Rules, let's try a slicker method. Add just the Scenario member to the Selection Rules (double-click on *Scenario* in the Properties panel),

In the Selection Rules box at the bottom, right-click on *Scenario* and choose *Select*. The choices that appear (*Children, Children and Member,* et al) are the same ones that you get when you right-click on a member in Member Select. Choose *Children*:

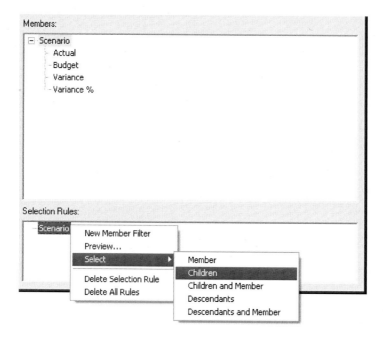

All of the selection options that are available in Member Select are available somewhere in EQD, but they're often called something else (and they probably look different too). For instance, in Member Select, we can right-click on a member and choose *Subset* to get to a window that lets us do things like limit ourselves to a specific UDA or pattern. In EQD, you get to "Subset" by right-clicking on a member in Selection Rules and choosing *New Member Filter*. If you choose *New Member Filter*, this window appears in the Properties panel:

Method:	UDA	▾

	Generation Name
	Level Name
Operator:	Pattern Matches
	UDA

Value:	

Just like the Subset in Member Select, you can create multiple new member filters and add AND/OR logic to the filters as well.

Try It! Create a new member filter, but remember to delete it afterwards so you can follow along with the next steps.

Our report doesn't need any member filters, so if you have correctly chosen the specified members, your Navigation panel should look like this:

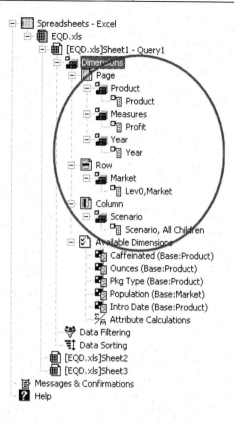

At this point, we have a complete query. Go ahead and run the query by right-clicking on the query name (in our example above, it's called Query1) and choosing *Apply Query*:

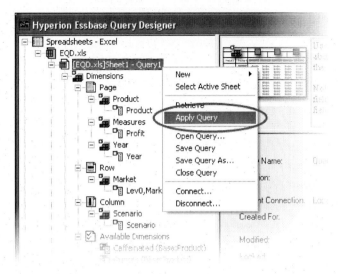

In Excel, you should now see:

	A	B	C	D	E
1			Product	Profit	Year
2		Actual	Budget	Variance	Variance %
3	New York	8,202	9,220	(1,018)	(11)
4	Massachusetts	6,712	7,300	(588)	(8)
5	Florida	5,029	5,900	(871)	(15)
6	Connecticut	3,093	3,960	(867)	(22)
7	New Hampshire	1,125	2,010	(885)	(44)
8	California	12,964	14,190	(1,226)	(9)
9	Oregon	5,062	6,270	(1,208)	(19)
10	Washington	4,641	6,150	(1,509)	(25)
11	Utah	3,155	5,240	(2,085)	(40)
12	Nevada	4,039	5,330	(1,291)	(24)
13	Texas	6,425	7,950	(1,525)	

Advanced Queries

It is admittedly true that this retrieve could have been done using the normal Essbase Add-In, but let's go back to EQD and do some things that would cause the Add-In to curl into a fetal position and bawl its eyes out.

Choose *Essbase >> QueryDesigner*. In the Navigation panel, click on *Data Sorting*:

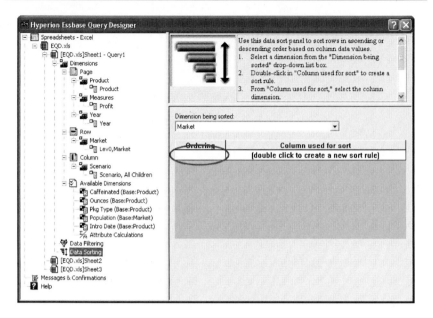

Notice that the tricky Hint panel is again trying to confuse us by renaming the Properties panel the "data sort panel." Do not be fooled by these Jedi mind tricks: the lower-right panel is always the Properties panel.

Let's begin by sorting our numbers from the highest actual profit to the lowest. In the dimension drop-down, the only dimension you'll see is Market, because this is the only dimension in the rows. Right below *Ordering* (the circled area in the image above), double-click. This should add the default first sort. The default sort is always to sort the first column (in our case, Actual) in ascending order:

Change the drop-down from *Ascending* to *Descending*. Rerun the query by right-clicking on the query name and choosing *Apply Query*. Your report in Excel should now look like:

	A	B	C	D	E
1			Product	Profit	Year
2		Actual	Budget	Variance	Variance %
3	California	12,964	14,190	(1,226)	(9)
4	Illinois	12,577	14,640	(2,063)	(14)
5	Iowa	9,061	9,170	(109)	(1)
6	New York	8,202	9,220	(1,018)	(11)
7	Colorado	7,227	8,810	(1,583)	(18)
8	Massachusetts	6,712	7,300	(588)	(8)
9	Texas	6,425	7,950	(1,525)	(19)
10	Oregon	5,062	6,270	(1,208)	(19)
11	Florida	5,029	5,900	(871)	(15)

Now California rightly takes it place at the top of the list as the beverage profitability capital of the USA. It's still difficult, though, to determine which states are missing their budgets by the most (and which ones are beating their budgets). Go back to EQD and click on *Data Filtering* in the Navigation panel:

In the Properties panel (or as the puckish Hint panel has taken to calling it, the "data filter panel"), you'll see options for ranking and restricting data. Ranking limits the data returned from the Essbase server to a specified number of top or bottom values. This is commonly called "Top Ten" reporting, though you can limit it to however many you want; the default is 25 rows.

Note! Data filtering and sorting are performed on the Essbase server before the data is ever returned to Excel. Filtering through thousands of records on the server and only returning the top ten to Excel is much faster than returning all the data to Excel and letting you filter on your desktop.

While California is the most profitable, that might just be because it's big (and people in California tend to overpay for soft drinks). Let's find out which five states exceeded their budget by the most (and the five that missed their budget by the most). Check the box next to *Top* and change the number of rows to 5. Check the box next to *Bottom* and also change the rows to 5.

The only dimension that will appear in the ranking is Market, because it's the only dimension in the rows. We don't want the top/bottom 5 based on actual. We want to know which states had the greatest percent difference between budget and actual. In the box underneath *Column used for ranking*, select *Variance %*. Your Properties panel should now look like this:

Rank: ☑ Top 5 Rows ☑ Bottom 5 Rows

Dimension being ranked:
Market

Column used for ranking:
Variance %

Data Restrictions:
(double click to create a new data restriction)

The greatest variances are going to be places where we had no budget (since we didn't plan on selling any beverages in that market) but we ended up having actual profit. We're going to restrict our data to just the variances where budgets are not #Missing. Double-click just below *Data Restrictions* (the circled area in the image above) to see the Properties panel turn into (per the psychotic Hint Panel) the data restrictions panel:

Use this data restrictions panel to filter data by comparing them to specific values.
1. Select one of the three options to specify the of value to compare the data against.
2. From the "Data" drop-down list box, select of comparison operator.
3. From the "Column used for filter" drop-down box, select the column dimension.

Retrieve rows where:

Data [is not ▼]

○ a value of [   ]

○ the data values in [Budget]

⦿ a #Missing value

Column used for filter:

[Budget ▼]

Combined with other Restrictions
○ And   ○ Or

Change the drop-down next to *Data* to say *is not* (since we want to only retrieve rows where the Budget *is not* #Missing). The check boxes below the drop-down are used to determine the type of restriction to perform:

- A value of - Use this when you want to compare values in one of your columns to a specific hard-coded value. For instance, if you only want to include rows with Actual profit of greater than 500, you would select ">" in the Data drop-down and type 500 in the box next to Value.

- The data values in - Use this when you want to compare one column of data against another column (such as, include all rows where Actual exceeded Budget).

- A #Missing value - Use this when you want to include or exclude rows that have no data in a specific column.

Since we want to exclude rows that have missing budgets, check the box next to *a #Missing value*. Set the *Column used for filter* drop-down to Budget. It is possible to set up multiple filters, but in our case, one is plenty. Your Navigation panel should now look like this:

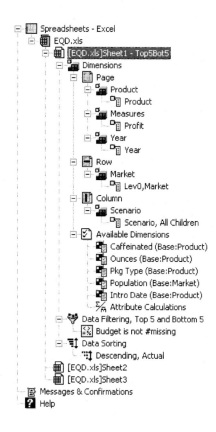

Rerun the query by again right-clicking on the query name and choosing *Apply Query* (see the image on page 107):

	A	B	C	D	E
1			Product	Profit	Year
2		Actual	Budget	Variance	Variance %
3	California	12,964	14,190	(1,226)	(9)
4	Illinois	12,577	14,640	(2,063)	(14)
5	Iowa	9,061	9,170	(109)	(1)
6	New York	8,202	9,220	(1,018)	(11)
7	Massachusetts	6,712	7,300	(588)	(8)
8	Wisconsin	3,547	4,950	(1,403)	(28)
9	Utah	3,155	5,240	(2,085)	(40)
10	Missouri	1,466	2,740	(1,274)	(46)
11	New Hampshire	1,125	2,010	(885)	(44)
12	New Mexico	330	1,330	(1,000)	(75)
13					

You'll immediately notice that not one of our states has met our budgeted profit for this year. Iowa came the closest, so we should probably send the Iowa manager a "thank you" note. New Mexico's profit is abysmal, so a "we hope you enjoy your next career" note would be more appropriate.

Before we continue, it would make sense to save our query in case we need to use it again in the future, because this is a pretty nifty query after all. Go back to EQD. At the moment, our query is called Query1 which isn't very descriptive, so right-click on Query1 and choose *Save Query As*:

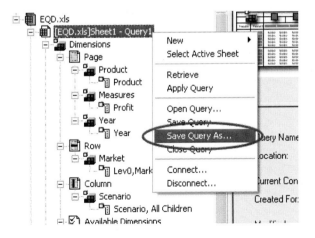

The Save As box that appears should look very similar to the one you saw before in Member Select when you wanted to save your list of members for later use:

If you want to share your query with others (and you have the necessary database privileges to do so), save your query to the server. For our purposes, select *Client*, give your query a name ("Top5Bot5" has a nice ring to it) and click *OK*.

To open and run up a saved query, follow these steps:

1. Open EQD.
2. Connect a worksheet to the appropriate database.
3. Right-click on the worksheet name and choose *Open Query*.
4. Right-click on the worksheet name and choose *Apply Query*.

Retrieving All Sheets

Before we conclude our discussion of the Essbase Query Designer, there is one neat trick to learn. Once you start creating retrieves in Excel, you'll start having workbooks with multiple sheets in them, each sheet containing a different Essbase retrieve. For instance, you might have a spreadsheet called FinancialReports.XLS that has tabs for Revenue, Expenses, PnL, BalanceSheet, CashFlow, and so on. When you open the workbook, you'll want a quick way to retrieve every worksheet in the workbook.

Many people solve this problem by writing a macro to select each sheet and retrieve before moving on to the next sheet, but EQD provides an easier way. Open up your spreadsheet with the multiple sheets in it. Open up EQD and right-click on the spreadsheet name:

Select *Retrieve All Worksheets* and EQD will zip through each of your sheets retrieving each along the way.

Note!

Each sheet needs to be connected to the correct database before running *Retrieve All Worksheets*.

Chapter 6:
Become a Smart View User

INTRODUCTION TO SMART VIEW

Many of you might think you're completely satisfied with the Essbase Add-In. Per Hyperion, you are wrong. Hyperion does have a point: among other things, the Essbase Add-In only works in Excel. What to do if you want to pull some Essbase data into a Word document? What if you need to make PowerPoint presentations with tables that automatically update from Essbase? Well, your problems are solved by the Hyperion Smart View Add-In.

Smart View is the new Add-In for Microsoft Office, integrating Hyperion products with Word, PowerPoint, Excel, and Outlook. It is the common Add-In for all Hyperion products including Essbase, Planning, Financial Management, Analyzer (Web Analysis), and Reports (Financial Reporting). It's Hyperion's version of the Swiss army knife and that makes you MacGyver.

When used in Excel, Smart View has similar functionality to the Essbase Add-In that we just covered. Yes: two different tools to do the same thing. The navigation is a bit different in Smart View but you can drill down, swap rows and columns, etc. Why do we need two tools? Since there is a world-wide problem of starving computer programmers, one might speculate that Hyperion is doing their part by keeping two development teams gainfully employed. But is there another reason?

Smart View brings Add-In functionality for all of the Hyperion products that need an Add-In. Yes, all of the products (okay, not Enterprise and Pillar, but all the major new products are there).

 If you're still using Pillar, upgrade to Hyperion Planning immediately. If you're content with Pillar, seek psychiatric help immediately.

Tip!

Smart View provides a single Excel interface for Hyperion Financial Management and Hyperion Planning, replacing the Planning Spreadsheet Add-In and HFM Spreadsheet Add-In. You can import BI+ documents (Analyzer, Reports, and other document images) into Microsoft Word or PowerPoint. You can import query ready or fully formatted grids into Microsoft Excel. Is there anyone at this point that doesn't want to toss the Essbase Add-In on the 8-track tape trash heap of obsolescence?

Actually, we know plenty of Luddites that are nowhere near ready to give up their Essbase Add-In. They've been using this tool for years and can use it blindfolded with one hand tied behind their back (yes, we've seen it done). The Essbase Add-In isn't going away for a long while.

If you install both the Essbase Add-In and the Smart View Add-In, you'll have two menu items in Excel. Here's a glimpse at the two menus:

Essbase	Help
Retrieve	
Keep Only	
Remove Only	
Zoom In	
Zoom Out	
Pivot	
Navigate Without Data	
Sample Data (Zoom In)	
Linked Objects...	
Query Designer...	
Visualize & Explore...	
FlashBack	
Options...	
Member Selection...	
Currency Report...	
Cascade...	
Retrieve & Lock	
Lock	
Unlock	
Send	
Calculation...	
Connect...	
Disconnect...	

Hyperion	Essbase	Help
Connection Manager...		
Active Connections	▶	
Reset Connection		
Ad Hoc Analysis	▶	
Forms	▶	
Functions	▶	
BI+ Content		
POV Manager...		
Undo		
Redo		
Member Selection...		
Refresh		
Refresh All		
Capture Formatting		
Submit Data		
Calculation Options	▶	
Cell Text		
Adjust		
Supporting Details		
Options...		
Help		
About...		

This section will focus on how the Smart View Add-In works with Essbase. We will show you how to perform Ad hoc analysis in Excel and how to bring data values into Word documents, Outlook e-mails, and PowerPoint presentations using SmartTags. While we will not show you how to scramble an egg while it's still inside its shell, Smart View probably could do that too.

DATABASE CONNECTION MANAGER

Before you can perform analysis using Smart View, you must first specify the database for which you want to connect. You will use the Database Connection Manager to do this. Ready, begin.

Connect to an Existing Database Connection

1. In Excel, select *Hyperion >> Connection Manager*:

A list of the existing database connections will display in the Connection Manager:

Connection Manager

Please select the data source you want to connect to. You can add or remove the data source by selecting the buttons below.

Name	Provider	Application/Cube	Descriptio
BPM_Forecast	Analytic Services Smart View Provider	EdenHPWF/Plan1	
EdenHFM	**Hyperion Financial Management**	**EdenHFM/Eden...**	**Eden Co**
EdenHP	Planning	EdenHP/Plan1	
EdenHPSA	Planning	EdenHPSA/Plan1	
EdenHPWF	Planning	EdenHPWF/Plan1	
EdenHVE	Analytic Services Smart View Provider	EdenHVE/Sales	
EdenSale	Analytic Services Smart View Provider	EdenSale/NewSale	
Hyperion System9 BI+	Hyperion Smart View Provider for Hyperion System 9 BI+		BI+ Repos

Help   Add   Delete   Edit   Connect   Change Password   Close

You can't help but notice that Smart View has a number of different types of database connections:

-   Analytic Services Smart View Provider – Use this provider to perform analysis against an Essbase database (e.g. swap rows and columns, drill down, etc.).
-   Financial Management Provider – Use this provider to connect to and perform Financial Management tasks.
-   Hyperion Smart View Provider for System 9 BI+ – Use this provider to import Financial Reporting, Web Analysis, or Interactive Reporting documents into Microsoft Office applications.

- Planning Provider – Use this provider to export Planning web forms and enter Planning data.

2. Select one of the Analytic Services Smart View Provider connections and click the *Connect* button.
3. Enter the user name and password:

Connect to Data Source ? X

User authentication needed. Please enter the user name and password for the connection entered earlier.

User Name: demoadmin

Password:

Help   Connect   Cancel

4. Click *Connect*.
5. Click *Close* to close the Connection Manager.
6. Make sure you are connected. Check the status in the lower left-hand corner of Excel.

Microsoft Excel - Book1

File Edit View Insert Format Tools Data Window Hyperion Essbase Help   Type a question for help

Connected [Online Connection: Sample_Basic] Application: Sample Cube: Basic

7. If you are not connected, set the connection via Active Connections (see next section).

View or Change Active Connections

1. Select *Hyperion >> Active Connections*.
2. Select the desired database connection:

Add a Database Connection via URL

The first time you use Smart View to connect to a database, you will need to create a new database connection.

1. In Excel, select *Hyperion >> Connection Manager:*

2. The Connection Manager will display.
3. Click the *Add* button.

There are two ways to add Database Connections: Registered Shared Services application and direct connection using a URL.

To use a direct connection via URL:

4. Select URL provider from the dropdown,
5. Select Hyperion Provider (for Essbase, Planning, and FM connections).
6. Enter the location URL:

For Analytic Services (Essbase), the default location URL is:

http(s)://<servername>:13080/smartview/SmartView

For Financial Management, the default location URL is:
http(s)://<servername>/hfmofficeprovider/
    hfmofficeprovider.aspx

For Planning, the default location URL is:
http(s)://<servername>:8300/HyperionPlanning/SmartVie
w

For Hyperion System 9 BI+ Provider, the default location URL is:
http(s)://<servername>:19000/workspace/browse/listxml

Check the Hyperion documentation to confirm the URLs for your version (yes, the URLS may change differ between System 9 versions).

7. Optionally, you can specify this connection to be the default connection. Click *Next* and the database repository window will display.
8. Select the desired Essbase server.
9. Enter a valid Essbase user name and password:

Select Database or Repository ✕

Please select the application you want to add to the connection. To select a different server, click Back and enter a new URL.

selecting the buttons

⊟ Servers
  ⊞ demodrive

e | Description ▲

n1

Connect to Data Source ? ✕

User authentication needed. Please enter the user name and password for the connection entered earlier.

User Name: demoadmin

Password: xxxxxx

Help | Help | Connect | Cancel

10. Click *Connect* and a list of the Essbase applications and databases will display.
11. Select Sample.Basic:

Select Database or Repository ✕

Please select the application you want to add to the connection. To select a different server, click Back and enter a new URL.

⊟ demodrive
  ⊞ Demo
  ⊟ Sample
    ◈ Basic
    ◈ Xchgrate
    ◈ Interntl
    ◈ Federal
  ⊞ Sample_U
  ⊞ Samppart
  ⊞ Sampeast
  ⊞ DMDemo
  ⊞ ASOsamp
  ⊞ EdenSale

Help | Back | Next | Cancel

12. Click *Next*.
13. Enter a name and description for the database connection:

14. Click *Finish*.
15. The new database connection will now be listed in the Connection Manager. Select the Connection and click *Connect*:

16. Click *Close* to close the Connection Manager.

Add a Database Connection via Shared Services

You will follow the same initial steps to create a database connection.

1. In Excel, select *Hyperion >> Connection Manager*.
2. The Connection Manager will display.
3. Click the *Add* button and select Shared Services:

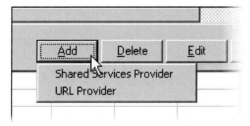

4. The Connection window will display. Verify the Shared Services URL:

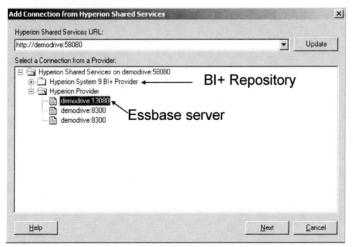

5. Click *Update* and a list of available providers in Shared Services will display.
6. Select the Essbase Server:

Note!

You will need to know the Essbase port number. The default port is 8300. Memorize this and impress your friends.

7. Click *Next*.

The remaining steps are the same as steps 8-16 of the URL database connection steps.

Tip!

Why should you use a Shared Services database connection versus a direct URL database connection?

Shared Services will store the provider URLs for all Hyperion products in one place (so you don't have to know each individual URL for each product; you only need to know the Shared Services connection information).

Try It!

Use the Connection Manager to edit and then delete the connection you just added.

READY TO ANALYZE

With Smart View, you can do most of the same tasks that you can in the Essbase Add-In. Let's take a look and see how things work in this new world of Smart View.

Turn Off Essbase Add-In

Before we get started, if you have both the Essbase Add-In and the Smart View Add-In installed, let's turn off some of the options for the Essbase Add-In.

1. Select *Essbase >> Options*.
2. Select the *Global* tab.
3. Uncheck *Enable Secondary Button* and *Enable Double-Clicking*:

Essbase Options

Display | Zoom | Mode | Global

— Mouse Actions —
☐ Limit to Connected Sheets
☐ Enable Secondary Button
☐ Enable Double-Clicking
   ☐ Enable Linked Object Browsing

If you leave these options checked, when you double-click or right click, the Essbase Add-In will attempt to launch.

Tip!

If you regularly use both Smart View and the Essbase Add-In, you can also check *Limit to Connected Sheets* and leave the two enable boxes checked. The Essbase Add-In will now only work on sheets that have been manually connected to Essbase.

Navigate Smart View in Excel

You have two options for navigating around in Smart View. The Hyperion menu provides an organized list of available actions:

Hyperion | Essbase | Help

Connection Manager...
Active Connections ▶
Reset Connection
Ad Hoc Analysis ▶   Zoom In
Forms   Zoom Out
Functions ▶   Pivot
BI+ Content   Keep Only
POV Manager...   Remove Only
Undo   Drill-Through Reports
Redo   View Qualified Member Name
Member Selection...   Change Alias Table
Refresh
Refresh All
Capture Formatting
Submit Data
Calculation Options

Tip!

You can get to this same list of actions by right clicking on a cell and choosing *Hyperion*.

Drilling, Pivoting, and More

Now we are ready to start using Smart View. Double-click into an empty spreadsheet. While this seems eerily familiar to the Essbase Add-In so far, we see that when data is retrieved, the spreadsheet looks a bit different with the Smart View Add-In. You only have two dimensions in the spreadsheet and a new object called the Point of View (POV). This is the default starting point for Smart View. The Point of View contains the remaining dimensions from the database.

Try It!

Open Excel and connect to Sample.Basic using the Smart View Add-In. Create a new database connection if necessary.

Double-click on *Year*, drilling down to the quarter level. Double-click on *Measures*, drilling down to the next level. Double-click on *Profit*.

You can also use the menus to drill down or up. Select *Hyperion >> Ad Hoc Analysis >> Zoom In* on the Year member and you'll see:

To those of you who actually played around with the Essbase Add-In during some of the earlier chapters, this should seem like déjà vu all over again. Now add *Product* to the spreadsheet. You can do this by selecting *Product* and dragging it to the spreadsheet:

You can also move *Product* to the spreadsheet by using the menu in the POV. Select *Options >> Pivot to Row (or Column) >> Product*:

[Book2]She ▼ ✕

Product ▼

Market ▼

Scenario ▼

Options ▼ ➡

🔧 Pivot to POV

Pivot to Row ▶ | Product

Pivot to Column ▶ | Market

Select Members ▶ | Scenario

In case two methods just aren't enough for you, the menus can also be used to pivot. Select *Hyperion >> Ad Hoc Analysis >> Pivot*:

	A	B	C	D	E	F	G	H	I	J	K
1			Margin	Total Expenses	Profit	Inventory	Ratios	Measures			
2	Product	Qtr1	52943	28240	24703	117405	55.25255688	24703			
3	Product	Qtr2	56317	29210	27107	119143	55.38705141	27107			
4	Product	Qtr3	57872	29960	27912	143458	55.00356413	27912			
5	Product	Qtr4	54387	28587	25800	141850	55.41720586	25800			
6	Product	Year	221519	115997	105522	117405	55.26162827	105522			

Double-click on *Product*, drilling down to the next level. Double-right-click (this might take some getting used to at first) on *Product* and you are returned to the Product dimension level (zoom up).

With my cursor still on *Product*, we can add Product back to the POV by dragging it to the POV or by using menu options. From the POV, select *Options >> Pivot to POV*:

Keep and Remove Only

To keep or remove specific members from your spreadsheet, use Keep / Remove Only functionality.

1. Select the desired member(s).
2. Select *Hyperion >> Ad Hoc Analysis >> Keep Only* (or *Remove Only*):

You can reach the same options via right click and selecting *Hyperion >> Ad Hoc Analysis >> Keep Only* (or *Remove Only*).

Ad Hoc Analysis

Let's create a Qtr1 income statement analysis spreadsheet.

1. Connect to Sample.Basic.
2. In a blank spreadsheet, double-click to perform an initial retrieve. Double-click on *Year*, drilling down to the quarter level.
3. Double-click on *Measures*, drilling down to the next level. Double-click on *Profit*.
4. Select *Qtr1* member. Right click and drag to columns.
5. Select *Margin*. Right click and drag to rows.
6. From the POV, select *Options >> Pivot to Column >> Scenario*.
7. Select *Qtr1* and drag to the top of the columns so that Time is above Scenario.
8. Double-click and zoom in on *Scenario*.
9. Select *Qtr1*. Select *Hyperion >> Ad Hoc Analysis >> Keep only* so that only Qtr1 is displayed in the spreadsheet.
10. Repeat *"Keep Only"* steps for the members *Margin, Total Expense*, and *Profit*.

The result should look like the following:

	A	B	C	D	E	F	G	H
1			Qtr1	Qtr1	Qtr1	Qtr1	Qtr1	
2			Actual	Budget	Variance	Variance %	Scenario	
3	Product	Margin	52943	51540	1403	2.722157548	52943	
4	Product	Total Expenses	28240	20960	-7280	-34.73282443	28240	
5	Product	Profit	24703	30580	-5877	-19.21844343	24703	
6								
7								
8								

Tip! If you know the exact member names, you can directly type into an Excel spreadsheet with the same layout. This is called Free Form Reporting and all the cool kids are doing it.

Refresh the Data

You can refresh the data in a spreadsheet at any time. Let's say that you've stared at the same screen for three hours while you count down the number of seconds until your next vacation. Suddenly, your boss approaches and you're worried that she will see three hour old data and reward you with a permanent vacation. To refresh the data to the current values in Essbase, select the green block arrow in the POV:

You can also refresh the data by selecting *Hyperion >> Refresh* or *Refresh All*. Refresh All will refresh all worksheets in a workbook for the database connection. This is really helpful in instances when you've created a workbook of reports that you run on a regular basis. For example, you create and update your monthly reporting package each month. With one menu item, you can refresh the data for all reports within your workbook.

Member Selection

You have a couple of different ways to change member selections. Again, this will look very similar to the Essbase Add-In.

1. Method 1, from the POV, select *Options >> Select Members >> Product* (or other dimension):

Method 2, select *Hyperion >> Member Selection*:

Hyperion   Essbase   Help

Connection Manager...

Active Connections ▶

Reset Connection

Ad Hoc Analysis ▶

Forms ▶

Functions ▶

BI+ Content

POV Manager...

Undo

Redo

Member Selection...

Refresh

2. The Member Selection Window displays. Select the desired dimension (if necessary):

Member Selection

Dimension

Product

Filter

Hierarchy - default

☐ Use Descriptions

☐ Dynamic Time Series Members

☐ Active Members

Members

☐ **Product**
 ☐ 100
  ☐ 100-10
  ☐ 100-20
  ☐ 100-30
 ☐ 200
 ☐ 300
 ☐ 400
 ☐ Diet

Selection

Product
100
100-10
100-20
100-30

Help   OK   Cancel

3. Select members by checking the box next to the desired member.
4. Click the arrows to move the items from left to right panels.

You can search for a member with the search icon (the binoculars) and you can clear selections with the clear icon (the open square with the dark border).

It's also possible to use functions for member selection by selecting the function icon (box with a checkmark in it) and choosing the desired function (Children or Base members):

"Base members" is yet another name for level-0 members.

Note!

    Notice Product is selected. The function Children automatically selected all of Product's children. You can then use the arrows to move over the selected members.

5. Click *OK* once the members are selected. You are returned to the spreadsheet.
6. Now, select the drop down for *Product* and you will see a list of the selected members:

Now let's move product back to the rows. The full list of selected products is added to the spreadsheet:

	A	B	C	D	E	F	G	H	I
1			Margin	Total Expenses	Profit	Inventory	Ratios	Measures	
2	Product	Qtr1	52943	28240	24703	117405	55.25255688	24703	
3	Product	Qtr2	56317	29210	27107	119143	55.38705141	27107	
4	Product	Qtr3	57872	29960	27912	143458	55.00356413	27912	
5	Product	Qtr4	54387	28587	25800	141850	55.41720586	25800	
6	Product	Year	221519	115997	105522	117405	55.26162827	105522	
7	100	Qtr1	14378	7330	7048	29448	57.40178857	7048	
8	100	Qtr2	15574	7702	7872	29860	57.28473167	7872	
9	100	Qtr3	16383	7872	8511	36461	57.39559978	8511	
10	100	Qtr4	14451	7414	7037	35811	56.99467561	7037	
11	100	Year	60786	30318	30468	29448	57.27288145	30468	
12	200	Qtr1	14748	8027	6721	33000	55.38738874	6721	
13	200	Qtr2	15207	8177	7030	31361	55.49797453	7030	
14	200	Qtr3	15387	8382	7005	35253	55.06764011	7005	
15	200	Qtr4	15244	8046	7198	32760	56.21773123	7198	
16	200	Year	60586	32632	27954	33000	55.53966595	27954	
17	300	Qtr1	12987	7058	5929	28865	54.11926491	5929	
18	300	Qtr2	14087	7318	6769	30334	54.7365558	6769	
19	300	Qtr3	14297	7599	6698	37331	53.64727955	6698	
20	300	Qtr4	13629	7226	6403	38142	54.4680681	6403	
21	300	Year	55000	29201	25799	28865	54.23795671	25799	
22	400	Qtr1	10830	5825	5005	26092	53.75223347	5005	
23	400	Qtr2	11449	6013	5436	27588	53.61273706	5436	
24	400	Qtr3	11805	6107	5698	34413	53.46709543	5698	
25	400	Qtr4	11063	5901	5162	35137	53.57903913	5162	
26	400	Year	45147	23846	21301	26092	53.59966758	21301	
27	Diet	Qtr1	14287	7270	7017	32834	55.52446465	7017	
28	Diet	Qtr2	14820	7484	7336	33641	55.32534438	7336	
29	Diet	Qtr3	15194	7662	7532	40652	55.26095654	7532	

Attribute Dimensions

To retrieve data for an attribute dimension, type the attribute dimension name over the base dimension name. In the case of Sample.Basic, type 'Ounces' over the top of Product (when Product is in the rows). Refresh the data and you might see something like this:

	A	B	C	D	E
1				Qtr1	
2				Actual	
3	Ounces	East	Sales	20621	
4		West	Sales	31674	
5					
6					

Now, double-click on *Ounces* to see sales by the Ounces attribute dimension:

	A	B	C	D	E
1				Qtr1	
2				Actual	
3	Ounces_32	East	Sales	3735	
4		West	Sales	8403	
5	Ounces_20	East	Sales	4536	
6		West	Sales	4997	
7	Ounces_16	East	Sales	4040	
8		West	Sales	4925	
9	Ounces_12	East	Sales	8310	
10		West	Sales	13349	
11	Ounces	East	Sales	20621	
12		West	Sales	31674	
13					

What if we wanted to then add a population breakdown to the grid above? Is it true that medium-sized states are especially fond of twelve ounce drinks? To satisfy your curiosity, insert a row in Excel above Qtr1. Type "Population" and then refresh the data. Double-click on *Population* to create a cross tab report using two attribute dimensions:

	A	B	C	D	E	F	G	H
1				Qtr1				
2				Small	Medium	Large	Population	
3	Ounces_32	East	Sales	853	986	1896	3735	
4		West	Sales	6658		1745	8403	
5	Ounces_20	East	Sales	1295	1208	2033	4536	
6		West	Sales	3040		1957	4997	
7	Ounces_16	East	Sales	893	1554	1593	4040	
8		West	Sales	2865		2060	4925	
9	Ounces_12	East	Sales	2083	4044	2183	8310	
10		West	Sales	8055		5294	13349	
11	Ounces	East	Sales	5124	7792	7705	20621	
12		West	Sales	20618		11056	31674	
13								
14								

Ad Hoc Analysis Options

If you read the Essbase Add-In chapters, this is going to sound *very* familiar (as such, we won't go into quite as much detail).

You can change your ad hoc analysis defaults, changing drill patterns, suppression options and much more. Select *Hyperion >> Options*. Select the *Ad Hoc* tab:

You can suppress no data (#missing) or zeroes from your spreadsheet. Let's say you are running a Qtr1 report for 5,000 products but only 500 products have data for Qtr1. You probably only want to list those products that have values, suppressing the remaining 4,500 "empty" products. To make a more legible report, suppressing underscores sometimes helps.

You can turn off or on *Repeated members*. Most of the time, you do not want to repeat members as this adds clutter to your analysis. Two notable exceptions are if you want to manually sort your data in Excel or if you're trying to create an export file that will be loaded into another system. Imagine how difficult to sort this file would be without repeated members turned on:

	A	B	C	D	E	F	G	H	I
1				Margin	Total Expenses	Profit	Inventory	Ratios	Measures
2	East	100	Year	18418	5762	12656	5384	66.39509733	12656
3	East	200	Year	12200	9666	2534	5957	51.53768165	2534
4	East	300	Year	9307	6680	2627	6278	45.9809298	2627
5	East	400	Year	9546	3202	6344	8125	60.62877104	6344
6	East	Diet	Year	4557	2149	2408	1867	57.54514459	2408
7	East	Product	Year	49471	25310	24161	25744	56.60427012	24161
8	West	100	Year	14139	10590	3549	8592	49.95054052	3549
9	West	200	Year	19056	9329	9727	11755	55.71929825	9727
10	West	300	Year	19949	9218	10731	8880	56.36743805	10731
11	West	400	Year	16882	11028	5854	9524	48.18747502	5854
12	West	Diet	Year	19392	11305	8087	11725	53.24108393	8087
13	West	Product	Year	70026	40165	29861	38751	52.67845724	29861
14	South	100	Year	8704	3931	4773	5483	53.46437346	4773
15	South	200	Year	13036	6921	6115	5336	59.23300618	6115
16	South	300	Year	7156	4806	2350	4466	56.98359611	2350
17	South	400	Year						
18	South	Diet	Year	10339	5427	4912	6531	55.35982009	4912
19	South	Product	Year	28896	15658	13238	15285	56.83042914	13238

On the "Indentation" section, you can switch the indentation from *Subitems* to *Totals* or *None*. *Navigate without data* allows you to set up your spreadsheet, defining the layout without the added time of retrieving data. This is helpful when first creating reports.

You can turn off double-clicking if you want (perhaps there is a conflict with another program) or maybe you're just a big fan of double-clicking bringing up in-cell editing. If you do turn it off, use menu navigation and right click options for zooming and drilling.

A nice improvement over the Essbase Add-In is that Smart View lets you have multiple levels of Undo. Although Flashback is a cooler name, we'll take multi-level Undo over a nice moniker any day. Someday, you'll accidentally zoom to the bottom level of your Product dimension, and you'll want a quick way to get back to the step before (or the step before that or the step before that).

One of the other things that might have been changed under your options is the "Zoom-In" definition. When you zoom in, you tend to want to see the members that make up the current member. When you zoom in Year, you want to see the quarters. Zooming on Qtr1 should show the first three months of the year. Some impatient people don't like passing

Hierarchy

Zoom-In

- ● Next Level
- ○ All Levels
- ○ Bottom Level
- ○ Sibling Level
- ○ Same Level
- ○ Same Generation
- ○ Formulas

through the levels in the middle on the way to the bottom-level of a dimension, so we have some alternatives to help us do this.

Right now, Zoom In (Smart View hyphenates it as "Zoom-In" and we have no idea why) is set to *Next Level*. This means that when you drill into Year, you see the quarters. If when you drill into Year, you want to see every single member in the Year dimension, set your Zoom In to *All Levels*. If you then drill on Year, you'd see every month and every quarter.

If you want to jump from the Year down to showing all the months without showing any of the quarters, select *Bottom Level*.

Try It!

Change your Zoom In level and then try zooming in and out on several dimensions. You can make an extremely large spreadsheet extremely quickly, and Essbase still remains extremely fast. Admittedly, Sample.Basic is extremely small.

Member retention works the same in Smart View as it does in the Essbase Add-In. If *Include Selection* is checked and you zoom in on Year, Year will still remain. If you uncheck this option, when you zoom in on Year, you will only see the children of Year:

Member Retention

☑ Include Selection

☐ Within Selected Group

☐ Remove Unselected Groups

FORMATTING

We've created our Qtr1 Income Statement Analysis spreadsheet, but it doesn't look that great. What we really need to do is apply some formatting to this spreadsheet.

Capture Formatting of Data Cells

We are in Excel so we can use all the power that is Microsoft for formatting our spreadsheets. One feature that Smart View adds to Microsoft functionality is the ability to save the formatting defined for data cells.

1. Select the cells with the formatting defined.
2. Select *Hyperion >> Capture Formatting*:

Hyperion	Essbase	Help

- Connection Manager...
- Active Connections ▶
- Reset Connection
- Ad Hoc Analysis ▶
- Forms ▶
- Functions ▶
- BI+ Content
- POV Manager...
- Undo
- Redo
- Member Selection...
- Refresh
- Refresh All
- **Capture Formatting**
- Submit Data

Now when you perform a refresh, the cell formatting will remain.

Captured formatting is tied to specific member combinations. If you drill down, next levels will not have the applied formatting.

Note!

Display and Cell Style Options

We can also set Display and Cell Styles that will help in the presentation of our spreadsheets. Select *Hyperion >> Options*. Select the *Display* tab:

Use this tab to define how you want missing data and "no access" cells to display. Determine if you want to show member names or aliases. Define scale and decimal places for the spreadsheet as well as define the thousands separator. Check *Use Excel Formatting* if you want to save any formatting defined in Microsoft Excel (and disable the use of Cell Styles).

Next, select the *Cell Styles* tab. You can define the default fonts and colors for member cells and data cells via Cell Styles. Follow the following steps with the utmost in caution:

1. Expand the *Analytic Services* Provider.
2. Expand *Member cells* to set member properties or expand *Data cells* to set data cell properties:

Options

Ad Hoc | Display | Cell Styles

Item position within the list determines its priority - topmost item has the highest priority

⊞ Expand   ⊟ Collapse   📝 Properties ▾   ⤴ Default Styles ▾   ⬆ Move Up   ⬇ Move Down

⊟–☐ 🗀 **Analytic Services**
  ⊟–☐ 🗀 Member cells
    ☐ Attribute
    ☐ Dynamic Calculations
    ☐ Contains Formula
    ☐ Shared
    ☐ Child
    ☐ Parent
    ☐ Duplicate Member
  ⊟–☐ 🗀 Data cells
    ☐ Drill-through
    ☐ Read-only
    ☐ Writable (lowest priority is recommended)
  ⊞–☑ 🗀 **Common**

OK   Cancel   Help

Let's change the cell style for parents.

Note! Make sure you uncheck *Use Excel Formatting* on the *Display* tab. If this option is selected, Cell Styles are ignored.

3. Check the box next to *Parent* to enable a properties box:

Options

Ad Hoc | Display | Cell Styles

Item position within the list determines its priority - topmost item has the highest priority

⊞ Expand   ⊟ Collapse   📝 Properties ▾   ⤴ Default Styles ▾   ⬆ Move Up   ⬇ Move D

⊟–☑ 🗀 **Analytic Services**
  ⊟–☑ 🗀 Member cells
    ☑ 𝐀 **Child**
    ☑ 𝐀 **Parent**
    ☐ Attribute

You can set the properties for *Font, Background,* and *Border*.

4. From the Properties drop down, select *Font*:

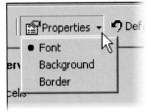

5. Change the font to bold and some nice earth tone (navy is the new black):

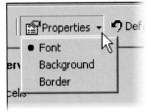

6. Click *OK* and then click *OK* again to save the settings and close the Options window.
7. Refresh data by selecting the green arrow on the POV.

    Here is the result:

	A	B	C	D	E	F
1		Qtr1	Qtr1	Qtr1	Qtr1	
2		Actual	Budget	Variance	Variance %	
3	Sales	6292	5870	422	7.189097104	
4	COGS	2164	1970	-194	-9.847715736	
5	**Margin**	#####	$3,900	$228	6	
6	**Total Expenses**	#####	$1,020	($361)	(35)	
7	**Profit**	#####	$2,880	($133)	(5)	
8						
9						
10						
11						

Notice for any member that is a parent, the font is now bold and a nice earth tone. Any member that is a child only (level-zero) is set to the default formatting. If you wanted all members to have the same formatting, go back to the *Options >> Cell Styles* tab and set the same font properties for the Child section.

A member can meet more than one criterion. Qtr1 is both a parent and a child. Yo Mamma is both a parent (yours) and a child (of yo Grandmamma). Use the *Move Up* or *Move Down* buttons to define the order of precedence for how cell styles should be applied:

The cells at the top of the list have higher precedence while cells at the bottom of the list have lower precedence.

On Data cells, you can set a background color for writable cells (along with font or border settings). Setting a background color is beneficial when developing budgeting input sheets for end user submissions. In the example below, read-only cells are set to gray and writable cells are set to yellow:

Options

Ad Hoc | Display | Cell Styles

Item position within the list determines its priority - topmost item has the highest priority

⊞ Expand   ⊟ Collapse | 🗗 Properties ▾ ↻ Default Styles ▾ | ⇧ Move Up   ⇩

☐-☑ 🗐 **Analytic Services**

   ⊞-☑ ☐ Member cells

   ☐-☑ 🗐 Data cells

      ☑ ■ Read-only

      ☑ ■ Writable (lowest priority is recommended)

      ☐ Drill-through

Here is an example of a budget entry spreadsheet with Cell Styles applied:

	A	B	C	D	E
1			Jan	Feb	Mar
2			Budget	Budget	Budget
3	New York	Sales	640	610	640
4	Massachusetts	Sales	460	440	460
5	Florida	Sales	190	190	190
6	Connecticut	Sales	290	300	290
7	New Hampshire	Sales	110	100	110
8	East	Sales	1690	1640	1690
9					
10					

Try It! Create your own budget entry spreadsheet for Sample.Basic. Show it to all your friends. See if you still have friends afterwards.

Preserving Formulas

We know you Excel gurus will want to add your own formulas into your spreadsheets. Can you do it? Yes, you can! You can add formulas within a grid of data cells as well as outside of the grid. You can retain these formulas upon refresh (to pull in new data) and when you drill down or up within the grid.

Let's add a formula to a spreadsheet. In this example, we've added a formula to calculate a percent of sales total for each state (highlighted yellow column):

		Qtr1				
		Actual	Budget	Variance	Variance %	% of Sales
New York	Sales	1998	1890	108	5.7	32%
	COGS	799	750	-49	-6.5	
	Margin	1199	1140	59	5.2	
	Total Expenses	433	360	-73	-20.3	
	Profit	766	780	-14	-1.8	
Massachusetts	Sales	1456	1360	96	7.1	23%
	COGS	219	190	-29	-15.3	
	Margin	1237	1170	67	5.7	
	Total Expenses	164	120	-44	-36.7	
	Profit	1073	1050	23	2.2	
Florida	Sales	1240	1150	90	7.8	20%
	COGS	507	470	-37	-7.9	
	Margin	733	680	53	7.8	
	Total Expenses	323	240	-83	-34.6	
	Profit	410	440	-30	-6.8	
Connecticut	Sales	944	880	64	7.3	15%
	COGS	377	340	-37	-10.9	
	Margin	567	540	27	5.0	
	Total Expenses	217	150	-67	-44.7	
	Profit	350	390	-40	-10.3	
New Hampshire	Sales	654	590	64	10.8	10%
	COGS	262	220	-42	-19.1	
	Margin	392	370	22	5.9	
	Total Expenses	244	150	-94	-62.7	
	Profit	148	220	-72	-32.7	
East	Sales	6292	5870	422	7.2	100%
	COGS	2164	1970	-194	-9.8	
	Margin	4128	3900	228	5.8	
	Total Expenses			361	35	

We can refresh and the formula remains, recalculated with the current data.

Note! Unlike the Essbase Add-In, formulas are preserved automatically with Smart View.

SUBMITTING AND CALCULATING

But wait: is Smart View only for reporting and analyzing data or can it change the data into better data than it ever was before? Good news, my friend (stop by anytime; we've got a fold-out couch in the den). Smart View provides the ability to submit data and run calc scripts just as the Essbase Add-In does.

To submit data, select *Hyperion >> Submit Data* on a spreadsheet that contains writable cells:

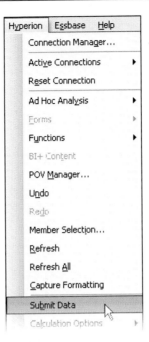

Calculating data is almost as easy. Select *Hyperion >> Calculation Options >> Calculate*:

This will pull up a list of calc scripts. You can filter this list by database. Select the calc script you wish to run and click *Launch*:

ADVANCED SMART VIEW

We've taught you the basics of Hyperion Smart View. There are some additional things that you can do with Smart View that we didn't necessarily cover in great detail. You can create highly formatted grids with Smart View (we introduced you to the basics of cell styles). You can create report templates which is helpful in the development and distribution of reports. You can add cell text (like LROs) to cells via Smart View. You can save point-of-views via the Point of View manager for future re-use.

INTEGRATING ESSBASE WITH OTHER OFFICE PRODUCTS

Have you ever sent an e-mail with a data value you pulled from Hyperion Essbase (manually copying and pasting from your spreadsheet)? Have you ever put together an executive presentation with Essbase numbers that you had to manually update each month?

Well, now this process will be much easier with the Smart View Add-In. Smart View uses Smart Tags to pull in data from Hyperion data sources (such as Essbase databases). Smart Tags are predefined properties that associate available actions with a keyword.

The best way to describe how this works is with an example. Let's learn how to pull an Essbase value into an Outlook e-mail.

1. Open Microsoft Outlook.
2. Select *Hyperion >> Connection Manager*.
3. Connect to the desired Essbase server (just like you did in Excel).
4. Once you are connected, type "smartview" anywhere in the document. "smartview" is the Smart Tag.
5. Move the mouse over the word and the Smart Tags Action icon will display. Select the icon:

6. From the Hyperion Smart View menu, select *Functions >> database_name >> HsGetValue*:

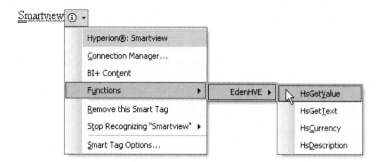

7. A member selection window is displayed. Select a dimension and then the desired member:

8. Click *OK* and the value is displayed in the e-mail.

You can also pull BI+ Content like a financial reporting document into the e-mail as well. Here's a particularly idyllic example:

Follow these same steps for integrating Essbase data into Word or PowerPoint. Here is another example where we've used smart tags within PowerPoint to pull data from Essbase to create our monthly executive presentation.

We first connect to the desired Essbase database. We then type "smartview" into the PowerPoint presentation (where we want the data value to appear). We mouse over the "smartview" tag. From the Hyperion Smart View menu, we select *Functions >> Sample_Basic >> HsGetValue:*

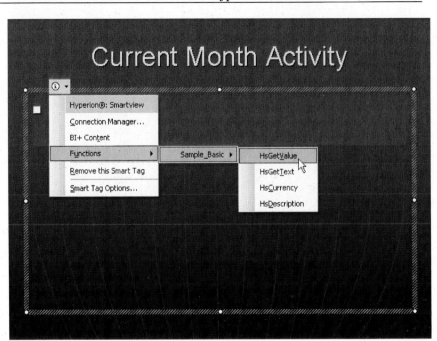

We specify the member selection information:

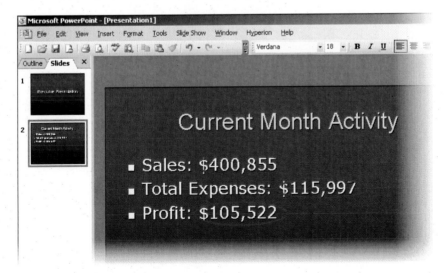

The following PowerPoint slide presents three Essbase data values (Sales, Total Expenses, and Profit):

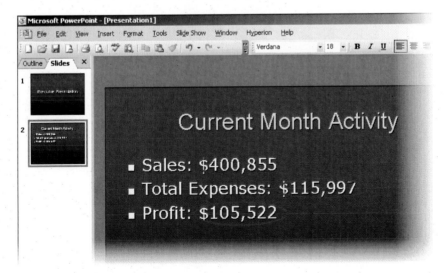

Because the data values are linked to Essbase, if the data changes in the database, all we have to do is refresh the data by selecting *Hyperion >> Refresh All*. The presentation will be updated with the current values (pretty cool for those last minute adjustments and journal entries). "Refresh all" will update all of the values in the presentation for the active database connection:

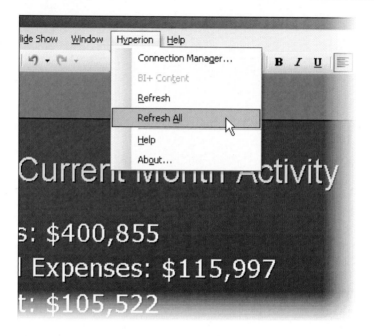

Now wouldn't it be nice to refresh this presentation each month for the current month automatically? We would use a substitution variable to select the current month within member selection so the presentation could dynamically refresh based on the variable's value.

Yes, this would be nice, but unfortunately it is *NOT* possible (yet). Substitution variables are not supported for the HsGetValue function.

There are a lot of other things you can do with Smart Tags. The key is typing in "smartview" and then right clicking on the Action icon.

Pull a data value from Sample.Basic into a Word document.

Try It!

Note! Smart Tags are used in the early System 9 versions. Beginning in version 9.3, an enhanced way of integrating data values into Microsoft was introduced, using linked data points.

Congratulations. You are now an Essbase (and Smart View) Add-In Master User. Now go out and act like it.

Chapter 7:
DIFFERENT APPLICATIONS

Everything we've done up to this point has been using the Sample.Basic database that comes with Essbase. While it's workable for exercises in this book, it's not terribly representative of databases in the real world. The goal for this chapter is to describe a few common types of databases in case you should ever run into them. For each application type, we'll review how the application is generally used and what the dimensions tend to be for that type of application.

Note! While an application can house one or more databases, most applications contain just one database. With that said, this chapter uses the terms "application" and "database" in the broader Information Technology sense.

COMMON DIMENSIONS

While every application will be different, most applications draw from a common set of dimension templates. The details within each dimension may change and the names of the dimensions may differ, but the same dimensions will keep appearing throughout many Essbase applications at your company. While we'll review later the differences for each specific application, it seems like a good idea to start with what we all have in common.

Time

All of us experience the constant effects of time and likewise (with very few exceptions), every Essbase database has one *or more* time dimensions. This is the dimension that contains the time periods for your database. Sample.Basic calls this dimension "Year":

```
⊟─Year (Alias: Period)
   ⊟─Qtr1 (+) (Alias: Q1)
      ├──Jan (+)
      ├──Feb (+)
      └──Mar (+)
   ⊟─Qtr2 (+) (Alias: Q2)
      ├──Apr (+)
      ├──May (+)
      └──Jun (+)
   ⊟─Qtr3 (+) (Alias: Q3)
      ├──Jul (+)
      ├──Aug (+)
      └──Sep (+)
   ⊟─Qtr4 (+) (Alias: Q4)
      ├──Oct (+)
      ├──Nov (+)
      └──Dec (+)
```

In addition to Year, other common names for this dimension include Periods, All Periods, Time (my personal favorite), Time Periods, Full Year, Year Total, and History. As you can tell from the plus signs above next to each member, this dimension generally aggregates from the bottom-up.

A Time dimension will usually have one or more of the following generations:

- Years
  - Seasons
    - Halves
      - Quarters
        - Months
          - Weeks
            - Days

While it is not unheard of to have an application that looks at hours or portions of hours, this is normally split off into its own dimension and called something like "Hours" or "Time of Day." Call center analysis applications and some retail sales applications analyze data by portions of a day.

It is quite common for an Essbase application to have two time dimensions. One dimension will house the quarters, months, days, and so forth. A separate dimension, generally called "Years" or "FY" (for Fiscal Year), will contain the calendar year. Here's an example of a Years dimension:

```
⊟ Years (Alias: Current Year)
   ├─ FY03 (~) (Alias: 2003)
   ├─ FY04 (~) (Alias: 2004)
   ├─ FY05 (~) (Alias: 2005)
   ├─ FY06 (+) (Alias: 2006)
   ├─ FY07 (~) (Alias: 2007)
   ├─ FY08 (~) (Alias: 2008)
   ├─ FY09 (~) (Alias: 2009)
   └─ FY10 (~) (Alias: 2010)
```

Unlike the Time dimensions that usually contain quarters and months, Years dimensions typically do not aggregate. Most often, the top member of a Years dimension is set to equal the data in the current year. In the above image, the tilde (~) signs (also called "no consolidate" tags) denote which years are not to be added into the total. As you can see, only FY06 has a plus next it, and therefore, is the only one to roll into Years. As such, Years equals FY06.

Some applications will combine a Time and Years dimension into one. This is often done when the Time dimension goes all the way down to the day-level and a company wants to do analysis by day of the week:

```
⊟ Time {Day of Week}
   ⊞ 2005 (+)
   ⊞ 2006 (+)
   ⊟ 2007 (+)
      ⊞ Jan, 2007 (+)
      ⊞ Feb, 2007 (+)
      ⊞ Mar, 2007 (+)
      ⊞ Apr, 2007 (+)
      ⊞ May, 2007 (+)
      ⊟ Jun, 2007 (+)
         ├─ Jun 1, 2007 (+) {Day of Week: Friday}
         ├─ Jun 2, 2007 (+) {Day of Week: Saturday}
         ├─ Jun 3, 2007 (+) {Day of Week: Sunday}
         ├─ Jun 4, 2007 (+) {Day of Week: Monday}
         ├─ Jun 5, 2007 (+) {Day of Week: Tuesday}
         ├─ Jun 6, 2007 (+) {Day of Week: Wednesday}
         ├─ Jun 7, 2007 (+) {Day of Week: Thursday}
         ├─ Jun 8, 2007 (+) {Day of Week: Friday}
         ├─ Jun 9, 2007 (+) {Day of Week: Saturday}
         ├─ Jun 10, 2007 (+) {Day of Week: Sunday}
         ├─ Jun 11, 2007 (+) {Day of Week: Monday}
         ├─ Jun 12, 2007 (+) {Day of Week: Tuesday}
         └─ Jun 13, 2007 (+) {Day of Week: Wednesday}
```

Each date in the dimension has a "Day of Week" user-defined attribute (UDA) assigned to it. "Jun 1, 2007," for instance, has a "Day of Week" attribute of Friday. If we had the years in a separate dimension, we would have to declare every June 1st to be a Friday. While the people born on June 1st would absolutely love this, the calendar makers would not. As such, we have to put the year in to specify a specific date as being a specific day of the week. Here is the "Day of Week" attribute dimension that is used in conjunction with the dimension above:

```
⊟ Day of Week [Type: Text]
    Sunday
    Monday
    Tuesday
    Wednesday
    Thursday
    Friday
    Saturday
```

While most Time dimensions use Essbase Dynamic Time Series functionality to calculate year-to-date and quarter-to-date members, it's not uncommon to come across an older Essbase outline that has actual YTD and QTD members. Usually, there will be a member called YTD (and/or QTD) in the Time dimension that will have a child for each month. For January, the member would be called either "Jan YTD" or "YTD Jan." Here's an example of a Time dimension with stored YTD members:

```
⊟··All Periods
   ⊟··MTD (+) (Alias: Full Year)
      ⊟·Qtr1 (+)
         ┌──Jan (+)
         ├──Feb (+)
         └──Mar (+)
      ⊞··Qtr2 (+)
      ⊞··Qtr3 (+)
      ⊞··Qtr4 (+)
   ⊟··YTD (~)
      ┌──Jan YTD (~)
      ├──Feb YTD (~)
      ├──Mar YTD (~)
      ├──Apr YTD (~)
      ├──May YTD (~)
      ├──Jun YTD (~)
      ├──Jul YTD (~)
      ├──Aug YTD (~)
      ├──Sep YTD (~)
      ├──Oct YTD (~)
      ├──Nov YTD (~)
      └──Dec YTD (~)
```

Measures

Like Time, almost every Essbase application has a dimension that lists the metrics for the database. While common practice is to call this dimension Measures (as Sample.Basic does), other frequently used names include Accounts and Metrics.

In Sample.Basic, the Measures dimension contains some profit and loss accounts, inventory metrics, and three calculated ratios:

```
⊟ Measures
   ⊟ Profit (+)
      ⊟ Margin (+)
         ┄ Sales (+)
         ┄ COGS (-)
      ⊟ Total Expenses (-)
         ┄ Marketing (+)
         ┄ Payroll (+)
         ┄ Misc (+)
   ⊟ Inventory (~)
      ┄ Opening Inventory (+)
      ┄ Additions (~)
      ┄ Ending Inventory (~)
   ⊟ Ratios (~)
      ┄ Margin % (+)
      ┄ Profit % (~)
      ┄ Profit per Ounce (~)
```

You'll notice that under "Profit," there are two members for "Margin" and "Total Expenses." Each one of these members has members below it. It's quite common for a Measures dimension to have many levels of hierarchy. A financial reporting application, for instance, might have hierarchy all the way down to a sub-account level.

While most every application will have a Measures dimension, what constitutes the Measures dimension will differ wildly:

- A financial reporting application will have accounts for income statement, balance sheet, and sometimes cash flow.
- An inventory analysis application will have measures for beginning inventory, ending inventory, additions, returns, adjustments, and so forth.
- A sales analysis application will have measures for sales dollars, units sold, and average sales price.
- A human capital analysis application will have metrics for payroll, FICA, FUTA, sick days, vacation days, years of employment, and so on.

The Measures dimension is the most important dimension in any application since it lets you define what metrics you're going to analyze, but you can safely expect every Measures dimension to be unique for every application.

It's worth pointing out that the Measures dimension in Sample.Basic is very odd. It's not normal to see inventory statistics along with profit and loss accounts in the same database. From what we can tell, this was only done to show in a sample database that Essbase can handle things beyond just financial metrics.

Scenario

This dimension is common to applications that in addition to actual data also have budget, forecast, or planning information. The "Scenario" dimension usually houses members such as Actual, Budget, Forecast, What-If, and several variances (differences between one scenario and another). While the most popular name for this dimension is Scenario (or Scenarios), other common names include Category, Ledger, Cases, and Versions.

As a general rule, we try to avoid calling my Scenario dimension "Versions," because Hyperion Planning also has a dimension called "Versions" in addition to a "Scenario" dimension. In Planning, the Versions dimension is used to differentiate between different drafts of budget and plan data. Members in a Versions dimension could be Initial, Draft 1, Draft 2, Draft 3, and Final. To avoid confusion in case you run across any lost Planning users at your company, don't name your Scenario dimension "Versions" when there are so many other good names from which to choose.

Here is Sample.Basic's Scenario dimension:

Most Scenario dimensions are non-aggregating (since it doesn't make a lot of sense to add Actual and Budget together). In Sample.Basic, the only child of Scenario to roll-up is Actual, in effect, setting Scenario equal to Actual.

```
⊟ Scenario
   Actual (+)
   Budget (~)
   Variance (~)
   Variance % (~)
```

Other Dimensions

Many applications have a dimension that differentiates between different organizational entities. Commonly, this dimension is called Entities (the name Hyperion Planning prefers), Organization (the name we prefer), Departments, Cost Centers, Companies, Locations, and other industry specific names (like Stores or Branches). The closest Sample.Basic has to an Organization dimension is the Market dimension.

Another common dimension that you might run across is Product which houses the relationships between products and their categories and families. This is one of the few dimensions where just about everyone calls it the same thing although the alias differs at the top of the dimension, containing something like "All Products" or "Total Products." The greatest difference in this dimension is the depth to which different applications go. Some Product dimensions stop at different classes of products while others will go all the way down to individual parts, items, or SKUs (Stock Keeping Units).

Other dimensions tend to be specific to different types of applications. For instance, a Customer dimension will tend to show up in Sales Analysis and Accounts Receivable applications. We'll cover some of the major applications you'll tend to see. This is by no means thorough, because every day, a company comes up with some new way to use Essbase that no one has ever tried before.

Please don't think that Essbase can only be used for financial applications. We once built an Essbase cube to track projects that families signed up for at our church Advent workshop. Okay, that's really geeky, but it goes to show you what you can do if get out of the finance realm.

FINANCIAL REPORTING

Financial reporting (often called General Ledger, or GL analysis) databases are by far the most common type of Essbase application. This goes back to the early days of Essbase when the Arbor Software sales team used to sell pretty much exclusively into finance and accounting departments. Even today, the first Essbase database most companies build is to facilitate general ledger analysis.

In all fairness, Essbase is very good at doing GL analysis. Essbase has hundreds of built-in financial functions that make it a good fit for GL reporting. The Essbase outline provides a user friendly view of how accounts, departments, and other entities roll up within hierarchies and dimensions. It is also very easy for finance-minded personnel to manage those hierarchies. The most attractive thing about Essbase to accountants, though, is that accountants love Excel and as you just saw from the earlier chapters, Excel loves Essbase (or is that the other way around?).

Financial Reporting applications generally receive data from one or more GL Systems (including those that are part of a larger ERP solution). Generally, this data is loaded monthly right after a financial close, but it is sometimes loaded more frequently during the close process.

Typical Financial Reporting dimensions include those common dimensions just discussed: Time, Measures, Scenario, Organization and Years. Measures will contain your account hierarchies for income statement, balance sheet, metrics, and cash flow. You can have alternate hierarchies to support different reporting requirements (more on that later).

In addition to the common dimensions, you will have those dimensions for which you'd like to perform analysis – by Geography, Product, Channel, or any other imaginable dimension that makes sense for your company. That's the beauty of Essbase: dimensionality is flexible and 100% customizable.

SALES ANALYSIS

Sales Analysis applications are a natural fit for Essbase, because they require fast retrievals at detailed levels. We once built a Sales Analysis application (sometimes called Flash Sales) that had data by store (for over 5,000 stores) by SKU (for over 100,000 products) by day for three years. It was an obscene amount of detail, but Essbase handled it flawlessly with retrievals measured in seconds.

Typical dimensions for this class of application such as Product, Location, and Geography. You can also view sales data by demographics like age and income level of buyer, by store information like store manager, square footage, store type, or location, or by product information like promotion or introduction date:

```
Income Level
    Under 20,000 (+)
    20,000-29,999 (+)        Payment Type
    30,000-49,999 (+)            Cash (+)
    50,000-69,999 (+)            ATM (+)
    70,000-99,999 (+)            Check (+)
    100,000 & Over (+)           Credit Card (+)

Age
    Teens (+)
        1 to 13 Years (+)
        14 to 19 Years (+)
    Adults (+)
        20 to 25 Years (+)
        26 to 30 Years (+)
        31 to 35 Years (+)
        36 to 45 Years (+)
        46 to 54 Years (+)
    Senior (+)
```

Time dimensions will often go to the day level (and be tracked across multiple years) and have attributes for day of week. Measures or accounts will often include units sold, cost of goods sold, price, revenue, and much more. Some sales applications have inventory data as well and include weeks of supply calculations.

With the introduction of Aggregate Storage Option (known in System 9 as "Enterprise Analytics"), the level of detail that can be loaded into Sales Analysis applications has grown exponentially. The advent of 64-bit Essbase has expanded the size of some of these databases even further since 64-bit Essbase allows far more RAM to be allocated to individual Essbase applications.

Unlike financial reporting applications which are generally fed from GLs or ERPs, Sales Analysis applications are generally fed from data warehouses, operational data stores, and legacy systems. It is not uncommon for Sales Analysis databases to be loaded every night with the prior day's sales data.

HUMAN CAPITAL ANALYSIS

Human Capital Analysis applications allow companies to analyze one of their most important assets: their people. (How important are certain people in your organization? Discuss.) Sometimes these applications are called Human Resources analysis, Employee analysis, or Salary analysis. We'll go with "Human Capital" analysis because it's trendy. "Human Resources" is *so* five minutes ago.

In addition to the ubiquitous Measures and Time, common dimensions for Human Capital applications include employee, employee status, job grade, and function. Detailed applications could also include title, start dates, and other employee-level information. It's also not uncommon to have Equal Employment Opportunity Commission attributes such as race, gender, age, and veteran status.

The Measures dimension will have accounts that tend to map to the General Ledger (particularly, the payroll or compensation section of the income statement).

```
501000 (+) (Alias: Total Compensation)
  501100 (+) (Alias: Salaries and Wages)
    501110 (+) (Alias: Total Salary)
    501120 (+) (Alias: Overtime)
    501130 (+) (Alias: Bonus Expense)
    501150 (+) (Alias: Auto Allowance)
  501200 (+) (Alias: Taxes and Benefits)
```

You can also use different drivers to budget and plan employee costs. Headcount, Start Month, Vacation Days, Sick Days, and many more can be used in calculations to complete accurate planning numbers.

These drivers can also provide invaluable insight into historical employee trends. We once knew a company that analyzed employee sick time patterns to find out which employees tended to be "sick" on Mondays more than any other day of the week. Apparently, the Monday morning flu was a big problem at their company.

CAPITAL EXPENDITURE ANALYSIS

Capital Expenditure applications (often abbreviated to "Cap Ex" and sometimes called Capital Equipment or Fixed Asset) are another frequent type of Essbase cube. Whether it is determining the rate of return on an investment or it is tracking capital equipment requests from your organization, you can implement a CapEx application to suit your company's needs. Dimensions include capital equipment item, equipment type, asset category, and asset life.

Here are some examples of capital equipment dimensions:

```
⊟ Category
    ── Capacity ( + )
    ── Capability ( + )
    ── Cost Reduction ( + )
    ── Maintenance ( + )
    ── Market Opportunity ( + )
    ── Quality ( + )
    └─ No Category ( + )
⊟ Projects
    ⊟ All Projects ( + )
        ── Laser Weld ( + )
        ── Plasma R&D ( + )
        ── Networking ( + )
        └─ BPM Implementation ( + )
    └─ No Project ( + )
```

```
⊟ Equip Type
   ⊟ All Equip Types (+)
      ⊢ Building (+)
      ⊢ Leasehold Improv (+)
      ⊢ Mfg Machinery (+)
      ⊢ Office Furniture (+)
      ⊢ Computer Equip (+)
      ⊢ New Software (+)
      ⊢ Auto (+)
   ⊢ No Equip Type (+)
```

The Account dimension for these applications usually contains a portion of your Balance Sheet:

```
⊟ BalanceSheet (~) (Alias: Balance Sheet)
   ⊟ 100000 (+) (Alias: Total Assets)
      ⊟ 150000 (+) (Alias: Fixed Assets)
         ⊟ 151000 (+) (Alias: Gross PPE)
            ⊢ 151100 (+) (Alias: Construction in Progress)
            ⊢ 151200 (+) (Alias: Land)
            ⊢ 151300 (+) (Alias: Buildings)
            ⊢ 151400 (+) (Alias: Leasehold Improvements)
            ⊢ 151500 (+) (Alias: Mfg Mach and Equip)
            ⊢ 151600 (+) (Alias: Office Furn and Fixtures)
            ⊢ 151700 (+) (Alias: Computer Equipment)
            ⊢ 151800 (+) (Alias: Computer Software)
            ⊢ 151900 (+) (Alias: Vehicles)
         ⊢ 152000 (+) (Alias: Accumulated Depreciation)
```

Other metrics that tend to show up in the Measures dimension include quantities, charges, months in service, asset life, and other drivers related to capital equipment.

Generally, CapEx applications are loaded from the Fixed Asset module from your ERP, but it is not uncommon for plan data for capital expenditures to be entered directly into Essbase (or via Hyperion Planning's Capital Expenditure model available in System 9.3).

BUDGETING, PLANNING, AND FORECASTING

With highly sophisticated write back capabilities, Essbase provides an excellent solution for budgeting, planning, and forecasting systems. Hyperion Planning was built on top of Essbase specifically to take advantage of Essbase's sublime ability to not only be used for reporting of data, but also multi-user submission of data.

Back in the days before Hyperion Planning was invented, many companies built Essbase cubes for budgeting purposes. They sent their data in via the Essbase Add-In and they were happy. Essbase security limited the dimensions and members for which data could be entered by users and calc scripts were used to calculate data if necessary.

If Essbase is perfect for budgeting, why was Planning created? The answer is simply due to the needs of planners and budgeters expanding beyond the abilities of Essbase. Modern forecasters require things like audit trails, integrated workflow, web-based data entry, and more. While Essbase can meet straight-forward budget needs, it doesn't have the built-in functionality that you get when you pay for Hyperion Planning.

Budgeting and forecasting applications written in Essbase (or built in Essbase via Hyperion Planning) will tend to look very similar to your reporting and analysis applications. For example, you may have a budgeting application to capture budget for income statement items, another application for capital equipment planning, and another application for salary planning. Though these applications will be similar to your reporting and analysis applications, they often do not contain the same level of detail. In general, budget data is not to the granular level that actual data is.

In the example below, budget is captured at the reporting line level of Market while actual data is captured by GL account:

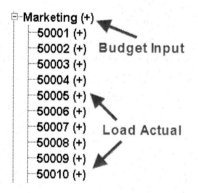

So...can we just capture budget and forecast information in my reporting and analysis applications? Yes, but there are some things to consider. First, understand the level of detail. If you are capturing budget at a higher level, you have to think carefully about how consolidations will take place in Essbase. If you enter data at an upper level and then run an aggregation, you could easily erase the data that was entered by users at the higher points in the dimension. There are ways to prevent this but the traditional work around is to use "dummy" members (see page below).

Second, we need to think about the dimensionality required for each purpose. In your reporting and analysis databases, you may want to analyze actual data by more dimensions or slices than you would for budget data. Too many dimensions can overly complicate the budgeting and planning process.

Third, you may also want to think about splitting reporting and budgeting for backup reasons. You'll want to backup your budgeting and planning applications more often as data changes far more frequently.

Even Dummies are Important in Essbase

Essbase dimensions are groups of members built into one or more hierarchies. Often times you might have data at different levels within the hierarchy. For example, in your financial reporting analysis application, you have actual data down to the account level, but your budget data is captured at a higher reporting level, one level above the account. How should you handle this?

As a rule in Essbase, always load to level-zero members. It is possible to load data at upper-level members in a hierarchy but avoid this if possible.

Helpful
Info

For the example that we are discussing, you can handle this requirement by adding "dummy" members. We've added a member "Marketing_Budget" that will be used for budget input. Actual data is still captured by GL account. The GL accounts and the dummy member both roll up to Marketing where we can perform budget vs. actual variance analysis:

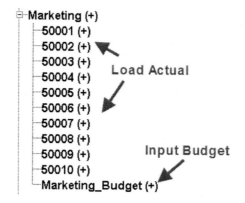

You can build "dummy" members automatically in your dimension build rules.

Become an Essbase Administrator

Chapter 8:
Create an Application

If you only plan on using existing Essbase applications and not building any new ones, you can skip the rest of this book. No, it's not that the remainder of the book is poorly written or that you wouldn't understand it (you're obviously smart since you bought this book), it's just not especially relevant to your daily job. Tear out the remaining pages (save the appendix, though) and give it to your favorite Essbase admin. On second thought, buy him his own copy of this book.

If you're still reading, you should thank the Essbase end user who bought you a copy of this book. As a fair bit of warning, the remainder of this book might not be quite as entertaining as the first seven chapters. This is because we know that few Essbase administrators have senses of humor. Just kidding! Lighten up, yeesh. Actually, we're going to shift the format to hopefully give you more of a step-by-step approach to doing your job. It might not be as fun, but boy will it be valuable.

ESSBASE ADMINISTRATION SERVICES

Essbase Administration Services (also known as EAS in versions 7x or under System 9, AAS for *Analytic* Administration Services) is the central administration tool for managing and maintaining all of Essbase. The goal of Administration Services is to make Essbase applications easier to maintain in a modernized interface that is fully cross-platform supported.

Administration Services replaces the Essbase Application Manager of prior Essbase versions. For those of you who enjoy living in the Paleolithic era, yes, you can still use Application Manager with Essbase 7x. Fear not, caveman: once you get used to the new interface, you will leave Application Manager and your pterodactyl phonograph player behind and never look back. Administration Services is now leaps and bounds better than Application Manager (no comments on the first few releases, though).

Administration Services consists of a client console (Administration Services Console). This is the graphical interface that Essbase administrators and designers use to build and manage Essbase applications. The Administration Services Console talks to a middle-tier application server (the "Administration Server").

The Administration Server is something that no one will see once it's working correctly. Administration Server serves as a centralized management point as it communicates directly with multiple Essbase servers, and allows multiple administrators to focus their work in a single shared environment.

Administration Server communicates directly with Essbase servers. One Administration Server can talk to multiple Essbase servers. All Administration Services components are J2EE-compliant. J2EE stands for Java 2 Enterprise Edition which in English-speak means that they're java-based. For those who believe a picture is worth a thousand words, here's a diagram to illustrate all those tiers:

Client Tier   Middle Tier   Database Tier

Spreadsheet Add In   Administration   Essbase
Administration Services   Services Server   Analytic
Console   (Data Store, App   Server
                            Server)

Administration Services Console is where you as the administrator or designer will build outlines, create dimensions, load data, calculate, assign security, define filters, manage all of your Essbase servers, and about 1.652 gazillion other things Essbase-related. This is *the* interface for all of your Essbase databases.

So, go ahead, start the Administration Console. Feel the power coursing through your veins.

Starting the Console

1. Double-click on the Admincon.exe icon.

    or

    Select *Start >> Programs >> Hyperion Solutions >> Essbase Administration Services >> Administration Console.*

2. Type or select the Administration Services server:
3. Type the user name and password and then click *OK*:

The Administration Services console will display:

In the console, you can view and manage all Administration servers installed in your environment. In most cases, you have one Administration Server that manages all of your Essbase servers including development and production:

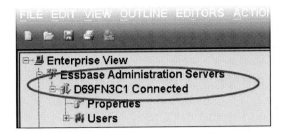

To view and manage all of the Essbase servers installed in your environment, expand the *Essbase Analytic Servers* section of the Enterprise View:

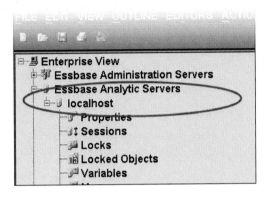

One of the big benefits of Administration Services is that you can manage development, QA, test, and production environments in one window. Copying objects across Essbase servers (even if they are different platforms like Unix and Windows) becomes child's play in Administration Services.

An Essbase administrator once deleted a production application, thinking he was connected to the development Essbase server. This same administrator also copied an unfinished development application from the development Essbase server to the production server, mixing up the 'to' and 'from' server during the copy. If you don't want to get fired, make sure you know which server you are connected to before you start performing potentially serious actions.

Navigate in Administration Services

There are three main ways to perform actions in the Administration Services console:

1. Menu items:

```
FILE  VIEW  EDITORS  ACTIONS  TOOLS  WIZARDS  WINDOW  HELP
```
Start all applications for "localhost"

Stop all applications for "localhost"

⊟ Enterprise View   Create application for "localhost" ▸
 ⊕ Essbase Admini
 ⊟ Essbase Analyti   Refresh application list for "localhost"
  ⊟ localhost   Status for all applications "localhost"
    ⌐ Properties   Show databases for "localhost"

2. Icons:

3. Right click:

⊟ Sample
 ├ Properties
 ⊕ Calcula⎯⎯⎯⎯⎯⎯⎯
 ⊕ Report   Start
 ⊕ Rules F   Stop
 ⊟ Databas   Set   ▸
   ⊟ Basi   Clear   ▸
    ├ Pr   Execute calculation...
    ├ Ou   Load data...
    ├ Lc   Export...
    ├ Li   Restructure...
    ├ Tr
    ⌐ Fi   Copy...
 View   Rename...
 ⎯⎯⎯⎯⎯ This ve Delete
 l051287
 cense will expir Edit properties
                  User/group access
                  Preview data
                  Add to   ▸

We personally prefer right clicking since it's an easy way not to have to remember which actions are available for a specific item. Right click on an object in the Enterprise View (the pane on the left) and you'll see all the relevant actions available to you.

Generally, when you open an item on the left (in the View pane), it will open in the pane to the right. There is another important pane in Administration Services: Messages. This section is found (unless you went to the *View* menu and turned it off) in the lower part of your window. Messages about whether actions are successful or not will be posted here:

Administration Services may not send up a big, flashy error message so be mindful of the information communicated in this section. Although messages will almost always be displayed here, the messages displayed here will almost always be highly summarized, and in computer-speak.

Stare at the messages a while and at least you'll be able to tell if the message is informational or it's a major error. For example, if a message was displayed saying "It's currently sunny with a chance of rain late in the day," this would be informational. If the message "Fatal error occurred: self-destruct sequence initiated" appears, stare at it for a nanosecond and then run.

You are very unlikely to see a "self-destruct" message.
Note!

What Can You Do in Administration Services?

Helpful
Info

- Define the database outline.
- Create dimension build rules.
- Create data load rules.
- Create calculation scripts.
- Create report scripts.
- Partition databases.
- Define security.
- Review log reports and database / server information.
- Manage Essbase servers.
- Manage users and groups.

CREATE AN ESSBASE APPLICATION

Creating new Applications and Databases using Administration Services is ridiculously simple.

Create an Application and Database

1. Select *File >> New.*
2. Choose either *Block Storage Application* or *Aggregate Storage Application.* For right now, select Block Storage since we won't be covering Aggregate Storage right now:

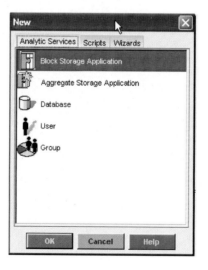

3. Select the Analytic Server and specify a new application name (Do not check "Unicode mode"; we'll cover this in a later section):

4. Click *OK*. You now have an application with no databases within it. This is completely useless, so don't stop now.
5. Right click on the application you just created and select *Create Database*:

6. Your server and application should already be selected, so type in a new database name:

Create Database

Analytic **S**erver:

localhost

Application:

Finrpt

Database name

Finrpt

Database type:

⦿ **N**ormal   ○ **C**urrency

OK   Cancel   Help

Note!

Select Normal for the database type. Don't select Currency, because you shouldn't be using Essbase's Currency Conversion module *ever*.

7. Click *OK*.

That's it. Creating the application is the easy part. Now it gets a bit more complicated, but we'll be here for you (imagine the Bon Jovi song playing in the background – "I'll Be There For You").

Try It!

Create a new application (Block Storage Option) and database (Normal type). Name both of them after yourself.

Essbase Outlines are *Very* Important

The single most important thing that you will work with in Essbase is the outline. Your Essbase outline contains *all* of the hierarchical information for your application and if your recall the earlier chapters on analyzing Essbase data you will know that hierarchies are EVERYTHING to an Essbase end-user. Unlike a relational database where the hierarchy is applied to data already stored in tables, in Essbase, the outline (and as such, the hierarchy) directly controls *how* data is stored and indexed. When you modify your outline, you restructure your database.

Note!

Essbase allows one and only one outline per database.

Building dimensions, ordering them, adding hierarchies, adding members with member attributes, and creating member formulas all drive the performance of your Essbase application. First and foremost, your outline needs to reflect your business requirements.

Tip! Do not commit the cardinal sin of looking at your source data first and then building an Essbase outline to hold it all. Do not turn every field in your relational table into a dimension in Essbase. This will result in a very flat Essbase cube that's extremely difficult to use and your users will burn your image in effigy.

We strongly recommend beginning this process by analyzing the reports that need to be created. Your reports will help you identify the dimensions for your database. What's in the rows and columns will become dimensions in your outline. If you're looking at an income statement that has accounts down the side and months across the top, you have an outline with at least two dimensions: Measures and Time. Pay attention to what applies to the whole report. If multiple copies of income statements are generated, one for each department in the company, then your outline will need an Organization dimension.

Let's start with baby steps and review some key outline concepts.

Dimensions are the common groupings of data elements for which we analyze and report. Examples include Time, Account, Product, and Market.

Dimensions are made up of members. Members will have a member name and alias: two ways to view the member. In the example below, we see product number is the member name and the product description is the alias:

```
⊟ Product
   ⊟ 100 (+) (Alias: Colas)          → Member Name
      ─ 100-10 (+) (Alias: Cola)
      ─ 100-20 (+) (Alias: Diet Cola)
      └ 100-30 (+) (Alias: Caffeine Free Cola)
   ⊞ 200 (+) (Alias: Root Beer)
   ⊞ 300 (+) (Alias: Cream Soda)
   ⊞ 400 (+) (Alias: Fruit Soda)          Alias
   ⊞ Diet (~) (Alias: Diet Drinks)
```

Note!
You can use either or both member name and alias when reporting against Essbase databases.

There are five dimension types that you will utilize in Essbase: Accounts, Time, Country, Currency Partition, and Attribute. You could also have "None" or no dimension type assigned. Essbase provides some built in functionality associated with each one of these dimension types. The Accounts dimension type has special account attributes like time balance and expense reporting. Time allows dynamic time series. Country and Currency Partition are important when using the Essbase Currency Conversion module (but as we already said, you should *never* use the Currency Conversion module).

Edit the Outline

Let's pretend for a second that you're starting your own business. No, it doesn't matter what type of company, but in the interest of simplicity, let's say your life long passion is to juggle wolverines. You run out and buy yourself some wolverines, a copy of Excel, and a copy of Essbase. Since you have a lot of venture capital (wolverine juggling is a growth industry), you pay to have a consultant come in and install Essbase and Administration Services.

Since the juggling business isn't that complicated (for instance, your only GL accounts are revenue, operating expenses, and other expenses), you've decided to create a simple, four-dimensional outline. While most outlines have five to nine dimensions, you're okay with four until your business starts to expand.

1. In Administration Services, navigate to the Database Outline beneath the database you've already created.
2. Right click and select *Edit*; the outline editor will open:

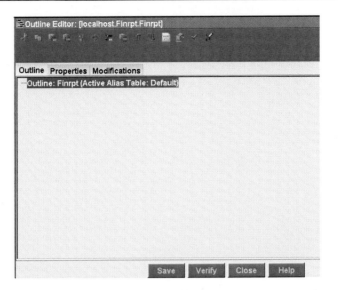

3. Right click and select *Add Child* or *Add Sibling*:

You can also click on the *Add Child* or *Add Sibling* icon in the Outline Editor Menu:

4. Begin adding dimensions and members.

For our cash cow company in the making, add Year, Period, Scenario, and Account dimensions to build an outline that looks like the following:

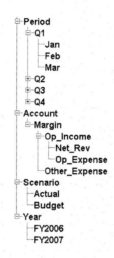

5. Select the *Account* dimension.
6. Right click and select *Edit Member Properties*.
7. On the Information Tab, set Dimension type for Account to *Accounts*:

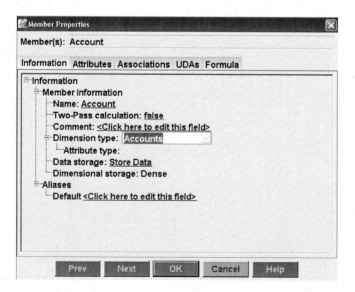

8. Repeat these same steps setting *Period* to the *Time* Dimension type.

Defining Member Properties

So you've built the basic structure of the outline with four dimensions and their hierarchies and members. Now let's discuss more member properties. There are common member properties that exist across all dimensions. We've already seen two – member name and alias. Other common member properties include consolidation, data storage, UDAs, and member formulas. Some member properties are specific to a dimension type like Expense Reporting and Time Balance.

Consolidation Operators

Consolidation operators tell the outline how to consolidate the member (yes, a user friendly description that accurately describes the property. Imagine that!) Should the members Dallas and Houston add together to reach a total for Texas? Should units sold be multiplied by price to calculate revenue? You can use consolidation operators to define how a member rolls up in the database.

Valid consolidation operators include:

- Addition (+) – This is the default consolidation property.
- Subtraction (-)
- Multiplication (*)
- Division (/)
- Percent (%)
- No consolidate (~)

Tip!

System 9.3 introduces a new consolidation type ^ which is similar to the no consolidate or ~ consolidation type. See Chapter 21, System 9 Mythbusters, for more details.

In most cases you will use the default Addition consolidation tag:

```
Outline  Properties  Modifications
⊟ Outline: Finrpt (Active Alias Table: Default)
   ⊟ Period
      ⊟ Q1 (+)
         ─ Jan (+)
         ─ Feb (+)
         └ Mar (+)
      ⊞ Q2 (+)
      ⊞ Q3 (+)
      ⊞ Q4 (+)
```

The second most common consolidation tag is "No consolidate". Use this in places where it doesn't make sense to add up members. Would we want to add Actual and Budget together for Scenario? No, so we would tag both Actual and Budget "no consolidate" or ~ in the outline.

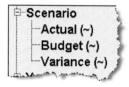

```
⊟ Scenario
   ─ Actual (~)
   ─ Budget (~)
   └ Variance (~)
```

Data Storage Property

The Data Storage property tells Essbase how the member should be stored. Valid data storage options include:

- Store: Store the data value with the member.
- Dynamic Calc and Store: Do not calculate the data value until a user requests it, but store the data value immediately after the retrieval.
- Dynamic Calc: Do not calculate the data value until a user requests it, and then discard the data value.
- Never share: Do not allow members to be shared implicitly (don't worry, a good explanation for this confusing concept is just below).
- Label Only: Create members for navigation and grouping. These members usually won't make sense from a logical consolidation standpoint.
- Shared Member: Share data between two or more members.

When should you set a member to Store? When you will need to load data or input data to that member. Set a member to store if that member has a large number of children. Most of the times, your large sparse dimensions will be set to Store. (What is a sparse dimension? We'll get there in just a few sections.)

When should you set a member to Dynamic Calc? In most cases, use the Dynamic calc property for your variances, ratios, and averages. You can also set upper level members of a hierarchy to dynamic calc when that member has just a few children. Often times you set upper levels of the Accounts and Time dimensions (and other dense dimensions) to Dynamic Calc to help reduce your database size.

When should you use Dynamic Calc and Store? Virtually never, actually. We recommend sticking to Dynamic Calc unless you have little used sparse members with very complicated formulas.

When should you use Never Share? When you have a parent that only has one child. Essbase has a built in feature called Implicit Sharing, a mischievous function that can cause confusion in your Essbase databases. Essbase tries to be smart for us. When a parent only has one child, the values for both the parent and the child will always be the same, right? So Essbase decides to only store one value, the child value, which reduces your database size. But this causes issues in loading or inputting data for the parent, who dynamically pulls the data value from the child.

When should you use Label Only? Use Label Only for members like "Scenario", "Ratios", or "Drivers", members whose sole purpose in life is to organize the dimension and hierarchy: members for which it never makes sense to add their children together. A member marked as Label Only will automatically pull the value of its first child when referenced. Because of this, when we make a member Label Only, we will often make its first child have a plus and the other children have a tilde to designate that only the first child is rolling to the member. This is entirely to help indicate what's going on in Essbase to a user who might not know that a Label Only member pulls the value from its first child.

In this example below, it makes no sense to add Actual and Budget together, so we flag Scenario as Label Only:

```
⊟ Scenario (Label Only)
   ┈ Actual (+)
   ┈ Budget (~)
   ┈ Variance (~) (Dynamic Calc) (Two Pass)
   ┈ Variance % (~) (Dynamic Calc) (Two Pass)
```

When should you use Shared Members? First, let's further define "Shared Members." Shared members have the same name as another member, belong to the same dimension and point to the same data values; however, shared members belong to different parents and participate in different roll-ups for alternate views of the same data. The original member contains the value and the Shared Member has a pointer to the original member. Members can be shared among many parents and can be shared with multiple generations.

Let's look at example from Sample.Basic, where products are organized by product category. An alternate hierarchy to obtain a total for all Diet drinks is present, utilizing Shared Members for all of the different diet products underneath the parent:

```
⊟ Product
   ⊟ 100 (+) (Alias: Colas)
      ┈ 100-10 (+) (Alias: Cola)
      ┈ 100-20 (+) (Alias: Diet Cola)
      ┈ 100-30 (+) (Alias: Caffeine Free Cola)
   ⊞ 200 (+) (Alias: Root Beer)
   ⊞ 300 (+) (Alias: Cream Soda)
   ⊞ 400 (+) (Alias: Fruit Soda)
   ⊟ Diet (~) (Alias: Diet Drinks)
      ┈ 100-20 (+) (Alias: Diet Cola) (Shared Member)
      ┈ 200-20 (+) (Alias: Diet Root Beer) (Shared Member)
      ┈ 300-30 (+) (Alias: Diet Cream) (Shared Member)
```

So back to the question at hand: when to use Shared Members? Use this feature when you'd like to create alternate rollups of data in the same dimension. For example, rolling up products both by Market and by Product Category; rolling up a department both by Manager and by Organization Structure; rolling up revenue both by standard income statement hierarchy and by a custom reporting hierarchy. Shared members provide powerful analysis capabilities by aggregating and analyzing values in many different ways, without creating a burden on either the end-user or the administrator.

User Defined Attributes (UDAs)

User defined attributes are tags assigned to outline members and are used to describe a member, to reference members for specific calculation purposes, or to isolate members for specialized reporting and analysis. A member can have more than one UDA associated with itself.

In the example below from Sample.Basic, a UDA describing each market's category has been assigned:

```
⊟-Market
    ⊟-East (+) (UDAS: Major Market)
        ─New York (+) (UDAS: Major Market)
        ─Massachusetts (+) (UDAS: Major Market)
        ─Florida (+) (UDAS: Major Market)
        ─Connecticut (+) (UDAS: Small Market)
        └─New Hampshire (+) (UDAS: Small Market)
    ⊞-West (+)
    ⊞-South (+) (UDAS: Small Market)
    ⊞-Central (+) (UDAS: Major Market)
```

This UDA can now be used in calculations (e.g. estimating budgeted product sales based on market size). We can even create a market category specific report, only pulling states with that are considered "Major Market."

Other examples of UDA usage include assigning Manager UDAs to a department or Product Start Date UDAs to products. UDAs can be used for almost anything that business requirements dictate, and do it without adding the storage requirements of extra dimensions or members.

User Defined Attributes are defined in the Member Properties window, when you click on the "UDA" tab.

Note!

Data cannot be summarized by UDA. To do this requires an attribute dimension.

Member Formulas

Member formulas allow you to define specific logic for calculating that member. This logic can range from very simple to highly complex. For most variance members, you will use a member formula for the variance calculation. Member formulas are utilized to calculate averages and ratios

Formulas are defined in the Member Properties window, under the rightmost tab labeled "Formula":

The different elements in a member formula could include mathematical operators, conditional operators, cross-dimensional operators, and functions.

The dimension reference area of the editor allows you to navigate the outline within the Formula window. You can search for a member and can insert a member name into the script area:

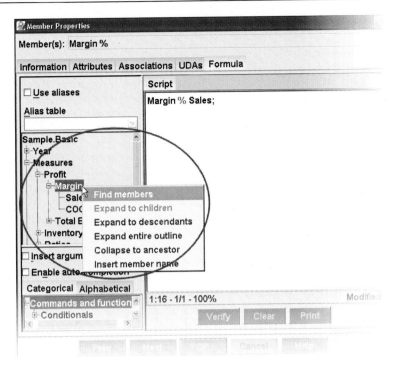

The functions section of the editor lists functions and operators available for member formulas. You can insert arguments into the script area, assisting the administrator with the formula syntax (trust me... this is very helpful). Turning on auto-completion will speed up the development of formulas:

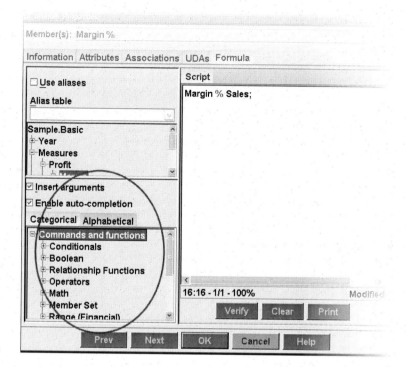

Here is a list of the available mathematical operators:
- Add, +
- Subtract, -
- Multiply, *
- Divide, /
- Evaluate a member as a percentage of another, %
- Control calculation order of nested equations, ()

For example, the member formula for the member "Margin Percent" is:

```
Margin % Sales;
```

Note! Note how the formula editor changes the formatting of keywords and operators to make the equation easier to read.

Mathematical functions define and return values based on selected member expressions. These functions include most standard statistical functions. An example with a mathematical function would be the member formula for the "Variance":

```
@VAR (Actual, Budget);
```

Conditional operators allow tests based on criteria. The member formula to calculate "Commission" is:

```
IF (Sales > 1000)
     Sales * .02;
ELSE
     10;
ENDIF
```

In English-speak, if Sales is greater than 1000, then Commission is equal to Sales times 2 percent, otherwise Commission is equal to 10.

Functions can also be used in member formulas. The member formula for the member "Market Share" uses an index function:

```
Sales % @PARENTVAL (Markets, Sales);
```

In other words, Market Share is equal to the Sales for the current member as a percent of the current member's parent data value for the Markets dimension.

The member formula for the member "Mar YTD" uses a financial function:

```
@PTD(Jan:Mar);
```

The member formula for "Payroll" shows how to use conditional or Boolean criteria:

```
IF (@ISIDESC (East) OR @ISIDESC (West))
     Sales * .15;
ELSEIF (@ISIDESC(Central))
     Sales * .11;
ELSE
     Sales * .10;
ENDIF
```

To put it in English, for all of the members under and including East and West, Payroll is equal to Sales times 15 percent, for all members under and including Central, Payroll is equal to

Sales times 11 percent, and for all other members, Payroll is equal to Sales times 10 percent.

Tip! The syntax for member formulas is almost identical to the syntax used in calc scripts. The calc script chapter provides a bit more detail on Essbase calc syntax.

Note! Member formulas must end with a semicolon. If the member name has spaces, you must enclose the member name in double quotes.

Time Balance Attributes

Time balance attributes are only available in the dimension tagged as Accounts, and are used to tell Essbase how a given member should be aggregated up the Time dimension. For example, should Headcount for January, February, and March be added together for Q1? This definitely wouldn't make sense.

	Actual	FY2007			
	Jan	Feb	Mar	Q1	Q2
Headcount	100	125	122	347	#Mis

In most cases you want Qtr1 to equal the March headcount, or in other words the last headcount in the period. To get Essbase to do this, you tag Headcount with the Time Balance Last ("TB Last") so that it will take the last member's value when aggregating time:

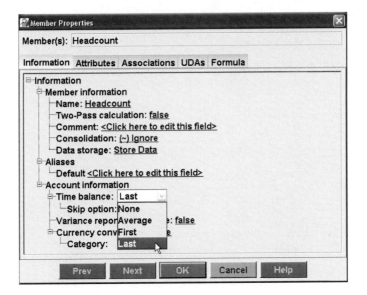

Depending on your requirements, you could also assign Time Balance First or Time Balance Average. Here is Q1's headcount now nicely equaling its last child, Mar:

What if we have just closed January? Then, showing the March headcount wouldn't be accurate because March is blank. A sub-property associated with Time Balance allows us to define how we handle missing and zero data values. In this example, we would want to ignore any blanks (or #missing). So we set Headcount to TB Last, and then select Skip "Missing":

Now Qtr1 will correctly show the January value:

	Actual	FY2007			
	Jan	Feb	Mar	Q1	Q2
Headcount	100	#Missing	#Missing	100	#M

Another example of Time Balance utilization is for inventory analysis members:

Tip!

```
Inventory (~) (Label Only)
    Opening Inventory (+) (TB First) (Expense Reporting)
    Additions (~) (Expense Reporting)
    Ending Inventory (~) (TB Last) (Expense Reporting)
```

Expense Reporting

Expense Reporting is a simple flag that tells downstream calculations and reports whether a positive variance is good or bad. If you're over your target on revenue, everyone is happy. Of course, the opposite is true when you spend too much on Office Supplies. Well, not everyone will be upset but you don't want to be making enemies in the Finance Department when it comes time for them to cut you the bonus check for those positive-variance Revenues, right?

Let's walk you through an example. If you budget $1,000,000 in revenue and you make $1,100,000, that's a favorable variance of $100,000. Expenses are quite the opposite: if you budget $1,000,000 in marketing expenses and you spend $1,100,000, that's an unfavorable variance of $100,000. In general, you want expense data to have lower actuals than budget.

To allow for this, Essbase uses the property called Expense Reporting. Tag all of your expense accounts with Expense Reporting and Essbase will calculate the variance correctly when using the @VAR or @VARPER functions. Essbase will show a positive variance when Actual data is higher than Budget for revenue or metric accounts. Essbase will show a negative variance for those expense accounts tagged with the "Expense Reporting" property:

	Jan	FY2007		
	Actual	Budget	Variance	
Net_Rev	100	75	25	
Op_Expense	100	75	-25	
Op_Income	#Missing	#Missing	#Missing	

Set the Variance Reporting Expense property to True for all measures where budget should be higher than actual.

The Expense Reporting tag is found on the first tab of the Member Properties window, second from the bottom:

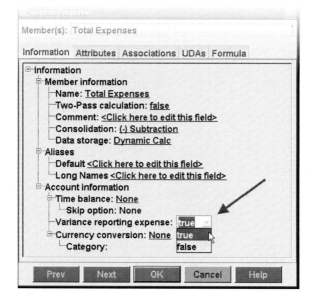

Two Pass

The two pass member property tells Essbase "come back and calculate this member at the end." Why is this important? Let's look at an example.

The Accounts dimension is calculated first (we'll learn this shortly) so Profit % is calculated based on input sales and profit. Once we roll up the Time dimension, the monthly Profit % is added together and placed in Q1's Profit %:

	A	B	C	D	E	F
1		Jan	Feb	Mar	Q1	
2	**Profit**	100	100	100	300	
3	**Sales**	1000	1000	1000	3000	
4	**Profit %**	10%	10%	10%	30%	
5						
6						

Hmmm... something's not right there. We want Profit % to recalculate once the quarter and year totals for Profit and sales have been calculated. Tag the Profit % member with the two pass member property and Essbase circles back to calculate the correct percent after it's finished everything else:

	A	B	C	D	E	F
1		Jan	Feb	Mar	Q1	
2	Profit	100	100	100	300	
3	Sales	1000	1000	1000	3000	
4	Profit % (tagged as two pass calc)	10%	10%	10%	10%	
5						
6						

Now that we've been through the different kinds of member properties, how do you actually define them?

Edit Member Properties

To edit member properties:

1. Right click on the member.
2. Select *Edit Member Properties*.
3. The Member Properties window will display:

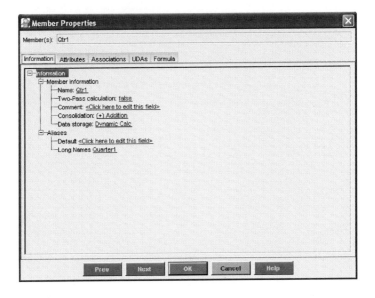

4. Assign the various member properties per your design on the Information tab or UDAs tab or Formula tab.
5. Click *OK* when you are finished.

Try It!

In our juggling wolverine application, tag Op_Expense and Other_Expense as expense reporting accounts. Assign "~" or non-consolidate for Actual and Budget members. Create a new member Variance. Make this member dynamic with the member formula @VAR(Actual, Budget);

You can select the *Previous* or *Next* buttons within the member properties window to move up and down the hierarchy. This will save you a few clicks when updating member properties for several members.

Tip!

Verify and Save Your Outline

You've now added dimensions, members and assigned member properties. You are ready to save your outline.

First, verify your outline and make sure you haven't broken any of the Essbase rules (see the next page). Click the *Verify* button to do this. Any errors or issues will display. In the case below, we have two members named "Jan" (we were playing around with Shared Members in the time dimension):

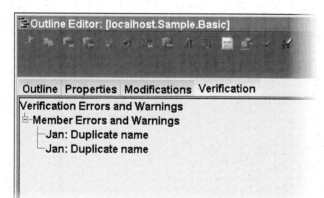

You can double-click on the issue, and you'll be taken directly to the place in the outline where the error occurs. Fix the issue and you are ready to verify once again. Once everything checks out ok, click the *Save* button to save the outline back to the server:

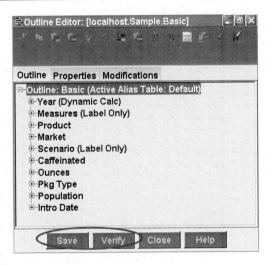

Essbase Outline Rules (Non-Unicode Applications*)

Helpful Info

- Member name limit is 80 characters.
- Alias limit is 80 characters.
- Member names and alias names must be unique across all dimensions.**
- Names are not case-sensitive unless case-sensitivity is enabled.
- Do not use " (quotation marks) or tabs anywhere.
- Do not use the following special characters at the beginning of a member name or alias: @\{},-=<().+'_|
- Do not use a space at the beginning or end of member name or alias.
- Do not use any of the key words used in calc scripts, report scripts, or other functions (see Technical Reference).
- Do not use Essbase specific words like ALL, MEMBERNAME, DIM, DYNAMIC, #MI (see DBA Guide for full list).

*Unicode applications are discussed in Chapter 20.
**Essbase allows duplicate member names in Hyperion System 9 – watch for this new feature.

Verify and save your wolverine juggling outline.

Try It!

Dynamic Time Series

Dynamic time series (DTS) allows end users to retrieve 'to-date' totals from the Essbase database. To enable DTS, you must tag a dimension Time. You then assign a description to the generation, identifying whether year-to-date, quarter-to-date, history-to-date, etc. should be used.

To set DTS,

1. Open the Outline Editor.
2. Right click and select *Dynamic Time Series*:

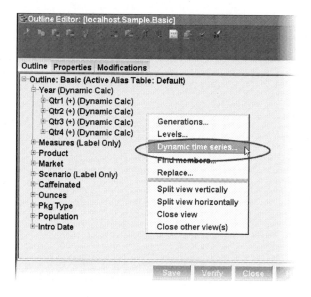

3. Check the box for the series you wish to enable.
4. Specify the generation number that correlates to the appropriate series.

    E.g., if quarters are at generation 2, then Q-T-D is 2.
5. Add a name if desired (this can be used in report queries):

Series	Enabled	Gen	Default	Long Names
H-T-D	☑	1		
Y-T-D	☐			
S-T-D	☐			
P-T-D	☐			
Q-T-D	☑	2	Quarter To Date	
M-T-D	☐			
W-T-D	☐			
D-T-D	☐			

Define Dynamic Time Series Members

[OK] [Cancel] [Help]

6. Click *OK.*
We covered how to retrieve DTS calculated data in the first part of the book, so we won't go over it again here.

For the wolverine juggling Finrpt outline, define DTS so that we can perform Q-T-D and Y-T-D analysis, then jump over to Excel and give it a test drive.

Try It!

Substitution Variables

Substitution variables are one of the best tools for Essbase administrators and report designers who live in a world where the clock advances (which is all of us, hopefully). Let's say you have 20 different current month reports across you Essbase applications. Do you want to modify all 20 reports each month to change the selected month? Do you want to modify all of your calc scripts that calculate current month each month? At year end, things are somewhat slow, so it won't be a problem to update all of your calc scripts and reports to reflect the new year, right? Trust me; you will be busy enough without adding those tasks to your plate.

Substitution variables are variables that serve as a placeholder for specific members. They are defined at the server, application, or database level. These variables can be utilized in calc scripts and reporting and analysis tools (the Essbase Add-In, Financial Reporting/Reports, and Web Analysis/Analyzer.). In System 9.3, you can also use substitution variables in member formulas and in rules files. Common substitution variables include curmth (current month), clsmth (closed month), CY (current year), and PY (prior year):

To define a substitution variable,

1. Under the Essbase Server name, right click on *Variables* and select *Create Variable.*

2. Specify the application and database for the substitution variable.

Tip! Define substitution variables for all applications and all databases when possible. For example, define 'curmth' current month substitution variable once for use in all applications and databases.

3. Specify the variable name.
4. Specify the variable value:

New Variable	✕
Analytic Server:	
localhost	
Application:	
(all apps)	▾
Database:	
(all dbs)	▾
Name:	
curmth	
Value:	
Jan	
OK Cancel Help	

5. Click *OK* to save the variable.

Try It! We plan to build 3 different current month reports to help us analyze revenue and expense for our wolverine juggling business. Because we want to spend our time on value added analysis versus time spent updating reports, let's create a substitution variable for current month called "curmo" (not to be confused with the long lost brother of that lovable monster Elmo).

Create Alternate Alias Tables

Outlines will always have the default alias table to store aliases, but you may have a requirement for different descriptions within your application. For your human capital analysis application, you might need a few more ways to report on a single employee:

- Last name, first name, title
- First name Last name
- Employee id, Last name, First Name

In order to meet all of these requirements, you will need to create some new alias tables. Jumping back to Sample.Basic, let's create an alternate alias table that will combine product number and name into the alias.

1. Open the Sample.Basic outline.
2. Select the Properties tab.
3. Right click on Alias table and select *Create alias table*:

4. Type in a name for the alias table that best describes the alias:

5. Right click on the new alias table and set the Product-Product Name table as active:

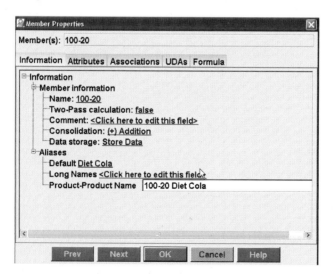

Note!

You can rename, copy, clear and delete alias tables. You can also import and export alias tables from and to other applications.

6. Select the Outline tab.
7. Right click on a product member and select *Edit Member Properties.*
8. Assign the alias for the new alias table:

Once the aliases have been assigned, the alias is ready for use in reporting and analysis.

Until now our wolverine juggling application has been pretty simple. We've decided to add a Customer dimension that lists the different customers or events that have paid for our juggling wolverine services:

```
⊟··Customer
     ⊟··Corporate Events (+)
          ⊢··1001 (+) (Alias: Hyperion User Conference)
          └··1002 (+) (Alias: Oracle User Conference)
     ⊟··Weddings (+)
          ⊢··1003 (+) (Alias: Hyperion-Oracle Happily Ever After Wedding)
          └··1004 (+) (Alias: Hyperion-Brio Happily Ever After Wedding)
     ⊟··Birthday Parties (+)
          ⊢··1005 (+) (Alias: interRel 10th Birthday Party)
          └··1006 (+) (Alias: Essbase 15th Birthday Party)
     ⊟··Street Peddling (+)
          ⊢··1007 (+) (Alias: Essbase 7th Street)
          └··1008 (+) (Alias: System 9th Ave)
```

We have eight wolverine juggling customers. OK, we can't track all of our street peddling customers individually so we'll track revenue and costs by street. Also there is a bit of confusion as to whether the Oracle and Hyperion User conferences are now the same thing. For simplicity's sake, we'll assume they are two events for now, not knowing what the future holds for this corporate event. And yes, Hyperion has had a few weddings – we don't have the most monogamous of customers but they sure love wolverine juggling.

 Add the customer dimension to the juggling wolverine application.

Try It!

Next we have a report that should display a second type of alias: customer number – customer name. We add an alternate alias table called "Long Names" and assign the new "Long Name" aliases for the customer dimension, concatenating customer number with customer name:

Member Properties

Member(s): 1001

Information Attributes Associations UDAs Formula

- Information
  - Member information
    - Name: 1001
    - Two-Pass calculation: false
    - Comment: <Click here to edit this field>
    - Consolidation: (+) Addition
    - Data storage: Store Data
  - Aliases
    - Default Hyperion User Conference
    - Long names | 1001 - Hyperion User Conference |

    Prev   Next   OK   Cancel   Help

Try It!

Add a new alternate alias table "Long Names" and manually populate the alias values for the juggling wolverine application.

ATTRIBUTE DIMENSIONS

What is an Attribute Dimension?

In early versions of Essbase, you were limited in the number of dimensions that you could have per database. Somewhere around seven dimensions was recommended and ten dimensions was stretching Essbase capabilities. But customers complained that they needed to be able to analyze data by more dimensions. Not just Product, but Product Start Date, Sales Manager, Packaging, Size, Weight, Target Group, and much more. So Hyperion introduced Attribute dimensions.

Attribute dimensions are dimensions just as we discussed in the prior section with some special considerations. Just like regular dimensions, they define characteristics about the data that is loaded to Essbase. They have hierarchies and members just like any other dimension. Think of the "attributes" of a can of apple juice, and that's exactly what Essbase can help you analyze using attribute dimensions:

The special aspect of attribute dimensions is that they do not impact the size of the Essbase database. You can add an unlimited number of attribute dimensions (yes, really, as many as you could possibly need). The other big benefit with attributes is the ability to develop really nice cross tab reports. For example, we can create a cross tab report of flavor attribute dimension and promotions dimension. If you remember the first part of the book, you can't do this with shared members from the same dimension, so attribute dimensions give you a great way to do detailed product and customer analysis that isn't possible otherwise. Lastly, you can analyze sum totals, minimum, maximum, average and count calculations by attribute members and hierarchies which isn't possible with UDAs.

But wait, before you get too excited, let's learn a bit more about attributes. There are four types of Attribute dimensions: Text, Numeric, Boolean, and Date.

Text attributes are the default type and are used to describe text characteristics.

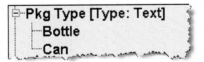

When *AND, OR NOT, <, >, =, >=, <=, <>, !=, IN,* and *NOT IN* operations are performed on text dimensions, Essbase makes logical comparisons for text attribute dimensions. Not always the most logical thing to do, but it's there all the same.

Numeric attribute dimensions contain numeric values at level 0. You can perform *AND, OR NOT, <, >, =, >=, <=, <>, !=, IN,* and *NOT IN* operations on numeric attribute dimensions. You can group numeric values into ranges (using the : symbol) and include these numeric values in calculations.

```
⊟ Ounces [Type: Numeric]
    ─32
    ─20
    ─16
    ─12
```

Boolean attribute dimensions contain exactly two members: True and False, Left and Right, or Yes and No. Once the two Boolean member names are defined, you must use same names for all Boolean attribute dimensions in database. When you perform *AND, OR NOT,* <, >, =, >=, <=, <>, !=, *IN,* and *NOT IN* operations on Boolean attribute dimensions, Essbase translates true to 1 and false to 0.

Date attribute members must contain date members at level 0 that are formatted properly. Valid date formats are mm-dd-yyyy or dd-mm-yyyy. All dates must be after 01-01-1970 and before 01-01-2038.

```
⊟ Intro Date [Type: Date]
    ─03-25-1996
    ─04-01-1996
    ─09-27-1995
    ─07-26-1996
    ─12-10-1996
    ─06-26-1996
    ─10-01-1996
```

AND, OR NOT, <, >, =, >=, <=, <>, !=, *IN,* and *NOT IN* operations can be performed on Date attribute dimensions. Date values can be also included in calculations.

There are five ways to calculate attribute data: Sum, Count, Average, Minimum, and Maximum. Sum is the default when you don't specify which one to use, but you can use the other calculations as though it was yet another dimension:

	A	B	C	D	E	F
1			Year	Product	Market	Actual
2			Bottle	Can	Pkg Type	
3	Sales	Sum	$ 270,593	$ 130,262	$ 400,855	
4		Min	$ 11,750	$ 30,469	$ 11,750	
5		Max	$ 46,956	$ 62,824	$ 62,824	
6		Avg	$ 27,059	$ 43,421	$ 30,835	
7		Count	10	3	13	
8						
9						

Note! Attribute dimensions are always dynamically calculated which could mean slower performance any time an attribute is referenced in a retrieval.

When should you use Attributes?

Use attributes when you need to create crosstab reports (examples include Product in the rows and Product Start Date across the columns or Product Packaging Type in rows and Product Start Date in the columns). Use attributes when you need to hide a level of detail in most reports but still want it available upon request (e.g. showing product revenue by packaging type vs. the entire list of products. Attributes are very helpful when performing comparisons based on certain type of data or when you performing calculations based on characteristics. Finally, use attributes when you need to add dimensionality to the database without increasing size of the database.

When should you NOT use Attributes?

Do not use attributes when you need to define characteristics of dense dimensions (no attribute dimensions are allowed on dense dimensions). Do not use attributes when you need to define characteristics that vary over time. An example - employee status is an attribute of employee. Roger Clemens is fired in September and his employee status is changed from "Active" to "Terminated" (who would ever fire Roger Clemens in September?). If we run reports for the month of January, it will look like Roger was terminated for that month. However, Roger was active for months January through October but Essbase has no way of knowing this because employee status is solely tied to the Employee dimension. If you need to track how an attribute changes over time, you must make it a stored dimension.

Do not use attributes when you need to calculate a value by placing a formula on a member (no member formulas are allowed on attribute members). Watch out for attributes when you need to improve retrieval performance (attributes are dynamically calculated and can be slow at times).

Build an Attribute Dimension

First, let's cover a few guidelines. Position attribute dimensions last in the outline. Consider the implication of Dynamic Calculations as reporting on Attribute dimensions can be slow. Define attribute dimensions on sparse dimensions only. When creating a member of an attribute dimension, you cannot perform any of the following actions:

- Tag the member as a shared member.
- Tag the member to use two-pass calculation.
- Define User-Defined Attributes (UDAs).
- Create alias combinations.
- Use consolidation symbols or formulas.

Now that we've gotten the rules out of the way, let's review the 5 steps to build an attribute dimension:

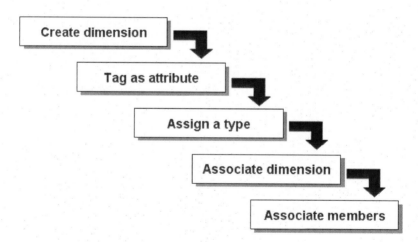

To build an attribute dimension,
1. Open the Outline Editor.
2. Right click on Outline and select *Add Child*.
   or
   Right click on an existing dimension and select *Add Sibling*.
3. Type in the new dimension name.
4. Right click on the new dimension and select *Edit Member Properties*.
5. Select *Attribute* for Dimension Type.

6. Select desired attribute type: Boolean, numeric, text, or date:

7. Click *OK*.
8. You may get a warning message - Click *Yes*. (Remember, attribute dimensions will always be placed last in the outline.)
9. Next add members and hierarchies to the dimension as you normally would by selecting *Add Child* or *Add Sibling*.

Let's add an attribute dimension for our customer dimension in the juggling wolverine application. We would like to further analyze customer by size of the event (so we can see how revenues and expenses relate to event size). Create a new text attribute dimension called Event Size with members: Small, Medium, and Large:

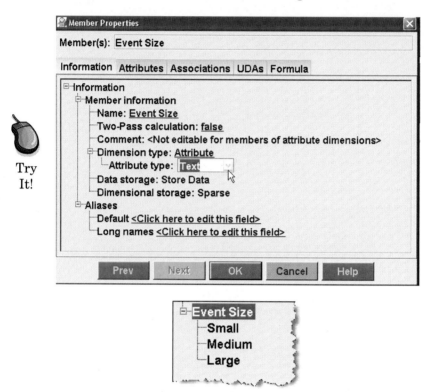

Try It!

Next you need to associate a base dimension. All attribute dimensions are associated with one and only one base dimension. Product Start Date is associated with the Product dimension. Department manager is associated with the Organization dimension.

Note! A base dimension can have one or more attribute dimensions.

10. On the base dimension, right click and select *Edit Member Properties*.

11. Select the *Attributes* tab.
12. Select the attribute dimension and click the *Assign* button to assign the base dimension:

```
┌─────────────────────────────────────────────────────────────┐
│ ▓ Member Properties                                      ☒  │
│ ┌─────────────────────────────────────────────────────────┐ │
│ │ Member(s):  Market                                      │ │
│ └─────────────────────────────────────────────────────────┘ │
│ Information  Attributes  Associations  UDAs  Formula        │
│ Associated attribute dimensions:      Other attribute dimensions: │
│ ┌──────────────────────┐  ┌─────────┐ ┌───────────────────┐ │
│ │ Market Size          │  │ Assign  │ │ Caffeinated (Product) │ │
│ │ Population           │  └─────────┘ │ Intro Date (Product) │ │
│ │                      │  ┌─────────┐ │ Ounces (Product)    │ │
│ │                      │  │Assign All│ │ Pkg Type (Product)  │ │
│ │                      │  └─────────┘ └───────────────────┘ │
│ │                      │  ┌─────────┐                       │ │
│ │                      │  │ Remove  │                       │ │
│ │                      │  └─────────┘                       │ │
│ │                      │  ┌──────────┐                      │ │
│ │                      │  │Remove All│                      │ │
│ └──────────────────────┘  └──────────┘                      │ │
│  ┌─────┐ ┌─────┐ ┌─────┐ ┌──────┐ ┌─────┐                   │
│  │ Prev│ │ Next│ │ OK  │ │Cancel│ │ Help│                   │
│  └─────┘ └─────┘ └─────┘ └──────┘ └─────┘                   │
└─────────────────────────────────────────────────────────────┘
```

13. Click *OK*.

After associating the base dimension, you then need to associate the attribute members. For example, assign an actual Product Start Date "3-14-2006" to the product "Diet Cola". Assign a Department Manager "Roger Clemens" to "Information Technology Department".

14. On base member, right click and select *Edit Member Properties*.
15. Select the *Associations* tab.
16. Select the attribute member and click the *Assign* button to assign the associated member:

Member Properties [X]

Member(s): Maine

Information Attributes **Associations** UDAs Formula

Associated attributes | Available attributes
Population: 3000000 | Attribute Dimensions And Members
Market Size: Major | Population
| Market Size
| Major
| Minor

Assign
Remove
Remove All

Full name of selected available attribute
Major

Prev | Next | OK | Cancel | Help

17. Click *OK*.

Tip!

You can define prefixes or suffixes for attribute members to ensure that all level 0 non-text member names are unique. A prefix is a value that Hyperion Essbase attaches to the beginning of a member name while a suffix is a value that Essbase attaches to the end of a member name. Right click and select *Edit Member Properties* to assign a prefix or suffix to an attribute member.

Associate the new attribute dimension Event Size with the customer dimension in the juggling wolverine application:

Member Properties   ☒

Member(s): Customer

Information | **Attributes** | Associations | UDAs | Formula

Associated attribute dimensions: Other attribute dimensions:

| Event Size |

[Assign]
[Assign All]
[Remove]
[Remove All]

[Prev] [Next] [OK] [Cancel] [Help]

Try It!

Then associate the attribute members (Small, Medium, and Large) with the base members of the customer dimension:

Member Properties   ☒

Member(s): 1003

Information | Attributes | **Associations** | UDAs | Formula

Associated attributes   Available attributes

| Event Size: Large | Attribute Dimensions And Members
                               ⊟ Event Size
[Assign]   ├ Small
[Remove]   ├ Medium
[Remove All]   └ **Large**

Full name of selected available attribute

Large

[Prev] [Next] [OK] [Cancel] [Help]

If you've been following along, your juggling wolverine customer dimension and event size attribute dimension should look like the following:

Customer {Event Size}
　Corporate Events (+)
　　1001 (+) (Alias: Hyperion User Conference) {Event Size: Medium}
　　1002 (+) (Alias: Oracle User Conference) {Event Size: Large}
　Weddings (+)
　　1003 (+) (Alias: Hyperion-Oracle Happily Ever After Wedding) {Event Size: Large}
　　1004 (+) (Alias: Hyperion-Brio Happily Ever After Wedding) {Event Size: Medium}
　Birthday Parties (+)
　Street Peddling (+)
　　1007 (+) (Alias: Essbase 7th Street) {Event Size: Small}
　　1008 (+) (Alias: System 9th Ave) {Event Size: Small}
Event Size [Type: Text]
　Small
　Medium
　Large

Recap – Steps to Build an Attribute Dimension

1. In Administration Services, open the outline.
2. Add a dimension in the Outline Editor.
3. Change the dimension type to attribute.
4. Set the Attribute type (Boolean, Number, Date, Text).
5. Add the Attribute members.
6. Associate the attribute dimension to a base dimension.
   a. Select the base dimension.
   b. Right click and select Edit Member Properties.
   c. Select on the Attributes Tab.
   d. Assign the attribute dimension.
7. Select the base members and associate the appropriate attribute members.
   a. Select the base dimension member.
   b. Right click and select Edit Member Properties.
   c. Select on the Associations Tab.
   d. Assign the attribute member.

Helpful
Info

Chapter 9:
Add Thousands of Members

You now know how to build an Essbase outline. Are you ready to manually build the product dimension with 7000 products? Then an Organization dimension with 10,000 cost centers? No way! Even the temp would give up halfway through the job. Fortunately, there is an easy way to automatically build dimensions using a text file or relational database query, and you use Essbase dimension build rules files to do it

DIMENSION BUILD RULES FILES OVERVIEW

Dimension build rules files contain the instructions to build dimensions dynamically in Essbase databases. With this handy tool, you can add new dimensions and members, remove or change existing dimensions and members, or modify attributes and calculations automatically. You can even create an outline from scratch. There are three different primary build methods for dimension rule files: Generation build, level build, and parent/child build. The build method you chose depends upon the format of your source system and determines the algorithm that Essbase uses to modify the outline.

A generation build data file looks like this:

```
Gen2     Gen3       Gen4
500      500-10     500-10-10
500      500-10     500-10-20
500      500-20     500-20-12
500      500-20     500-20-15
500      500-20     500-20-20
```

A generation build rules file will translate the data file above into this hierarchy:

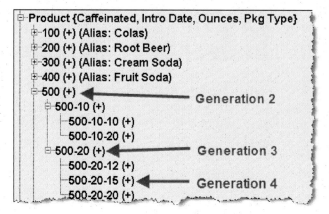

A file suitable for a level build looks like this:

```
Level0          Level1    Level2
600-10-11       600-10    600
600-20-10       600-20    600
600-20-18       600-20    600
```

A level build rules file will translate the data file above into this hierarchy:

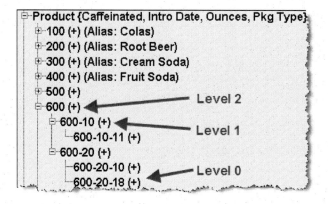

A parent/child build data file looks like this:

```
Parent    Child     Alias
200       200-10    Old Fashioned
200       200-20    Diet Root Beer
200       200-30    Sasparilla
200       200-40    Birch Beer
200       200-50    With Caffeine
```

A parent/child rules file will translate the data file above into this hierarchy:

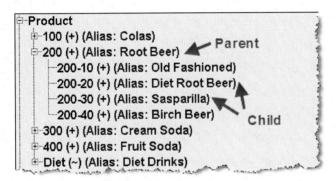

There are five steps in building a dimension build rules file:

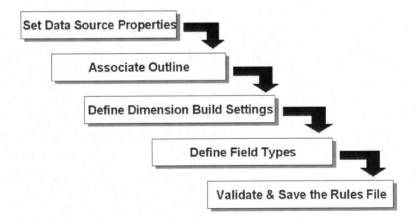

The Data Prep Editor is where you build all rules files:

So now that you understand the basics, let's jump into the details and walk through the steps to create a dimension build rules file.

CREATE A DIMENSION BUILD RULES FILE

1. In the Administration Services Enterprise View panel, navigate to the *Rules Files* section under the Sample.Basic database.
2. Right click on the Rules Files and select *Create Rules File*:

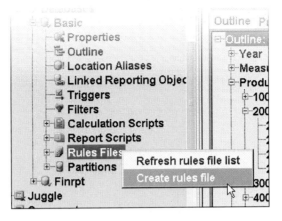

3. Select *File >> Open Data File.*
4. Browse to and open the dimension data source file. For this example, open the genref.txt file from the Sample.Basic database:

5. Click *OK.*
6. Select *Options >> Data Source Properties.*
7. The Data Source properties window will open.

Data source properties will tell Essbase the source file delimiters, what field edits have been made in the rules file, and what header rows may exist. On the Delimiter tab, specify Comma, Tab, Spaces, Custom, or Column Width delimiter for the dimension build data source file:

On the Header tab, you can specify how many lines to skip or define any records that may have header information and field information:

Next, let's associate the outline,

8. Select the *Associate Outline* button in the toolbar or if you prefer menus, choose *Options >> Associate Outline*.
9. The Associate Outline window will open.
10. Select the desired database:

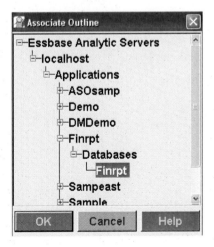

There are two modes for rules files: dimension building and data loading (we'll talk about data loading soon enough).

Note!   When working on a dimension build rules file, select the Dimension Building mode:

When working on a data load rules file, select the Data Load mode:

Next, to define the dimension build settings,
11. Select *Options >> Dimension Build Settings.*
12. The Dimension Build Settings window will open.

The Global tab of the Dimension Build Settings window allows you to define which alias table to update, autoconfiguration for sparse/dense, and exactly how the rules for selecting or rejecting should behave. Remember those three alias tables that we created in the previous chapter? Well, this is where we can specify which alias table to update from this source file. In most cases, you'll want to leave the defaults alone for this tab:

Dimension Build Settings

Dimension Build Settings | Dimension Definition
Global Settings

⊟ Global properties
   ⊢ Update alias table <u>Default</u>
   ⊟ Data configuration
     ⊢ ⊙ Use dimension property settings
     ⌐ ○ Autoconfigure dense/sparse
   ⊢ ☐ Arrange dimensions by size and type to an hourglass shɛ
   ⊟ Global select/reject Boolean
     ⊢ ⊙ And
     ⌐ ○ Or

[Outline...] [OK] [Cancel] [Help]

Tip!

Don't use "Autoconfigure dense/sparse", as it's almost always the surest way to de-optimize your database (meaning it's not even a good starting point!) We'll provide some good tips on how to set dense and sparse settings in a later chapter.

Next select the Dimension Build Settings tab to (drum roll, please) define the dimension build settings. Select the dimension that will be updated in the rules file. In this example, double-click on Product to select Product (so that Product displays next to Dimension):

After selecting the dimension, you will define how existing members in that dimension should be handled: "Allow moves", "Allow property changes", "Allow formula changes", "Allow UDA changes", and "Do not share".

"Allow moves" enables children to be moved from one parent to another. An example where you might use this: you want to reorganize your market dimension via a dimension build rules file, splitting Southwest into South and West.

This is what the dimension looks like before:

Southwest (+)
    Texas (+) (UDAS: Major Market) {Population: 21000000}
    Oklahoma (+) (UDAS: Small Market) {Population: 6000000}
    Louisiana (+) (UDAS: Small Market, New Market) {Population: 6000000}
    New Mexico (+) (UDAS: Small Market) {Population: 3000000}
    California (+) (UDAS: Major Market) {Population: 33000000}
    Oregon (+) (UDAS: Small Market) {Population: 6000000}
    Washington (+) (UDAS: Small Market) {Population: 6000000}
    Utah (+) (UDAS: Small Market) {Population: 3000000}
    Nevada (+) (UDAS: Small Market, New Market) {Population: 3000000}

After the dimension build rule (with "Allow Moves"):

West (+)
    California (+) (UDAS: Major Market) {Population: 33000000}
    Oregon (+) (UDAS: Small Market) {Population: 6000000}
    Washington (+) (UDAS: Small Market) {Population: 6000000}
    Utah (+) (UDAS: Small Market) {Population: 3000000}
    Nevada (+) (UDAS: Small Market, New Market) {Population: 3000000}
South (+) (UDAS: Small Market)
    Texas (+) (UDAS: Major Market) {Population: 21000000}
    Oklahoma (+) (UDAS: Small Market) {Population: 6000000}
    Louisiana (+) (UDAS: Small Market, New Market) {Population: 6000000}
    New Mexico (+) (UDAS: Small Market) {Population: 3000000}
Central (+) (UDAS: Major Market)

"Allow property changes" enables Essbase to update member properties based on the source file. For example, if you build your Accounts dimension from the GL and an account description changes, you will want to make sure the account alias is updated so that it is consistent with the description in the GL. Without this option selected, Essbase will not allow any alias changes.

Selecting the build method is a critical item – don't forget to do this, even though it's hidden at the bottom. You must specify the appropriate build method for the dimension selected that matches the dimension data file. Build options include:

Build method
    ⊙ Use generation references
    ○ Use level references
    ○ Use parent/child references
    ○ Add as sibling of member with matching string
    ○ Add as sibling of lowest level
    ○ Add as child of:
    ☐ Process null values

The three core Generation, level and parent/child build methods were discussed earlier, but there is also the flexibility to add a list of members as:

- A sibling of a member with a matching string
- A sibling of the lowest level
- A child of a specific member that you choose

For example, you may have a list of new cost centers that have not yet been mapped to a correct parent. You can add these cost centers to a specific parent called "New Cost Centers" so your aggregated data will be up-to-date even though the outline may not be.

The next step in the process is to define the properties of each of the data columns. Every column in the source file must either be explicitly ignored by the rules file, or assigned a specific generation, level, parent, child, or member property.

To define the field properties,

13. Select the first column in the data file.
14. Select *Field >> Properties*.
15. The Field Properties window will open.

The Global Properties tab allows you to translate text to upper / lower case, add prefixes and suffixes, convert spaces to underscores, and perform a find and replace:

For example, let's say your Account number structure and Product number structure could have the exact same number. Essbase won't allow you to have a member with the same name (remember the Essbase outline rules). You can add a prefix "Product_" to the Product dimension build so that the members will be unique.

Next we will select the Dimension Build Properties tab. (Ignore the Data Load Properties tab for now since we are focusing on dimension building).

Since we are looking at the first column of the genref.txt file for Sample.Basic, we will define the following field properties:

16. Select the dimension that maps to the field. Choose Product.
17. Select the dimension build type for the field. Choose Generation.
18. Enter the reference number which is 2 in this case (we want this value being added as generation 2):

Field Properties ☒

Global Properties   Data Load Properties   Dimension Build Properties

Field number:1

```
⊟ Dimension build
   ⊟ Field definition
      ⊞ Dimension: Product
      ⊟ Field
         ⊟ Type Generation
            ── Generation
            ── Duplicate generation
            ── Alias
            ── Property
            ── Formula
            ── Level
            ── Duplicate level
            ── Parent
            ── Child
            ── Duplicate generation alias
            ── Duplicate level alias
            ── Currency name
            ── Currency category
            ── UDA
            ── Solve order
            ── Attribute parent
         ⊞ Attribute dimensions
      └ Number 2
```

Outline...

OK

Cancel

Next>>

<< Prev

Help

Use this dialog to set dimension build field properties.

19. Click *Next* to move to the next column in the data file.
20. Select the dimension that maps to the second field, in this case it is still Product.
21. Select the dimension build type for the field. Choose Generation.
22. Enter the reference number, in this case 3.
23. Click *Next*.
24. Select the dimension that maps to the field. Still Product,
25. Select the dimension build type for the field. Choose Generation.
26. Enter the reference number, in this case 4.

Tip!

When navigating in the field property window, to select, you can Double-click a particular item. Make sure the item shows up in blue next to Dimension or Type. If you single click, the item may not be selected.

27. Click *OK* once all of the fields have been defined.

Here is a completed example of a generation build rules file:

Data Prep Editor [localhost.Sample.Basic.Genref]
Encoding:English_UnitedStates.Latin1@Binary

1	500	500-10	500-10-10
2	500	500-10	500-10-20
3	500	500-20	500-20-12
4	500	500-20	500-20-15
5	500	500-20	500-20-20

	GEN2,Product	GEN3,Product	GEN4,Product
1	500	500-10	500-10-10
2	500	500-10	500-10-20
3	500	500-20	500-20-12
4	500	500-20	500-20-15
5	500	500-20	500-20-20
6			

Note how generations must be listed from highest generation to lowest– Gen2,Product; Gen3,Product; Gen4,Product.

Here is a completed example of a level build rules file:

Data Prep Editor [localhost.Sample.Basic.Level]
Encoding:English_UnitedStates.Latin1@Binary

1	600-10-11	600-10	600
2	600-20-10	600-20	600
3	600-20-18	600-20	600

	LEVEL0,Product	LEVEL1,Product	LEVEL2,Product
1	600-10-11	600-10	600
2	600-20-10	600-20	600
3	600-20-18	600-20	600
4			
5			

Note how levels must be listed from level zero to upper levels in sequential order – Level0,Product; Level1,Product; Level2,Product.

Here is a completed example of a parent/child rules file:

Data Prep Editor [localhost.Sample.Basic.Parchil]			
Encoding:English_UnitedStates.Latin1@Binary			
1	200	200-10	Old Fashioned
2	200	200-20	Diet Root Beer
3	200	200-30	Sasparilla
4	200	200-40	Birch Beer
5	200	200-50	With Caffeine

	PARENT0,Product	CHILD0,Product	ALIAS0,Product
1	200	200-10	Old Fashioned
2	200	200-20	Diet Root Beer
3	200	200-30	Sasparilla
4	200	200-40	Birch Beer
5	200	200-50	With Caffeine
6			

The parent column must always precede the child column.

Note! You can choose to "Ignore a field during dimension building". This checkbox can be found at the bottom of the Dimension Build Properties tab under *Options >> Dimension Build Settings.*

The last steps are to validate and save the rules file. Rules files are validated to ensure member and dimension mappings jive with the associated outline.

28. Select the *Validate* icon (or select *Options >> Validate).*

My Rules File won't Validate – What Should You Check?

Helpful Info

- Is every field name valid?
- Are the reference numbers sequential?
- Are there repeated generations?
- Is the field type valid for the build method?
- Are the fields in correct order?
- Does the child field have a parent field?
- Do all dimension names exist in the outline?
- Are all dimensions referenced in the rules file?

29. Select the Save icon (or select *File >> Save*).
30. Specify the rules file name (must be 8 characters).

UPDATE THE OUTLINE

Now that you've created the rules file and you have your dimension data file, you are ready to update the outline.

1. Open the outline in the Outline Editor.
2. Select *Outline >> Update outline*.
3. The Update Outline window will open:

4. Specify SQL if loading directly from a relational source or Data files if loading from a file.
5. Select *Find Data File* and navigate to the dimension data file.
6. Select *Find Rules File* and navigate to the dimension build rules file.
7. Specify the error file location and name.
8. Optionally, you can check the option to "Overwrite". This will overwrite any error file that may already exist.
9. Click *OK* to update the outline.

DYNAMICALLY BUILD ALTERNATE HIERARCHIES

The examples we've seen so far have been pretty straightforward. Now let's look at how you can build alternate hierarchies with shared members.

A generation build data file with a column for adding an alternative hierarchy looks like the following:

The DUPGEN, "duplicate generation", column must follow the generation at which members are shared. The rules file will translate this data file into the following dimension hierarchy:

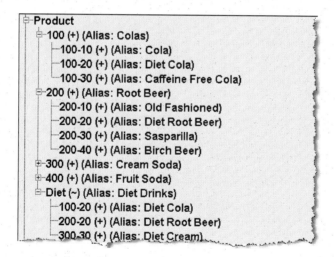

A different way to build the same hierarchy with shared members would be to use a level dimension build method. The level build data file with a column for adding an alternative hierarchy looks like the following:

```
Level0              Level1   Level1
100-20              100      Diet
200-20              200      Diet
300-20              300      Diet
```

You could also use a parent/child build method to build alternate hierarchies. The parent/child dimension build data file looks like the following (make sure to uncheck "Allow Moves"):

```
Parent              Child
100                 100-20
200                 200-20
300                 300-20
Diet                100-20
Diet                200-20
Diet                300-20
```

DYNAMICALLY ASSIGN MEMBER PROPERTIES

Under Field properties, you can update aliases, member properties, member formulas, and UDAs. If your dimension source file contains valid values, then the rules file can update any of these properties.

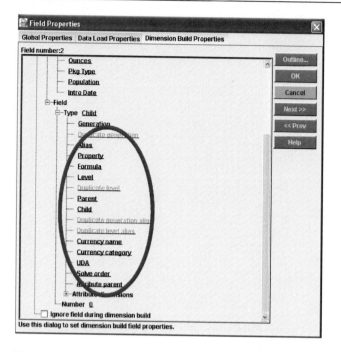

Here is a list of valid codes for assigning Essbase member properties:

%	Set consolidation to express as a percentage of current total.
*	Set consolidation to multiply by the current total.
+	Set consolidation to add to the current total.
-	Set consolidation to subtract from the current total.
/	Set consolidation to divide by the current total.
~	Set to no consolidation.
A -	Set to Time Balance Average (applies to accounts dimensions).
B	Exclude data values of zero or #MISSING in time balance.
E	Assign expense reporting tag (applies to accounts dimensions).
F	Set to Time Balance First (applies to accounts dimensions).
L	Set to Time Balance Last (applies to accounts dimensions).
M	Exclude data values of #MISSING from the time balance.
N	Set data storage to Never Share.
O	Set data storage to Label Only (store no data).

S	Set data storage to Store (non-Dynamic Calc and not label).
T	Assign two-pass calculation (applies to accounts dimensions).
V	Set data storage to Dynamic Calc and Store.
X	Set data storage to Dynamic Calc.
Z	Exclude data values of zero from the time balance.

As an example, the following file will build an accounts dimension using a source file set up in Parent/Child format. Member properties are also assigned in the source file. The rules file has defined the following field properties:

- Parent, Account
- Child, Account
- Alias, Account
- and Property, Account for the remaining property fields.

The resulting hierarchy will look like this:

Note!

If a member property is not specified in the source file, Essbase will assume the default value.

Tip!

The sample applications that are installed with Essbase have some great examples of different types of dimension build rules files. Use these as you create your own dimension build rules.

We've decided to add members to the Accounts dimension in our wolverine juggling application to track key metrics and drivers. We've been supplied the following file (you can easily create this file using notepad) for the new metrics (yes, there are only three but let's pretend we have a long list of metrics):

```
Account,Metrics,,0,~
Metrics,Avg_Wolverines_Juggled,Average Wolverines Juggled,S,~
Metrics,Avg_Dropped_Wolverines,Average Dropped Wolverines,S,~
Metrics,Headcount,,S,~
```

Then we build the following rules file to update the outline:

Data Prep Editor [localhost.Finrpt.Finrpt.wolvacct]

Encoding:English_UnitedStates.Latin1@Binary

1	Account,Metrics,,0,~
2	Metrics,Avg_Wolverines_Juggled,Average Wolverines Juggled,S,~
3	Metrics,Avg_Dropped_Wolverines,Average Dropped Wolverines,S,~

	PARENT0,Account	CHILD0,Account	ALIAS0,Account	PROPERTY0,Account	PROPERTY0,A
1	Account	Metrics			~
2	Metrics	Avg_Wolverines_Juggled	Average Wolverines Juggled	O S	~
3	Metrics	Avg_Dropped_Wolverines	Average Dropped Wolverines	S	~
4					
5					

Try It!

Build a rules file to update the Accounts dimension in the juggling wolverine application.

RULES FILES FOR ATTRIBUTE DIMENSIONS

You can use rules files to build attribute dimensions and associate base members. Let's see how.

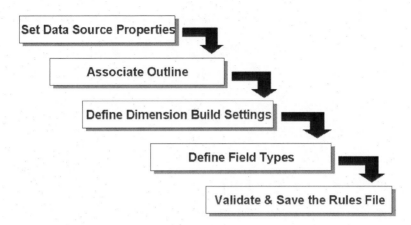

Does this process look familiar? It should. The process to build an attribute dimension is the same process for building a regular dimension.

Now what if you want to associate members in the base dimension with the attribute member? Here's an example: assigning packaging or size to a product member. To do this, you just need to accurately map the field definition.

See in the example below, columns three and four have been mapped to the correct attribute member. Notice the generation number of the attribute members matches the generation of the product member that is the associated base member:

P Data Prep Editor [localhost.Sample.Basic.Attrprod]				
Encoding:English_UnitedStates.Latin1@Binary				
1	500	500-10	64	True
2	500	500-20	64	False

	GEN2,Product	GEN3,Product	Ounces3,Product	Caffeinated3,Product
1	500	500-10	64	True
2	500	500-20	64	False
3				
4				

To assign the field properties to associate base dimension members,
1. Select *Field >> Properties*.
2. Click *Next* until you get to column 3.

3. For dimension, double click to select Product (if not already done).
4. Under Field Type, select the attribute dimension for column 3 (in this case Ounces).
5. Click *Next* to assign the next field property:

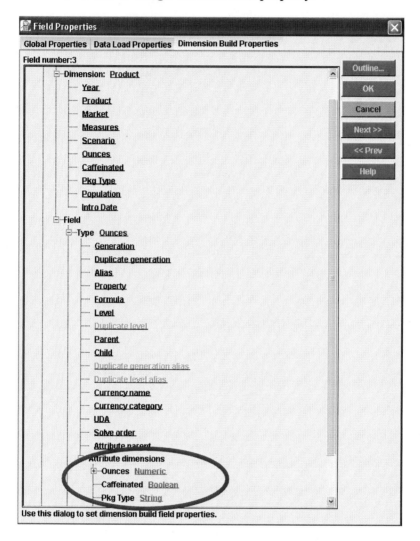

You can also add ranges to an attribute dimension. Ranges functionality allows you to use a model where numeric attribute members represent a range of values.

Note! Query processing, calculation and data load have no notion about a range model.

Let's walk through an example to help clarify what ranges look like and how to set them up using a rules file. In this example, we will change the Ounces dimension to use ranges vs. just a list of numbers. We will use a copy of the Sample.Basic application and the attrprod.rul rules file.

To define a rules file using ranges,

1. Open the attrprod.rule file for this example.
2. Select the Ounces field and select *Field >> Properties*.
3. On the Dimension Build Settings tab, expand the field type for Attributes.
4. Expand Ounces by selecting the + icon.
5. Check the option "Place attribute members within a numeric range".
6. Define a range size and a start value.
7. Check "Delete all members of this attribute dimension" (in this case, because we removing the list and adding in range members):

```
⊟···Attribute dimensions
   ⊟···Ounces  Numeric
      ⊟···☑ Place attribute members within a numeric range
         ⊞···Range Size:  10.0
         ⊞···Start Value:  0.0
         ⊞···☑ Delete all members of this attribute dimension
```

8. Click *OK*.
9. Select *File >> Save As* and save the updated rules file as 'attrrng':

10. Open the outline.
11. Select *Outline >> Update Outline*.
12. Find and select the attrng.rul rules file.
13. Find and select the attprod.txt source file.
14. Specify the location for any error files.
15. Check the "Overwrite" option:

Update Outline

[localhost.Finrpt.Basic]

Type
○ SQL
◉ Data files

SQL user: [   ]   SQL password: [   ]

Data files

Find Data File   Delete

localhost.Finrpt.Basic.Attrprod

Use rules   Find Rules File

Rules file
localhost.Finrpt.Basic.attrrul

Error file
C:\Hyperion\eas\client\dimbuild.err   ☐ Overwrite

OK   Cancel   Help

16. Click *OK*.
17. Optional – you can add aliases to the range members as we did in this example.

Here is the attribute dimension with the numeric list (before):

⊟ **Ounces Attribute [Type: Numeric]**
    ├─32
    ├─20
    ├─16
    └─12

Here is the attribute dimension with the numeric range (after):

⊟··**Ounces Attribute [Type: Numeric]**
 ┊ ├····**0 (Alias: 0-9 oz)**
 ┊ ├····**10 (Alias: 10-19 oz)**
 ┊ ├····**20 (Alias: 20-29 oz)**
 ┊ ├····**30 (Alias: 30-39 oz)**
 ┊ ├····**40 (Alias: 40-49 oz)**
 ┊ ├····**50 (Alias: 50-59 oz)**
 ┊ └····**60 (Alias: 60-69 oz)**

SELECT / REJECT RECORDS

Say your dimension data file has every possible account, but you have special hierarchy logic to apply to the revenue accounts. This requires a filter using wildcards to only load the revenue account range. Using Sample.Basic as an example, we want to update the level.rul to only build products that begin with 600-20.

To add a filter to your load rule,
1. Select *Record* >> *Select* or *Reject*:

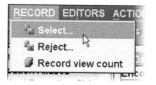

2. Define the type: *String* or *Number*.
3. Type in the value.
4. Select the criterion: equals, does not equal, greater than, greater than or equal to, less than, less than or equal to, contains, or does not contain.
5. Check whether the filter should be case sensitive:

Select Record

Field: LEVEL0,Product

Boolean

○ And ⊙ Or

Type	String/Nu...	Condition	Case-sen...
String	600-20	Contains	■

New   Delete   OK   Cancel   Help

6. Click *OK*.

Try It!

Make a copy of gen.rul in Sample.Basic. Update the copied rules file to reject all records containing the value "500-10-10". This product has been discontinued but the source that provides the dimension hierarchy keeps sending the complete dimension list (those pesky IT administrators).

Note!

You can add multiple lines of criteria for Select or Reject records in a rules file.

CREATE COLUMNS USING TEXT OR JOIN

Often times we need to do some manipulation with the dimension build source file (or even the data load file). The file may be missing some information or you may need to join columns to create the desired member names.

For example, we have the following requirements for our product dimension. We want the alias value set to product number joined with the product description. And for level 1, we want to add on the words "Product Category" to the category number.

Here is the data file that we are provided:

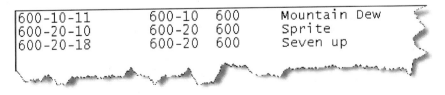

```
600-10-11       600-10   600      Mountain Dew
600-20-10       600-20   600      Sprite
600-20-18       600-20   600      Seven up
```

Note this file doesn't meet our dimension build requirements so we are going to need to do some further manipulation in the rules file. There are lots of changes, so let's get started. First we want to move the level zero alias field to directly behind the level zero product number.

1. Select *Field >> Move*.
2. Select the desired field to move and click the *Up* or *Down* buttons to order the columns appropriately:

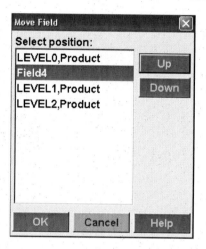

3. Click *OK*.
4. Select *Field >> Create Using Text*:

5. Type in the text " – " because we would like to have a hyphen between product number and alias.
6. Click *OK*.
7. Select *Field >> Create Using Join*:

8. Select the desired columns to join:

Create Field Using Join

Fields to join for create:

LEVEL0,Product
Field2
Field3
LEVEL1,Product
LEVEL2,Product

OK   Cancel   Help

9. Click *OK*.

Note!

The fields will be joined in the order they are listed in the "Create Field Using Joins" window.

10. Notice the new field created with the three concatenated columns. We now need to move this new column to just after the product number. Select *Field >> Move* and move the column.
11. Next assign the field property alias to the new column.
12. Assign "Ignore during dimension build" to the two extra columns.

Tip!

Select *Field >> Properties* to find the "Ignore during dimension build" option.

Data Prep Editor [localhost.Sample.Basic.Level]
Encoding:English_UnitedStates.Latin1@Binary

1	600-10-11	600-10	600	Mountain Dew
2	600-20-10	600-20	600	Sprite
3	600-20-18	600-20	600	Seven up

	LEVEL0.Prod...	ALIAS0.Product	Field3	Field4	LEVEL...	LEVEL...
1	600-10-11	600-10-11 - Mountain Dew	-	Mounta...	600-10	600
2	600-20-10	600-20-10 - Sprite	-	Sprite	600-20	600
3	600-20-18	600-20-18 - Seven up	-	Seven up	600-20	600
4						
5						
6						
7						
8						
9						
10						
11						
12						
13						

You can view and undo these field edits. Select *Options >> Data Source Properties*. Select the Field Edits tab:

Data Source Properties

Delimiter | Field Edits | Header | Ignore Tokens

Split / Join / Create / Move

Operation:	Columns:	Split Char...
Move	4	2
Create [text]	2	-
Create [join]	1 2 3	
Move	1	2

Move
Join
Split
Create Using Text
Create Using Join

Delete | OK | Cancel | Help

Try It!

Make a copy of the parchil rules file in Sample.Basic. In the copy, update the rules file using "Create using Text/Join" functionality to assign product number concatenated with a hyphen concatenated with product description (e.g. 200-10-10 – Old Fashioned) as the alias.

PRINT A RULES FILE

You can print a rules file via Administration Services. This is helpful for documentation purposes or if you are just trying to understand what the rules file does (vs. opening all of the various windows to view the rules settings).

To print a rules file,
1. Select *File >> Print*.
2. Define what should be printed:

3. Click *OK*.

Recap – Steps to Building Dimensions via Rules File

Helpful Info

1. In Administration Services, navigate to the Rules Files section under the application or database.
2. Right click and *Create Rules File*.
3. Once the data prep editor is open, select *File >> Open Data File*.
4. Navigate to the appropriate folder on the Essbase Analytic server. Find the dimension data file.
5. Make sure you've selected Dimension Build mode (dimension build icon).
6. Select *Options >> Data Source Properties*. Update any of the data source properties for the applicable file (e.g. skip first line).
7. Select *Options >> Dimension Build Settings*.
8. Update the Field Properties for each column (Select *Field >> Properties*).
9. Validate the rules file.
10. Save the rules file.
11. Open the outline in the outline editor.
12. Select *Outline >> Update Outline*.

Chapter 10:
Load Data

Now that our outline is ready, we can start loading data into Essbase. Thinking that you're going to have to learn a whole new interface? Not so... You will load data via ...wait, drumroll please... a rules file. The last chapter covered dimension build rules files, and thankfully creating data load rules files are very similar.

Before we get into the data load rules files, let's take a step back for a moment. There are many different ways to load data to Essbase:

- Spreadsheet lock and send
- Free-form and drag and drop
- Data load rules
- Data load rules using SQL interface
- Essbase Integration Services

In this chapter we will cover free form data loading and data load rules.

FREE FORM DATA LOADING

Free-form data loading is a simple process to load data to Essbase. The data file can be loaded as is without any explicit description of its contents (i.e. no load rule), but the data <u>must</u> be in the natural order for Essbase. So what is the natural order for Essbase? It is really the same rules that apply to the Excel add-in so go back and review Chapters 2 and 4 if you need a quick refresher. Any valid dimension/member/alias name combination is acceptable. Data is read according to the member names Essbase finds.

Free Form Data Load Example 1:

Markets Products Scenario Year Measures

East	Cola	Actual	Jan	Sales	$10
East	Cola	Actual	Feb	Sales	$21
East	Cola	Actual	Mar	Sales	$30
East	Cola	Actual	Apr	Sales	$35
East	Cola	Actual	May	Sales	$40
East	Cola	Actual	Jun	Sales	$45
East	Cola	Actual	Jan	Marketing	$8
East	Cola	Actual	Feb	Marketing	$16
East	Cola	Actual	Mar	Marketing	$20

Free Form Data Load Example 2:

Measures Markets Products Year Scenario

	East	"100-10"		Actual
	Jan Feb Mar Apr May Jun			
Sales	10 21 30 35 40 45			
Marketing	8 16 20 33 38 40			

To load a free form data file,
1. Select *Actions >> Load data for "dbname"*.
2. The Load Data window will open.
3. Specify Data files (this is the default option).
4. Select *Find Data File* and navigate to the data file.
5. DO NOT select *Find Rules File*. A rules file is not necessary for a free form load:

6. Click *OK*.

That's it for Free Form Data loading. If all your input files are formatted that nicely, then your job as an Essbase Administrator is going to be very easy indeed.

DATA LOAD RULES OVERVIEW

Just as we used dimension build rules, we can use data load rules to perform transformations and define information in a text file for Essbase, but in this case to load data. We have to define what columns map to what dimensions, which columns contain data, and any necessary header information.

So when should you use a data load rule?

- You need to ignore fields or strings in data file.
- You need to change the order of fields by moving, joining, splitting or creating.
- You need to map the data in the data source to the database by changing strings.
- You need to change the data values in the data source by scaling data values or adding them to existing values in the data source.
- You need to set header records for missing values.

- You need to reject an invalid record and continue loading data.
- You want to add new dimensions and members in the database along with the data load.
- You want to change existing dimensions and members in the database along with the data load.

So what we are really saying is that in most cases you will use a data load rule to load data to Essbase.

Here is what a data load rule will look like in the Data Prep Editor:

Look familiar? Yes. The same interface as dimension build rules files. So let's create a data load rules file.

CREATE A DATA LOAD RULES FILE

1. In Administration Services, navigate to the *Rules Files* option under the application or database.
2. Right click and select *Create Rules File*:

3. Select *File >> Open Data File*.
4. Browse to and open the data file. For this example, open the act1.txt from the Sample.Basic application:

5. Select *Options >> Data Source Properties*.
6. The Data Source properties window will open.

Data source properties will tell Essbase the data source delimiters, what field edits have been made in the rules file, and what header rows may exist.

On the Delimiter tab, specify Comma, Tab, Spaces, Custom, or Column Width delimiter for the data file (if someone with a wacky sense of humor gave you a data file with @ or ~ as the delimiter, Essbase can handle this with the custom option):

Specify how many lines to skip or define any records that may have header information and field information on the header tab:

Next, associate the outline,

7. Select Associate Outline icon or *Options >> Associate Outline*.

8. The Associate Outline window will open.
9. Select the desired database:

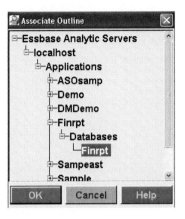

To define the data load settings,
10. Select *Options >> Data Load Settings*.
11. The Data Load Settings window will open:

On the Data Load Values tab, define whether this rules file should overwrite, add to, or subtract from existing values. In most cases, you want to overwrite, but there are some exceptions.

Here's one: the source file you load to Essbase contains daily data but your Essbase database contains aggregated monthly data. You would want to specify "Add To Existing Values" for the following text file to get Essbase to calculate the total for the month. If the data load rule is set to overwrite, then only the final value in the file will be stored:

```
01/01/2007, Jan, California,Caffeine Free Cola, Sales, 145
01/02/2007, Jan, California,Caffeine Free Cola, Sales, 123
01/03/2007, Jan, California,Caffeine Free Cola, Sales, 132
01/04/2007, Jan, California,Caffeine Free Cola, Sales, 145
01/05/2007, Jan, California,Caffeine Free Cola, Sales, 102
01/06/2007, Jan, California,Caffeine Free Cola, Sales, 116|
```

You can also specify whether to flip a sign based on an assigned User Defined Attribute on the Data Load Values tab. If your source file contains debits and credits, you will want to load only positive values because you will be handling the sign flipping in Essbase using Unary Operators. To do this, you can assign a UDA of "Flip Input" (or something else descriptive of the task) to all of your accounts that will be arriving as negative values. Check the "Sign Flip on UDA" check box and select the "Flip Input" UDA. The sign will be flipped for all records in the data file for the accounts tagged "Flip Input".

To clear data for a specific intersection before loading the data file, utilize the Clear Data Combinations tab. This is helpful if you load actual data on a daily basis and want to automatically clear out the month being loaded before loading the daily data. In the example below, the rules file will clear all January Actual data before loading the new data file:

The Header Definition tab allows you to define any dimension not represented in the data file. In the example below, we've defined a header of 'Actual' because there isn't a column in the file that identifies the scenario. Essbase needs to know exactly where you want to load data for every dimension. Should it load data to Actual, or Budget, or both?

Note!

A data load rules file must reference every dimension, either in the fields section or in the header section.

Next, define the Field properties, mapping the columns to dimensions or members and identifying data values.

12. Select *Field >> Properties.*
13. The Field Properties window will open.

The Global Properties tab allows you to translate text to upper / lower case, add prefix and suffixes, convert spaces to underscores, and perform a find and replace. This is used to make sure that the values specified in the data load match what is in the outline, especially if you've used a dimension build file to add prefixes or suffixes to member names.

For example, let's say your Account number structure and Product number structure could have the exact same number. Essbase won't allow you to have a member with the same name so you built your Product dimension to include a prefix "Product_". Now your source file only has the product number. You need add the prefix "Product_" to the Product column so that data will load to the correct product member.

Members in the data file must match the members in your outline exactly! If the Objects_Juggled dimension in our juggling wolverine application has the member "Super-sonic silver wolverine" but our data file has "Super sonic silver wolverine" with no hyphen, data will not be loaded for those records. But (whine) its close enough. Can't Essbase figure it out? Nope. Members in the data file must match member names in the outline.

Tip!

Next we will select the Data Load Properties tab. (Ignore the Dimension Build Properties tab since we are focusing on data loading).

14. Select the dimension that maps to the field
    or select a specific member
    or select "Data Field"
    or select "Ignore field during a data load":

![Field Properties dialog box with Global Properties, Data Load Properties, and Dimension Build Properties tabs. Field number:1. A tree showing Data load > Field definition > Field name Market, Dimension with Year, Measures, Product, Market, Scenario; Data field; Ignore field during data load; Scale with 0.0. Buttons: Outline..., OK, Cancel, Next>>, <<Prev, Help. At bottom: "Use this dialog to set data load field properties"]

Tip!

When navigating in the field property window, double-click to select a particular item. Make sure the item shows up in blue next to Field Name. If you single click, the item will not be selected. This can be an annoying little feature that will test your memory and patience... "but I know I set that property" and you probably did but you single clicked instead of double clicked.

Note!

You can only have one column assigned "Data Field" within a data load rules file.

15. Click *Next* to move to next field.
16. Click *OK* once all of the fields have been defined.

Note!

There are two modes for rules files: dimension building and data loading. When working on a dimension build rules file, select the Dimension Building mode:

When working on a data load rules file, select the Data Load mode:

Here is an example of a data load rules file where the first three columns map to a dimension and the remaining columns map to a specific member in the Period dimension:

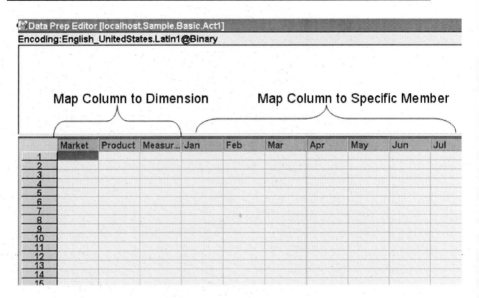

The last step before saving is to validate the rules file. Rules files are validated to ensure the member and dimension mapping defined in the rules file maps to the associated outline. Validation cannot ensure that the data source will load properly. For example, you've defined the rules file, setting source file and data load properties, assigned field columns, and everything validates successfully. But what if your source file contains the member "Forecast" but "Forecast" doesn't exist in the outline. Any records containing members that do not exist in the outline will not be loaded to Essbase. These invalid or "fallout" records are sent to an exception file that you can review after the load has finished.

17. Select the Validate icon (or select *Options >> Validate*).

My Data Load Rules File won't Validate – What Should You Check?

Helpful Info

- Is the field name valid?
- Are the file delimiters correctly placed?
- Is there a member in the field name?
- Is the dimension name used in another field name or the header?
- Are you using a member as member combination in one place and a single member in another?
- Is more than one field defined as the data field?
- Is the dimension used for sign flipping in the associated outline?
- Is the rules file associated with the correct outline?

18. Select the *Save* icon (or select *File >> Save*).

Within a rules file you can filter records from a source file using either Select or Reject. Say your data file had all accounts but you only wanted to load data for revenue accounts. You could define a filter using wildcards to only load data for the revenue account range.

To add a filter to your load rule,
1. Select *Record >> Select* or *Reject*.
2. Define the type: *String* or *Number*.
3. Type in the value.
4. Select the criterion: equals, does not equal, greater than, greater than or equal to, less than, less than or equal to, contains, or does not contain.
5. Check whether it is case sensitive.
6. Click *OK*.

LOAD DATA

We have the data file, we have the data load rules file. Let's load some data (Is it sad that we are really excited about getting to this step? Ok, yes, we are complete geeks).

To load data using a rules file,
1. Within Administration Services, select *Actions >> Load data for "dbname"*.
2. The Load Data window will open.

3. Specify SQL if loading directly from a relational source or Data files if loading from a file.
4. Select *Find Data File* and navigate to the dimension data file.
5. Select *Find Rules File* and navigate to the dimension build rules file.
6. Specify the error file location and name.
7. Check the "Overwrite" check box if you want the error file replace an error file that may already exist:

Data Load	☒

[localhost.Sample.Basic]

Type
- ○ **S**QL
- ⦿ **D**ata files

Options
- ☐ **M**odify outline
- ☐ **A**bort on error during data load
- ☐ Execute in the **b**ackground
- ☑ **L**oad data
- ☑ **I**nteractive

SQL **u**ser: [   ]   SQL **p**assword: [   ]

Data files

[Find Data File] [Dele**t**e]

localhost.Sample.Basic.Act1

☑ Use **r**ules   [Find Rules File]

Rules file

localhost.Sample.Basic.Act1

Error file

C:\Hyperion\eas\client\dataload.err   ☐ **O**verwrite

[OK] [Cancel] [Help]

8. Click *OK* to update the outline.

Tip!

You can load more than one load file with the same rules file if needed.

Other options available on the Data Load window include *Modify Outline, Abort, and Execute in the Background*:

Options

☐ Modify outline   ☑ **Load data**

☐ Abort on error during data load ☑ **Interactive**

☐ **Execute in the background**

You can perform two operations on the data as it is loaded. During a data load, you can modify a database outline using a rules file and load data at the same time. Use the *Modify outline* option on the Data Load window to do this.

Abort on error during data load will stop the data load process if an error is found with the data file. If this is not selected, Essbase will load the valid records and send the invalid records to the error file.

Execute in the background will run the process in the background on your desktop, freeing up Administration Services to perform other tasks. If this is not selected and your data load takes 3 hours, you can't do anything else in Administration Services until the data load is complete (while the break would really do you some good, this will most likely frustrate the heck out of you).

Recap – Steps to Load Data via Rules File

1. In Administration Services, navigate to the Rules Files section under the application or database.
2. Right click and *Create Rules File*.
3. Once the data prep editor is open, select *File >> Open Data File*.
4. Navigate to find the data file
5. Make sure you've selected Data Load mode (use the data load icon to do this).
6. Select *Options >> Data Source Properties*. Update any of the data source properties for the applicable file (e.g. skip first line).
7. Select *Options >> Data Load Settings*.
8. Update the Field Properties for each column (Select *Field >> Properties*).
9. Validate the rules file.
10. Save the rules file.
11. Select the Database.
12. Right click and select *Load Data*.
13. Navigate to the data file and select.
14. Select the new rules file you just created.
15. Click *OK* to load data.

Helpful Info

Let's get ready load data to our juggling wolverine application. We've been supplied the following data file. (You can easily create this file in Excel, saving as tab delimited text.)

		Jan	Feb	Mar	Apr	May	Jun	Jul	Aug	Sep	Oct	Nov	Dec
1001	Net_Rev	100	100	100	100	100	100	100	100	100	100	100	100
1001	Op_Expense	20	20	20	20	20	20	20	20	20	20	20	20
1001	Other_Expense	5	5	5	5	5	5	5	5	5	5	5	5
1002	Net_Rev	200	200	200	200	200	200	200	200	200	200	200	200
1002	Op_Expense	35	35	35	35	35	35	35	35	35	35	35	35

What two dimensions are missing from this data file and where do we define them in the load rule? If you guessed Year and Scenario to part 1 of the question and "Header Definition" for part 2, you are right! Move forward one page and collect $200 (kidding). If not, please go back to the beginning of this chapter, do not stop and do not collect any money.

Create a data load rule to load the data file above to the juggling wolverine application. Then load the data!

Try It!

Chapter 11:
Calculate Data

We've created applications, built dimensions, and loaded data. We're almost to the end of the road of making you a knowledge Essbase administrator. The next step in the process is to consolidate and calculate Essbase data. This chapter will make calculations in Essbase seem very basic but trust me, we are just skimming over the iceberg here (there is a reason why Essbase administrators get paid big bucks). Later chapters will cover more advanced topics related to calculations in Essbase.

DENSE AND SPARSE

Before we get into consolidations and calculations, we need to review some key concepts related to the Essbase structure. Get ready to impress your coworkers with complicated concepts like "dense" and "sparse" and "optimized block structure".

First, let's define member combination. A member combination is the intersection of members from each dimension. See the following examples of member combinations for the Sample.Basic outline:

```
⊟ Year Time (Active Dynamic Time Series Members: H-T-D, Q-T-D) (Dynamic Calc)
   ⊞ Qtr1 (+) (Dynamic Calc)
   ⊞ Qtr2 (+) (Dynamic Calc)
   ⊞ Qtr3 (+) (Dynamic Calc)
   ⊞ Qtr4 (+) (Dynamic Calc)
⊟ Measures Accounts (Label Only)
   ⊞ Profit (+) (Dynamic Calc)
   ⊞ Inventory (~) (Label Only)
   ⊞ Ratios (~) (Label Only)
⊟ Product {Caffeinated, Intro Date, Ounces, Pkg Type}
   ⊞ 100 (+) (Alias: Colas)
   ⊞ 200 (+) (Alias: Root Beer)
   ⊞ 300 (+) (Alias: Cream Soda)
   ⊞ 400 (+) (Alias: Fruit Soda)
   ⊞ Diet (~) (Alias: Diet Drinks)
⊟ Market {Population}
   ⊞ East (+) (UDAS: Major Market)
   ⊞ West (+)
```

Example member combinations:
- Qtr1->Profit->100->East->Actual

- Year->Profit->100->East->Actual
- Jan->Sales->100-10->New York->Budget
- Jan->Sales->100->New York->Budget

Tip!

The symbol "->" is known as a cross dimensional operator in Essbase (more on this later). For now, when you see the "->", think of the word "at". We are referencing the data value at Qtr1 at Profit at 100 at East at Actual.

Dense data is data that occurs often or repeatedly across the intersection of all member combinations. For example, you will most likely have data for all periods for most member combinations. You will most likely have data for most of your accounts for member combinations. Time and accounts are naturally dense.

Sparse data is data that occurs only periodically or sparsely across member combinations. Product, Market, and Employee dimensions are usually sparse:

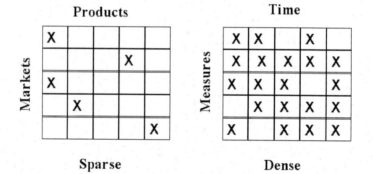

You as the administrator will assign a dense / sparse setting to each dimension. This will dictate how the Essbase database is structured.

To define dense or sparse for a dimension,
1. In Administration Services, open the outline.
2. Select the Properties tab.
3. Scroll down to the Data Storage section:

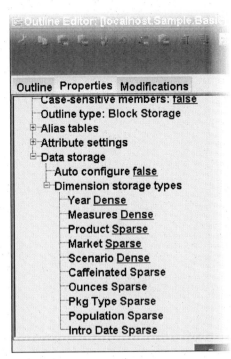

4. Choose the Dense and Sparse settings from the drop down box for each dimension:

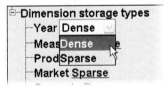

Tip!

Disable Autoconfiguration. Autoconfiguration of dense and sparse dimension provides only an approximation and cannot take in account the nature of the data loaded into the database or the requirements of calc scripts.

BLOCK STRUCTURE

The Essbase database is composed of a number of blocks. A block is created for each intersection of the sparse dimensions. In the example below, Market and Product are sparse. See a block for each sparse member combination in the example below:

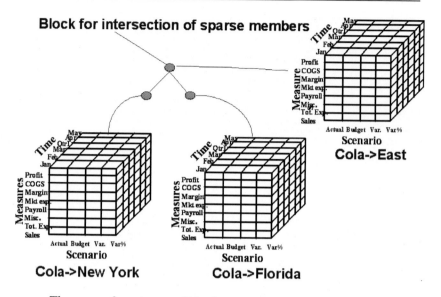

Block for intersection of sparse members

Scenario
Cola->East

Scenario
Cola->New York

Scenario
Cola->Florida

There are four types of blocks:

- Input blocks are blocks where data is loaded or input.
- Calculated blocks are blocks are created through consolidation or calculation.
- Level zero blocks are blocks are created from the level zero members of all dimensions.
- Upper-level blocks are all blocks that contain at least one upper level member (non-level zero).

Each block is made up of cells. These cells are created for each intersection of the dense dimensions. In the example below, Time, Measures, and Scenario are dense dimensions. See the cells for each dense member combination in the example below:

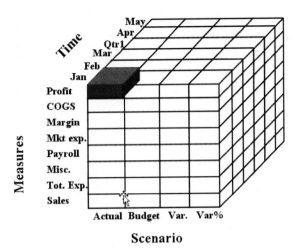

Set the following dense / sparse settings for the dimensions in our juggling wolverine application:

Account: Dense
Period: Dense
Scenario: Dense
Customer: Sparse

Try It!   Why can't you change the dense / sparse setting for the Event Size dimension? If you answered "Event Size is an attribute dimension and attribute dimensions are always sparse", pat yourself on the back. You're coming along, my fledgling administrator.

Outline Consolidation

Essbase is built to perform outline consolidations. You assigned a consolidation attribute to each member that tells Essbase how to perform the consolidation, whether it should add to the total, subtract from the total, and so forth. Unary operators include +, -, *, /, %, and ~. The consolidation will use these operators and follow the path of the hierarchies for each dimension.

So what does outline consolidation and dense/sparse have to do with each other? Essbase will perform dense calculations first and then sparse calculations. The default calculation order for Essbase is the following:

- First, Accounts
- Second, Time
- Third, remaining dense dimensions

- Fourth, remaining sparse dimensions
- Two Pass Calculation (covered in a later chapter)

Let's follow the path of an Essbase consolidation to help you better understand. In the example below, the cells in the lower left corner of the block indicate cells loaded with data. The cells in the lower right hand corner of the block represent those cells populated with the Accounts dimension calculation. The cells in the upper portion of the block represent those cells populated with the Time dimension calculation.

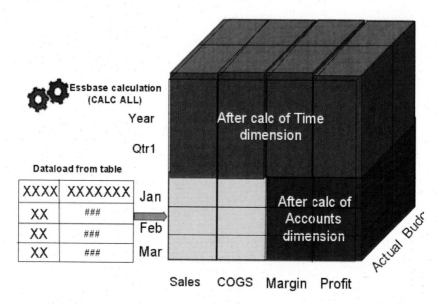

Here is another view of this dense calculation. Data is loaded to Sales and COGS members for each month. We are looking at the block for Vermont, Cola, and Actual (there's that cross dimensional symbol that means "at").

Vermont -> Cola -> Actual

Accounts	Jan	Feb	Mar	Qtr1
Sales	124.71	119.43	161.93	
COGS	42.37	38.77	47.28	
Margin				

First we consolidate the Accounts dimension, calculating the Margin member.

Vermont -> Cola -> Actual

Accounts	Jan	Feb	Mar	Qtr1
Sales	124.71	119.43	161.93	
COGS	42.37	38.77	47.28	
Margin	82.34	80.66	114.65	

Next we consolidate the Time dimension, calculating the Qtr1 member.

Vermont -> Cola -> Actual

Accounts	Jan	Feb	Mar	Qtr1
Sales	124.71	119.43	161.93	406.07
COGS	42.37	38.77	47.28	128.42
Margin	82.34	80.66	114.65	277.65

Once the Dense calculation is complete, the sparse calculation is next. The Vermont -> Cola -> Actual block and the New York -> Cola -> Actual block are added together to create the East -> Cola -> Actual block.

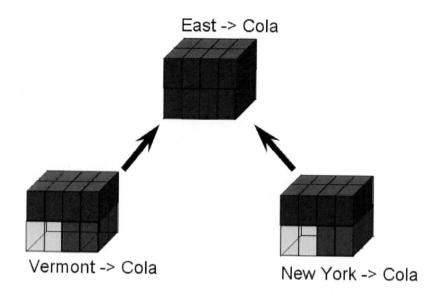

East -> Cola

Vermont -> Cola

New York -> Cola

DEFAULT CALC

The default calc will is the simplest method for calculating Essbase databases, performing outline consolidations and calculating formulas as they appear in the outline. The default calc runs a "Calc All" calc script against the Essbase database.

Outline consolidations (sometimes called "unary operators") are those little plus, minus, divide, multiply, percent, and "no consolidate" signs that you place on individual members in the outline:

⊟ **Measures**
  ⊞ **Profit (+)**
    ⊞ **Margin (+)**
    ⊞ **Total Expenses (-)**
  ⊞ **Inventory (~)**

In this snippet of Sample.Basic, you see that "Margin" has a plus sign next to it and "Total Expenses" has a minus sign. These are unary operators. When a default calculation occurs on Sample.Basic, the data in these two members will consolidate together and be saved in the Profit member. "Inventory" has a tilde next to it (AKA "No Consolidate") so it won't be added to the data from "Profit" and stored in Measures.

The other type of calculation that occurs during a default calculation is the members in the outline with formulas will have their formulas evaluated:

⊟ **Ratios (~)**
　├─ **Margin % (+) [Formula: Margin % Sales;]**
　└─ **Profit % (~) [Formula: Profit % Sales;]**

When the default calculation occurs, the formula on "Margin %" will evaluate and take margin as a percentage of sales.

Note!　In Sample.Basic, Margin %, Profit, and Measures are not actually stored members, so no data is really stored into these members.

To launch the default calc,

1. Select the database.
2. Right click and select *Execute Calculation*:

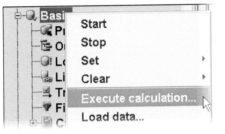

3. Select Default calc.
4. Check "Execute in Background" (this frees up the Administration Services console for other tasks):

Execute Database Calculation ☒

[localhost.Sample.Basic]
State: Data values have been modified since the last calculation
Calculation script

(default)

☑ **Execute in the background**

OK   Cancel   Help

5. Click *OK*.

Data will be consolidated for all dimensions and members.

Run the default calc for the wolverine juggling application.
Try It!

You are now ready to retrieve, report, and analyze. You jump into the Essbase Add-In or Smart View Add-In and click "Retrieve". The anticipation is killing you. Finally we are ready for analysis. But all you see is #Noaccess. Oh, that's right. We haven't covered one of the most important parts of Essbase, security. Let's do that next.

Chapter 12:
Assign Security

SECURITY OVERVIEW

Essbase provides flexible security that can be implemented from a high level down to the individual cell level. Cell level? Yes, you can define write access for product 100 for January for gross revenue for actual for FY07 for the west region. Do we recommend this level of security? No because this would be a nightmare to maintain. But it is still possible if your requirements dictated this madness. This section will teach you how.

First, we'll review the different types of users within Essbase. Essbase has four different kinds of users: supervisors, user managers, application creators, and end users:

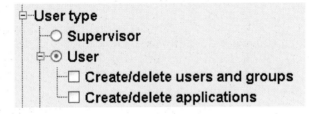

Supervisors (think god-like supreme beings) have full access to all Essbase components and applications. User managers can manage security access but cannot update or access applications. Application creators (think 2nd-in-command god-like beings) can manage applications but they cannot update security (although one user could be assigned both of these roles). An application creator can be defined at the application level and the database level. The Application designer can perform the following:

- Modify or delete the application.
- Create, modify or delete the database within application.
- Assign user access privileges at the application or database level.
- Define and assign filter objects anywhere in the application.

Database designers are the low-people-on-the-totem pole in the world of Essbase administrators. Don't feel too bad, database designers. You still have full control of your own database world and you don't have the headaches that come with being a god-like supervisor. The database level, also called Database designer, can perform the following:

- Modify or delete the database.
- Assign user access privileges at the database level.
- Define and assign filter objects anywhere in the database.
- Remove data locks within the database.

With Essbase 7x, you create and maintain users and groups in Essbase Administration Services. Beginning in version 7.1.3 and System 9, Essbase security is maintained in a product called Shared Services. You complete the same basic processes that you do in Administration Services with slightly different navigation. That statement sounds pretty simple but trust me, Shared Services security, while it provides huge benefits (discussed later in the System 9 chapter), is a bit more complex than Administration Services security.

SET DEFAULT MINIMUM ACCESS

You can set a default level of access for an application or database that will apply for all users. For example, all users have read access to the wolverine juggling Finrpt database. Define this at the database level and you are done with security for most users. Then you may add a filter with write access to the Budget scenario for the Budget office so they can update the enterprise budget.

To set application or database default access,
1. Right click on the application or database.
2. Select *Edit Properties*.
3. On the General tab, set the Minimum access level to either: None, Read, Write, Calculate or Database Designer:

Database Properties: [localhost.Sample.Basic]

Database: | Status:
localhost.Sample.Basic | Loaded

General | Dimensions | Statistics | Caches | Transactions | Storage | Currency | Modifications

- General
  - Description Click here to edit
  - Database type Normal
  - Startup
    - ☑ Allow users to start database
    - ☑ Start database when application starts
  - Calculation
    - ☐ Aggregate missing values
    - ☐ Create blocks on equations
    - ☑ Two-Pass calculation
  - **Minimum access level** | None
    - | None
  - Data retrieval buffers | Read
    - Buffer size (KB) 10 | Write
    - Sort buffer size (KB) | Calculate
    - | Database Designer

Apply | Refresh | Close | Help

4. Click *Apply* to save the change.

CREATE A GROUP AND ASSIGN SECURITY

In Essbase you will want to use Group security assignments as much as possible. Groups reduce the overall maintenance for your security application. You define security once and as users come and go, they can be added and removed to groups. If security requirements change, you update the group security once vs. many times for many users.

Note! The same group can be used across multiple applications and databases.

Let's walk through an example. End users of the Sample.Basic application will only have access to their market. We will create a group and assign security for the West market.

1. Within Administration Services, select *File >> New >> Group*
    or
    Right Click on *Groups* and select *Create Group*:

2. The Create Group window displays.
3. Type in the group name.
4. Specify Group Type:
   - Supervisor
   - User
   - Application access type

5. Select the Users tab.
6. Select desired available users.
7. Select the < (or the << to assign all groups):

At this point in the example we don't have any users to assign so we'll continue to the next step.

8. Click the App/Db Access tab. By default, users do not have access to any application or database:

At this point in the example we don't have any users to assign so we'll continue to the next step.

To assign access,

9. Select the application for and select *"Access Databases"* from the drop down box next to the desired application:

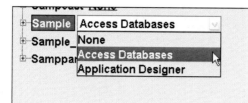

10. Select the database and then the desired access from the drop down box (e.g. Filter access):

Available options include:
- None – Assign no access.
- Filter – Assign a specific security filter (e.g. a filter that allows read access to a certain member or members).
- Read – Assign read access to the entire database.
- Write – Assign read and write access to the entire database.
- Calculate – Assign read, write, and calculate access for the entire database.
- Database designer – Allow users to update the Essbase database in Administration Services (e.g. change dimensions, write calc scripts, create load rules).

In this example, we are creating a group that has read access to the West market. What access should we assign? If you answered 'Filter', you are correct.

11. Select the filter to assign to the user (more on filters in just a few pages).
12. Click *Apply* and the group should be created successfully.

CREATE A USER AND ASSIGN SECURITY

Roger Clemens has finally decided to retire from major league baseball and pursue a career in business performance management. While the baseball world is devastated, this is good news for us. Our hugely successful wolverine juggling business has recruited Roger to be the manager for the West Region (pretend that we've added a Market dimension to our juggling wolverine application). Let's create a new user, 'rclemens' and assign him to the West Region group.

1. Within Administration Services, select *File >> New >> User* or
   Right click on Users and select *Create User*:

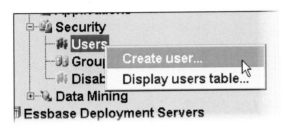

2. The Create User window displays:

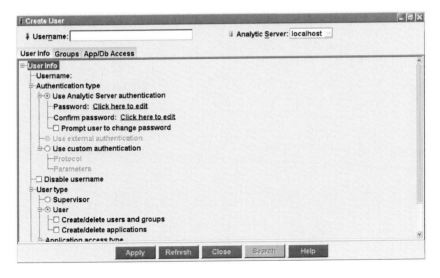

3. Type in the user name "rclemens".
4. Specify authentication method and enter password if necessary.

With Essbase 7x, you can authenticate against the Essbase server or an external provider like Microsoft Active Directory or LDAP. There are additional configuration steps required for external authentication (see the Hyperion installation guides for more information). For this example, we will choose Essbase authentication.

5. Specify User Type.
    *   Supervisor
    *   User
    *   Application access type

In this example, we choose 'User'.

6. Select the Groups tab.
7. Select desired available groups.
8. Select the < (or the << to assign all groups). We'll assign the rclemens to the West group:

9. Click *Apply*.

Now if we wanted to assign user specific security to an application, we could do so by selecting the App/Db Access tab and follow the same steps for assigning database access security. But we are leveraging groups for all security assignments (remember that best practice tip). So we are done with the process of creating the user, rclemens.

Roger will need to input budgets for the West region in the Sample.Basic application. Create a new "Budget" group and assign Roger to this group.

Try It!

Roger has recruited the recently retired Jeff Bagwell to join the juggling wolverine business. Create a new user jbagwell but don't assign him to any groups at this point.

Try It!

INHERITANCE RULES

Users inherit all privileges defined for their group. Though, sometimes group security assignments may conflict with each other. How does Essbase handle conflicting security group and user assignments?

Let's use the following scenario to explain. The minimum access for the database is set to Read. The Budget group has write access to the Budget scenario and all regions via the F_Budget filter. Rclemens is a member of the Budget office group. Rclemens is assigned write access to the West Region. Jbagwell is an Essbase user and is not a member of any group.

So here are the rules of inheritance:

Default minimum access will apply for all users. So Jbagwell has read access to the entire database.

If a user has higher access privileges than the default, those assignments will take precedence. Rclemens is a user so by default has read access to the entire database. But he is a member of the Budget group which has a higher level of security – filter access with Write to the Budget scenario. So this write access will take precedence over the default Read setting.

User access will override group access. The Budget group has write access to all Regions but rclemens only has write access to West. The individual security takes precedence so rclemens will be able to write to the West region.

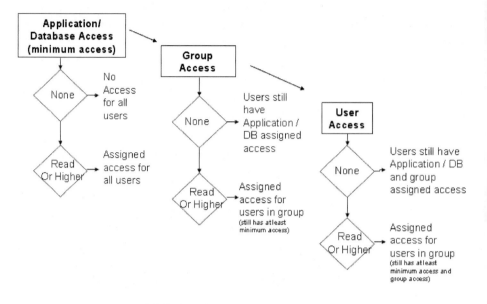

DATABASE FILTERS

In our example, we assigned the West Region filter to the West group. Before we create the filter, let's review a few concepts.

Database filters provide cell level security for Essbase. Filters can define access for multiple dimensions with either none, read, write, or metaread security access. None, read, and write access rights are pretty straightforward. Metaread security adds a layer of security for metadata (dimensions and members) in outlines, similar to read-only security for data cells. This level restricts access to dimensions or members during retrieval of an outline in a report.

In the example below, a user only has access to the West Region. Because metaread security has been implemented, they only see the West portion of the hierarchy:

If the user had read access to the descendants of West, they would be able to see the full Market hierarchy but would receive a message "#noaccess" for data points other than the West region descendants.

The user can see the full hierarchy:

But the user can only see data values for the descendants of West:

	A	B	C	D	E	
1			Sales	Product	Actual	
2	East	Year	#NoAccess			
3	California	Year	47442			
4	Oregon	Year	19992			
5	Washingto	Year	19036			
6	Utah	Year	17305			
7	Nevada	Year	29156			
8	West	Year	#NoAccess			
9	South	Year	#NoAccess			
10	Central	Year	#NoAccess			
11	Mar	Year	#NoAccess			
12						
13						

Metaread security offers the following benefits:
- Improves the ease of use when users can only see a small number of the members
- Provides privacy so extranet users can't see the existence of other extranet users (such as vendors)

- Provides privacy so that users of sensitive applications (i.e., Payroll) can't see the existence or *non-existence* of specific members (like a company reorganization where a department may be eliminated)

CREATE A DATABASE FILTER

Let's create the database filter for the West group. This filter should only allow access to the West dimension. We do not want the West users to be able to see the other members of the Market dimension. What type of filter access should be assigned? That's right – metaread.

1. Within Administration Services, navigate to the application and database where you will be creating the filter.

Note! Be aware! Filters are created in the Application / database section of Administration Services; not Security. This is because filters are always associated with an application and database.

2. Right click on Filters and select *Create Filter*:

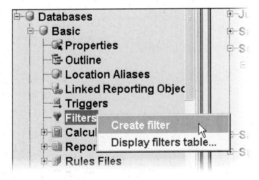

3. The Filter Editor window will open.
4. Type in the name of a filter; in this case 'F_West'.
5. Under Access, select *"Metaread"*:

Filter Editor [localhost.Sample.Basic.untitled]

Use aliases

Alias table

Sample.Basic
- Year
- Measures
- Product
- Market
- Scenario
- Caffeinated

Insert arguments

Alphabetical
Categorical

Commands and functions
- Member Set

Filter Definition

Filter name

F_West

Filter rows

Access	Member Specification
	Click here to add
None	
Read	
Write	
MetaRead	

Verify | Delete Row | Save | Close | Help

Dimension References in the Filter Editor

Helpful
Info

- The dimension reference area allows you to navigate the outline within the Filter editor window.
- You can search for member.
- You can insert a member name into the filter definition area.

Filter Editor [localhost.Sample.Basic.F_West]

Use aliases

Alias table

Sample.Basic
- Year
- Measures
- Product
- Market
  - East
    - New

Insert argu

Categorical

Commands and functions
- Member Set

Find members
- Expand to children
- Expand to descendants
- Expand entire outline
- Collapse to ancestor
- Insert member name

Filter Definition

Filter name

F_West

Filter rows

Access	Member Specification
MetaRead	@DESCENDANTS ("West")
Click here to add	Click here to add

Verify | Delete Row | Save | Close | Help

Available Functions in the Filter Editor

- Lists available functions and operators available for filters.
- You can insert arguments assists the administrator with the formula syntax.
- You can enable auto-completion speeds up filter generation.

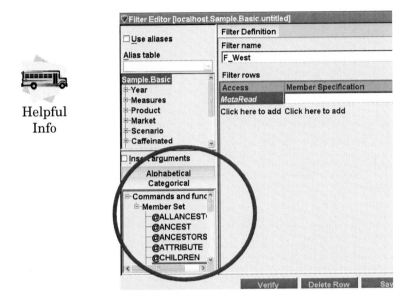

Helpful Info

6. Next, place your cursor in the Member Specification box.
7. Under the Commands and functions section of the Filter Editor, expand the Member Set grouping and look for '@DESCENDANTS':

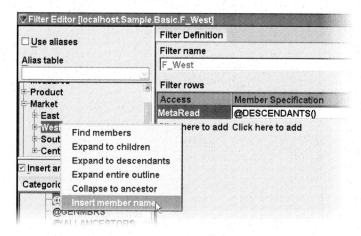

8. Double-click on '@DESCENDANTS' when you find it. This should insert the function into the Member Specification box.
9. Place your cursor in between the two brackets. We need to insert the desired member in between the brackets – in this case, West.
10. In the dimension reference portion of the Filter editor, expand the Market dimension to find the West member.
11. Right click on West and select *Insert Member Name*:

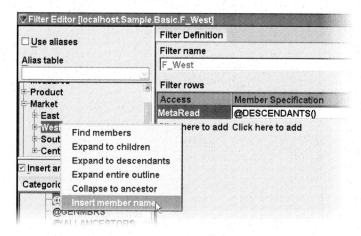

12. This should insert the function into the Member Specification box.

We are choosing descendants in this case because we want this filter to allow metaread access to West's descendants.

The "I" in the function means inclusive. @IDESCENDANTS would give access to West and West's descendants. Depending on your security requirements, Tip! you may choose the "I" instead of no "I".

You don't have to use the dimension reference or available functions sections in the Filter editor. If you know the syntax and exact member name, you can type directly into Note! the Member Specification box.

13. Click on the *Verify* button.

14. Check the message panel for any errors.

15. Select *File >> Save* or the *Save* button to save the filter.

In our example, we only defined access on one dimension but you could define access on multiple dimensions. We could have also locked down Accounts, giving read access to Net Income accounts but not balance sheet accounts. We could have granted write access to the budget scenario and read access to Actual.

If a filter has overlapping member specifications, access is set by the following rules:

- A Filter that defines a more detailed dimension combination list takes precedence over a filter with less detail.
- If the preceding rule does not resolve the overlap conflict, the highest access level among overlapping filter rows is applied.

The access level for unspecified members is the inherited access level of the database.

MAINTAINING ESSBASE SECURITY

In the Administration Services console, you can easily maintain your Essbase security (for versions 7x). Use "Copy" functionality when you need to create a group (or user) that is exactly the same as another group (or user) with one or two slight changes. Use the "Edit" functionality when you need to edit group (or user) access. You can delete groups (or users) as necessary.

Double-click on Groups or right click on Groups in the Enterprise View panel. Select *Display Groups table* to maintain Essbase groups. Double-click on Users or right click on Users and select *Display Users table* to maintain Essbase users:

From time to time users can become disabled (e.g., they've entered in the wrong password three times). To re-enable (or if you wanted to manually disable a user), double-click on *Disabled Usernames* under Security in the Enterprise View panel. The Disabled User window will display. Move the users from Disabled to Enabled (or vice versa depending on your objective) and click *Apply*:

Now you are ready to retrieve and report. Happy analyzing!

Chapter 13:
A Day in the Life ...

We've taken you through the process of creating an application and assigning security but what about the day to day tasks of an Essbase administrator? Sipping pina coladas, napping on the beach... If only that were true. Now let's jump into what your job will really be like. Here are some of the daily tasks you will perform.

MANAGE THE ESSBASE SERVER

You will definitely need to know how to start and stop the Essbase server. Essbase will stop responding at some point no matter how good of an administrator you are.

Note! There will be many, many times when something happens in Essbase and you just don't know what caused it. Prepare yourself for the unknown at times. Let the force guide you (not really, let the knowledge you gain from this book guide you).

To start Essbase, type "`essbase password`" at any command line or double-click on Essbase.exe in Windows environment. You can also start the Essbase Server from the Hyperion Solutions program group in the start menu. Any of these steps will start the Essbase server in the foreground. You can create a script to start Essbase in the background which is recommended for production instances. You don't want anyone to see an open command line window on the server and hit the X button. No more Essbase.

Other commands that you might use for managing the Essbase Server:

START *appname*	Starts the specified application.
STOP *appname*	Stops the specified application.
USERS	Displays a list of all users connected to the Analytic Server.

PORTS	Displays the number of ports installed on the Analytic Server and the number of ports in use.
LOGOUTUSER user	Disconnects a user from the Analytic Server and frees a port. This command requires the Analytic Services system password.
PASSWORD	Changes the system password that is required to start the Analytic Server. This command requires the Analytic Services system password.
COMPACT	Enables compaction of the security file when the Agent is running. Essbase compacts the security file automatically each time the Agent is stopped.
DUMP filename	Dumps information from the Analytic Services security system to a specified file in ASCII format. If you do not supply a path with the file name, the file is saved to the bin directory. Requires the Essbase system password.
VERSION	Displays the Analytic Server software version number.
HELP	Lists all valid Agent commands and their respective functions.
QUIT and EXIT	Shuts down all open applications and stops Analytic Server.

START AND STOP AN APPLICATION

Before users can connect to an application, it must be started. There are a few different ways to start an application.

- Using the Essbase Server Agent window, type `Start application_name`
- Using Administration Services, right click on the application and select *Start Application.*
- Using MaxL, type `alter system load application application_name`
- Applications can be configured to startup automatically with the Essbase Server. Update this property under Application Properties in Administration Services.

Once the application has been started, data and user security is enabled and each database can be started. Users can connect to the application and administrators can change settings of the application.

At times you will want to stop an application. Careful! Stopping applications while actions are in progress could cause database corruption. The steps to stop an application are similar to the Start steps:

- In the Essbase Server Agent window, type `Stop application_name`
- Using Administration Services, right click on the application and select *Stop Application.*
- Using MaxL, type `alter system unload application application_name`

START AND STOP A DATABASE

You must also start a database to allow users to connect. When the database is started, the entire index cache is committed to memory. What is an index cache? Don't worry about this for now. We'll cover index caches in an upcoming *master* chapter.

To start a database, use one of the following methods:
- Using the Essbase Server Agent window, type `Start application_name database_name`
- Using Administration Services, right click on the database and select *Start Database.*
- Using MaxL, type `alter system load database database_name`
- Databases can be configured to startup automatically with the Essbase Server. Update this property under Database Properties in Administration Services.

The same caution we noted above related to stopping an application applies to databases as well. Stopping databases while actions are in progress could cause database corruption. Once the database is stopped, all data is unloaded from memory and committed to disk. The steps to stop an application are similar to the Start steps:

- In the Essbase Server Agent window, type `Stop database_name`
- Using Administration Services, right click on the application and select *Stop Database.*
- Using MaxL, type `alter system unload database database_name`

Try It!

Roger Clemens has kicked off a huge query against our juggling wolverine application and the application has stopped responding. Stop and restart the application to resolve the issue (note – this may not always work but it is one of the first things you try).

VIEW THE SERVER LOG FILE

You are going to have to troubleshoot at some point. Really? Errors? Issues with Essbase? Yes, yes, and yes. The Essbase Server log file is one of your first starting points when investigating an issue. The server log file is stored in the main Essbase folder as ESSBASE.log. This log file captures all server activity, including user logins, application level activities, and database activities. We can see that Roger Clemens, the end user, logged in at 7am on Tuesday. We can see that Jeff Bagwell renamed an application at 10am (glad we're paying the big bucks for those hardworking users).

You can view this log file through Administration Services. Select the Essbase server from the Enterprise View panel in Administration Services. Right click and select *View Log*:

Choose Starting Date and enter the desired start date in most cases. Your log files will get really big and if you open the entire log file, be prepared to wait.

Have you ever tried to read text in a foreign language? Just a little confusing, right? Well, prepare yourself for a similar experience with the Essbase server log files:

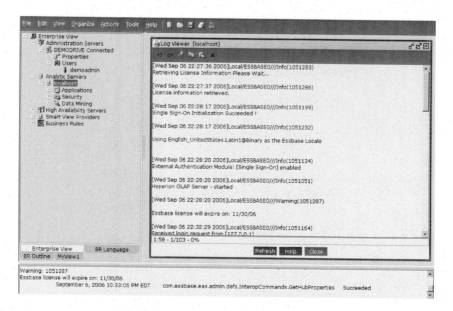

Actually, interpreting the log files isn't that bad. We'll give you a brief translation course on some of the common messages. Here are some example Startup Messages that you will see in the Essbase.log. We see the Sample application is loaded and started, and then the database Basic is loaded.

```
[Tue Nov 06 07:54:16
    2006]Local/ESSBASE0///Info(1051061)
    Application Sample loaded - connection
    established
[Tue Nov 06 07:54:16
    2006]Local/ESSBASE0///Info(1054027)
    Application [Sample] started with process id
    [1300]
[Tue Nov 06 07:54:18
    2006]Local/ESSBASE0///Info(1054014) Database
    Basic loaded
```

Here is an error message captured in the log file when user admin tried to rename an application. He received an error message stating that an application already existed with the name 'Testing'.

```
[Tue Nov 06 08:00:04
    2006]Local/ESSBASE0///Info(1051001) Received
```

```
            client request: Rename Application (from user
            admin)
[Tue Nov 06 08:00:04
            2006]Local/ESSBASE0///Error(1051031)
            Application Testing already exists
[Tue Nov 06 08:00:04
            2006]Local/ESSBASE0///Warning(1051003) Error
            1051031 processing request [Rename
            Application] - disconnecting
```

Here is an example of the messages you will see when you stop the Sample application and shutdown the Essbase server.

```
[Tue Nov 06 08:00:46
            2006]Local/ESSBASE0///Info(1054005) Shutting
            down application Sample
[Tue Nov 06 08:00:52
            2006]Local/ESSBASE0///Info(1051052) Hyperion
            Essbase Analytic Server - finished
```

Congratulations! You now speak Essbase-log-ish.

Tip!

Periodically archive off the Essbase.log file. Smaller log files can help with performance

Try It!

Take a look at your Essbase.log file. Look for instances where applications are started and users have logged into the server. Find them?

VIEW ESSBASE SERVER PROPERTIES

Within Administration Services you can view Essbase server level properties like username and password management settings, version information, server statistics, and OS/CPU and Memory information.

Within Administration Services, right click on the Essbase server. Select *Edit Properties*. Select the Security tab:

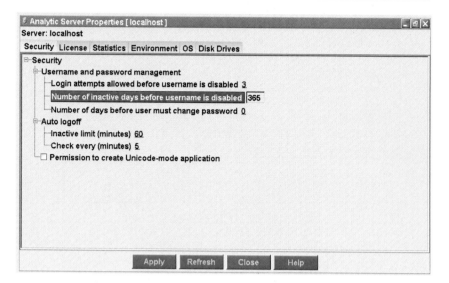

Set "Login attempts allowed before username disabled" to 3 and set "Number of inactive days before username disabled" to 365. If a user enters an invalid password, after three tries, the username is disabled. If a user hasn't logged into the server in a year, their username is disabled (don't waste those precious, costly Essbase licenses).

Select the License tab. Want to see what version you've installed, what additional components are installed, and when does the license expire (pretty important to know)? You can view this information on the License tab:

On the remaining tabs, you can view server statistics, environment information, and other hardware related information.

What is the inactive limit on your server? What version of Essbase are you running? Check out these settings and more for the Essbase server.

Try It!

VIEW SERVER SESSIONS

You can view current activity for the server: Who's connected? For how long? And more importantly, what are they doing? It is fun to be big brother. For example, you receive a call from a user complaining that performance has slowed significantly on the Essbase server. You check out the current sessions and see that Roger Clemens kicked off an application copy that has brought the system to its knees.

To view Sessions, select Sessions under the Essbase server in the Enterprise View panel:

From the Sessions module, you can log off and kill users from their sessions. Why would you want to kill someone? No matter how much of a pacifist you may be, you will want to kill someone in your Essbase world.

You will definitely receive this call at some point. "I just accidentally drilled down to Dimbottom on the Product dimension which has 10,000 products. Now my computer is frozen." What is the resolution to this problem? View sessions and log off or kill this particular user. Killing may be a bit drastic but sometimes it's required. Don't worry – killing a user is Essbase is quite legal.

To log off or kill, select the desired option from the dropdown at the top of the Sessions window:

| Log off | selected user | only | ☐ Use Force |

| Log off | | | |
| Kill | | | |

| | ... | Applica... | Databa... | Db Con... | Request | Reques... | Conne... | Connec... | Reques... |
| rclemens 1951399... 00:00:09 | Sample | Basic | 00:00:08 | none | 00:00:00 | localhost | 127.0.0.1 |

Select User, All Users or All Instances of User:

| Log off | selected user | only | ☐ Use Force |

User	Session	Login T...	A				Request	Reques...	Conne...	Connec...	Reques...
			selected user							
rclemens	1951399...	00:00:09	all users				none	00:00:00	localhost	127.0.0.1
			all instances of user							

Select On Server, On selected Application, or On selected Database. Select Use Force (if necessary):

| Log off | all users | on selected server | ☐ Use Force |

User	Session	Login T...	Applica...	Databa...	Db Con...	R	on selected server		Connec...	Reques...
rclemens	1951399...	00:00:09	Sample	Basic	00:00:08	no	on selected application		127.0.0.1
							on selected database		

So we have some flexibility with logging off or killing. In our request above, we may only have to kill the user for a specific database. You may need to log all users off of a particular application just before the monthly load and calc takes place. You may need to log all users off of a server before nightly backups run.

Try It! As an almighty Essbase administrator, see what the minions in your domain are doing right now. View the current sessions for your Essbase server.

SERVER DATA LOCKS

Essbase will lock cells when they are being updated whether it is through Essbase Add-In lock and send, data load, or calculation. Once the update is complete, the lock is released. Occasionally locks are not released. You select *Essbase >> Lock* in the Essbase Add-In and then Excel crashes. You may want to periodically check for data locks or you may get a call from a user saying that Essbase won't accept their data changes.

To view data locks, select Locks under the Essbase server:

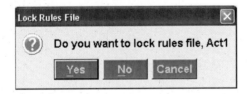

From the Locks window, you can view locks by application, database, and user. You can unlock locks by selecting *Unlock* (very tricky, we know).

LOCKED OBJECTS

Similar to data locks, you can also have locks on Essbase objects. Remember how you are prompted with the following message each time you edit an object:

Most of the time we say "Yes" because we don't want anyone else to change the object while we are viewing or editing it. Once we save our changes and close the object, the object lock is released. But what happens if your computer freezes and causes you to reboot while you had the act.rul data load rule open? You weren't able to successfully close the rules file within Administration Services so the lock remains on the rules file.

You can unlock the rules file in the Locked Objects window. To view locked objects, select Locked Objects under the Essbase server.

From the Locked Objects window, you can view locked objects by application, database, and user. You can unlock locked objects by selecting *Unlock*.

See if you have any data locks or locked objects on your Essbase server.

Try It!

VIEW AND EDIT APPLICATION PROPERTIES

The application properties and statistics tabs provide some helpful options to administrators. Remember, this is where we set the default minimum security for an application. You may want to enable "Allow Users to Start Application" for rarely used applications. This way the application and database won't take up precious memory if it is not being used. When the application is needed, it will start when the user tries to connect via the Essbase Add-In or other reporting tool. This will, however, add a bit more initial response time for the user. Alternatively, if you have a highly used application, you can check "Start application when Analytic Server starts" because you know this application will need to be started and you can save some time for the first user to connect. This is also where you can define an application as a Unicode application (more on this later).

To view and edit application properties,
1. Select the application.
2. Right click and select *Edit >> Properties*.
3. The Application properties window will display:

Application Properties [localhost.Sample]

Application: Status:
[localhost.Sample]   Loaded

General Statistics

- **General**
  - Description Click here to edit
  - Startup
    - ☑ Allow users to start application
    - ☐ Start application when Analytic Server starts
  - Security
    - ☑ Allow commands
    - ☑ Allow connects
    - ☑ Allow updates
    - ☑ Enable security
  - Minimum access level None
  - Timeout on data block locks (minutes) 60
  - Max attachment file size (KB) Unlimited
  - Data storage type Default
  - ☐ Unicode mode

Apply   Refresh   Close   Help

Change the minimum access to our wolverine juggling application to Read. Allow the application to start when Essbase starts.

Try It!

VIEW APPLICATION LOG FILE

The Application log file displays all activity for an application and its databases. There is a different application log file for each application. The log file name is the *application_name.log* and is stored in the application App file. This file tracks activity for the specific application, including the "who" and "when" of an operation and any errors of operations. For example, we can see Roger Clemens ran a calc script on Monday at 12 p.m. You we can see that Jeff Bagwell performed a series of retrievals on Tuesday at 1 p.m. (more big brother capabilities).

You can view this log file through Administration Services. Select the application in Administration Services. Right click and select *View Log*:

Choose Starting Date and enter the desired date in most cases. Your log files will get really big and if you open the entire log file, be prepared to wait.

The application log file will display:

Let's learn more Essbase-log-ish. Here are some example Startup Messages that you will see in the application log file.

Essbase writes information about the dimensions and members in the outline, such as the dimension sizes and dynamic calculation information, to the application log.

```
[Tue Nov 06 08:47:14
       2006]Local/Sample///Info(1002035) Starting
       Essbase Server - Application [Sample]
[Tue Nov 06 08:47:15
       2006]Local/Sample///Info(1200480) Loaded and
       initialized JVM module
[Tue Nov 06 08:47:15
       2006]Local/Sample///Info(1019008) Reading
       Application Definition For [Sample]
[Tue Nov 06 08:47:15
       2006]Local/Sample///Info(1019009) Reading
       Database Definition For [Basic]
[Tue Nov 06 08:47:15
       2006]Local/Sample///Info(1019021) Reading
       Database Mapping For [Sample]
[Tue Nov 06 08:47:15
       2006]Local/Sample///Info(1019010) Writing
       Application Definition For [Sample]
[Tue Nov 06 08:47:15
       2006]Local/Sample///Info(1019011) Writing
       Database Definition For [Basic]
[Tue Nov 06 08:47:15
       2006]Local/Sample///Info(1019022) Writing
       Database Mapping For [Sample]
[Tue Nov 06 08:47:15
       2006]Local/Sample///Info(1013202) Waiting for
       Login Requests
[Tue Nov 06 08:47:15
       2006]Local/Sample///Info(1013205) Received
       Command [Load Database]
[Tue Nov 06 08:47:15
       2006]Local/Sample///Info(1019018) Writing
       Parameters For Database [Basic]
[Tue Nov 06 08:47:15
       2006]Local/Sample///Info(1019017) Reading
       Parameters For Database [Basic
```

Essbase also writes information about the outlines for each database to the application log.

```
[Tue Nov 06 08:47:15
    2006]Local/Sample///Info(1019012) Reading
    Outline For Database [Basic]
[Tue Nov 06 08:47:15
    2006]Local/Sample///Info(1007043) Declared
    Dimension Sizes = [20 17 23 25 5 3 5 3 15 8 6
    ]
[Tue Nov 06 08:47:15
    2006]Local/Sample///Info(1007042) Actual
    Dimension Sizes = [20 14 20 25 4 3 5 3 15 8 5
    ]
[Tue Nov 06 08:47:15
    2006]Local/Sample///Info(1007125) The number
    of Dynamic Calc Non-Store Members = [8 6 0 0 2
    ]
[Tue Nov 06 08:47:15
    2006]Local/Sample///Info(1007126) The number
    of Dynamic Calc Store Members = [0 0 0 0 ]
```

Here is an example of an error message in an application log file. The user Admin tried to load data to the Sample.Basic but the data file contained the member '500-10' which does not exist in the outline. We are told that zero records were loaded (the rules file was most likely set to abort on error).

```
[Tue Nov 06 08:49:52
    2001]Local/Sample///Info(1013210) User [admin]
    set active on database [Basic]
[Tue Nov 06 08:49:52 2001]
    Local/Sample/Basic/admin/Info(1013091)
    Received Command [DataLoad] from user [admin]
[Tue Nov 06 08:49:52 2001]
    Local/Sample/Basic/admin/Info(1003040)
    Parallel dataload enabled: [1] block prepare
    threads, [1] block write threads.
[Tue Nov 06 08:49:52 2001]
    Local/Sample/Basic/admin/Error(1003000)
    Unknown Item [500-10] in Data Load, [0]
    Records Completed
[Tue Nov 06 08:49:52 2001]
    Local/Sample/Basic/admin/Warning(1003035) No
    data values modified by load of this data file
[Tue Nov 06 08:49:52 2001]
    Local/Sample/Basic/admin/Info(1003024) Data
    Load Elapsed Time : [0.11] seconds
[Tue Nov 06 08:49:52 2001]
    Local/Sample/Basic/admin/Info(1019018) Writing
    Parameters For Database [Basic]
```

Take a look at the wolverine juggling application log file. What date and time did we load data most recently? How long did the default calculation take place?

Try It!

Managing Log Files

We recommend you archive log files on a periodic basis (depends on the level of activity on an application). These files can become quite large and could slow performance. Within Administration Services, after you've made a backup of the file, you can clear the file.

View Log Charts

A new enhancement in Essbase 7x, log charts, will help you review and understand Essbase activity much better than those easy-to-read log files (we are kidding about the easy-to-read part). No Essbase-log-ish required.

To view the log file in chart format, select the application in Administration Services. Right click and select *View Log Chart:*

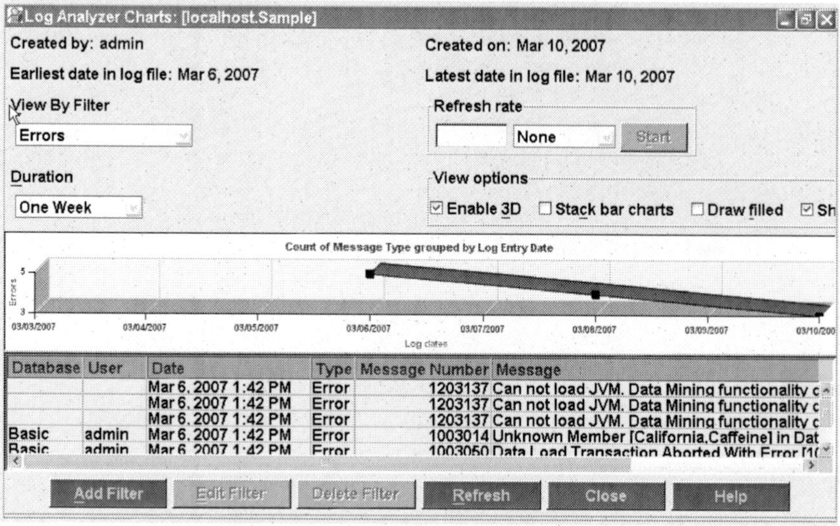

You can filter Log charts by predefined filters: errors, warnings, calculations, data loads, and spreadsheet queries:

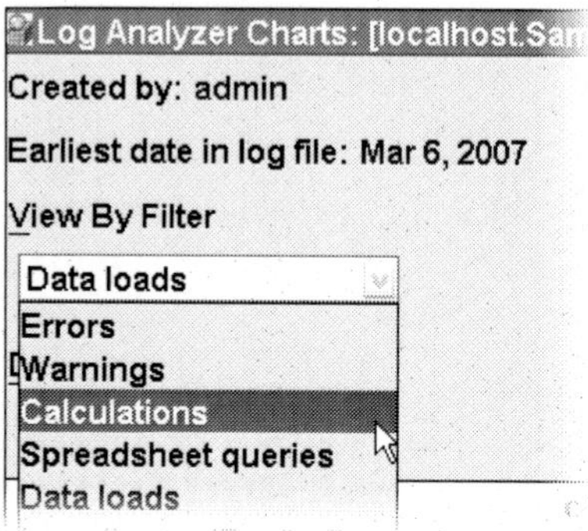

The following log chart shows all data loads that have occurred, when they occurred, how long the data load lasted, and who performed the load:

You can also create your own custom filter. Click the *Add Filter* button. Jbagwell has been acting a bit suspiciously and we're wondering if that shoulder injury is interfering with the juggling business. You want to track his activity in Essbase for the wolverine juggling application for the next month.

First, define the following information for the filter: a name for the filter, the application, the database, the user, either "All message numbers" or a specific message number, start date, and end date. Utilize "Look Up" functionality to see the description associated with a message number (honestly, who is going to memorize all of the different Essbase message codes?). The "Text contains" provides search capabilities for a specific string. Lastly, define the X and Y axis for the chart. Most of the fields within the log file filter definition are optional.

In our case, we create the following filter to track jbagwell's activity:

Now the Investigate_Jbagwell filter is added to the filter list and we can view a chart detailing jbagwell's activity.

Try creating your own custom log file filter.

Try It!

OTHER APPLICATION TASKS

Via Administration Services, several other actions for applications are available. Select an application in the Enterprise View panel and right click. These are the other actions you can perform on applications. You can copy, rename, and delete applications from Administration Services:

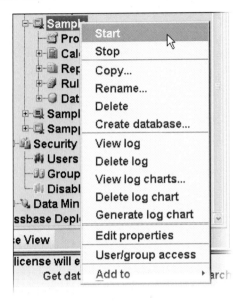

When you copy an application, all objects will be copied within Essbase including the outline, rules files, report scripts, calc scripts, and data. During the copy process, users are prohibited from accessing both the 'from' and the 'to' applications. You can copy across servers if desired.

We need to create a development version of the wolverine juggling application. Copy the wolverine juggling application, creating devjug (we love to be creative with our 8 character limit for application and database naming).

Try It!

VIEW AND EDIT DATABASE PROPERTIES

Get to know your database properties! You can define startup options and default access privileges for databases just as you can applications. Important information is displayed including dimension dense / sparse settings, member counts, and other helpful ratios and statistics. You can manage commit settings, cache settings, data storage volumes, and much more via database properties.

To view and edit database properties,
1. Select the database.
2. Right Click and select *Edit >> Properties*.
3. Select the General tab:

Database Properties: [localhost.Sample.Basic]

Database:
localhost.Sample.Basic

Status:
Loaded

General **Dimensions** Statistics Caches Transactions Storage Currency Modifications

- **General**
  - Description Click here to edit
  - Database type Normal
  - Startup
    - ☑ Allow users to start database
    - ☑ Start database when application starts
  - Calculation
    - ☐ Aggregate missing values
    - ☐ Create blocks on equations
    - ☑ Two-Pass calculation
  - Minimum access level None
  - Data retrieval buffers
    - Buffer size (KB) 10
    - Sort buffer size (KB) 10

Apply   Refresh   Close   Help

The Dimensions tab presents the dimensions in a helpful table, labeling dense and sparse settings and giving you a count of all members and stored members:

Database Properties: [localhost.Sample.Basic]

Database:
localhost.Sample.Basic

Status:
Loaded

General **Dimensions** Statistics Caches Transactions Storage Currency Modifications

Number of dimensions 10

Dimension	Type	Members in Dimension	Members Stored
Year	Dense	19	12
Measures	Dense	17	8
Product	Sparse	22	19
Market	Sparse	25	25
Scenario	Dense	5	2
Caffeinated	Sparse	3	3
Ounces	Sparse	5	5
Pkg Type	Sparse	3	3
Population	Sparse	15	15
Intro Date	Sparse	8	8

Apply   Refresh   Close   Help

The remaining tabs for Database properties will be discussed in upcoming chapters.

OTHER DATABASE TASKS

Via Administration Services, you can perform several other actions for databases. Select the database and right click. These are the other actions you can perform on databases. You can copy, rename, and delete databases from Administration Services. You can clear data from a database, clearing either upper levels blocks, non-input blocks, or all blocks. You can load data, calculate, export, or restructure data:

Those same notes we mentioned about copying applications also apply to copying databases. All objects will be copied within Essbase including the outline, rules files, report scripts, calc scripts, and data. During the copy process, users are prohibited from accessing both the "from" and the "to" databases. You can copy across servers if desired.

BACKUPS AND RECOVERY

We can't stress how important it is to backup your applications. Listen to me – this is REALLY important. There are two ways to backup Essbase. We recommend doing both.

The first method is to prepare the Essbase server and applications for file system backup. To do this,

1. Place database in read-only ("archive") mode. Using MaxL, type **alter database begin archive**
2. Perform backup using third-party backup utility, backing up the entire Essbase directory or specific files.
3. Return database to read-write mode. Using MaxL, type **alter database end archive**

BEGINARCHIVE commits any modified data to disk, switches the database to read-only mode, reopens the database files in shared, read-only mode and creates a file containing a list of files that need to be backed up. By default, the file is called archive.lst and is stored in the *ARBORPATH*\app\appname\dbname directory. ENDARCHIVE switches the database back to read-write mode.

It is important to back up all .ind and .pag files related to a database because a single database can have multiple .ind and .pag files. These files could be placed on different volumes so make sure you are backing up everything.

These are the key files to backup:

ess*n*.ind	*ARBORPATH*\app*appname**dbname*
ess*n*.pag	*ARBORPATH*\app*appname**dbname*
dbname.esm	*ARBORPATH*\app*appname**dbname*
dbname.tct	*ARBORPATH*\app*appname**dbname*
dbname.ind	*ARBORPATH*\app*appname**dbname*
dbname.app	*ARBORPATH*\app
dbname.db	*ARBORPATH*\app*appname**dbname*
x.lro	*ARBORPATH*\app*appname**dbname*
dbname.otl	*ARBORPATH*\app*appname**dbname*
essbase.sec	*ARBORPATH*\bin
essbase.bak	*ARBORPATH*\bin
essbase.cfg	*ARBORPATH*\bin
Database object files (.otl, .csc, .rul)	*ARBORPATH*\app*appname**dbname*

ESSCMD or MaxL scripts	No defined storage location

To restore files from a backup,
1. Stop the application and databases.
2. Replace the files on disk with the corresponding files from the backup.

Now let's review a few rules for file system backups. You can use the file system backup to restore application files (same server, same application name, same database name). You can not use the platform file system to copy, move, rename, or delete applications and databases. When an application or database is altered through the file system, the Essbase security file is unable to recognize the changes (more on the Essbase.sec shortly). Do not move, copy, modify, or delete any of the following files: essn.ind, essn.pag, dbname.ind, dbname.esm, dbname.tct. Doing so may result in data corruption.

You can however manage the following files through the file system:

- Rules files for dimension builds and data loads (.rul)
- Data load or dimension build text files
- Calculation scripts (.csc)
- Report scripts (.rep)
- MaxL scripts (.mxl or any extension)

The second method for backups is data exports. Exporting will copy data to a text file that you specify. You can export all data, level zero data, or input-level data. The thing with exports is that it only exports data. Essbase objects like outline files, rules files, etc. are not included so you will need to use file system backups for those items.

So if we have to do a file system backup anyway, why export? Use exports when you want to transfer data across platforms, when you want to back up only a certain portion of the data (level 0 blocks), or when you want to create an exported file in text format, rather than binary format. If you have a copy of the outline and data export, this can be a quick way to recover a corrupted database.

To perform a data export,
1. Select the database.
2. Right click and select *Export* or Select *Actions >> Export "dbname"*:

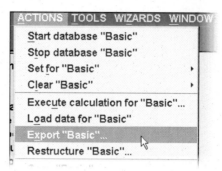

3. Specify the name for the exported data file.
4. Choose the export option.
   - All data
   - Level 0 blocks
   - Input blocks
5. Choose either column or non-column format. Column format often facilitates loads to relational databases or other systems. Non-column format is faster for loading or reloading to the Essbase database.
6. Select "Execute in the background" in most cases:

The export file is by default placed in the \arborpath\essbase\app directory.

To reload an exported file, you will follow the same steps to load any data file though you won't need a rules file.
1. Right click on the database and select *Load Data*.

2. Select *Find Data File* and navigate to the exported data file.
3. Specify the error file location and name.
4. Click *OK* to load the data.

If you are reloading a level zero export or input level export file, the database must be recalculated.

Man, we were really serious in the backup and recovery section. No jokes, no humor? That's right. There is no joking in the backup process.

And with that, we'll conclude the "Become an Essbase Administrator" section. You made it! Congratulations, Essbase Administrator. But we're not done yet. We're not satisfied with making you a knowledgeable Essbase administrator. We want to make you a *Master* Essbase administrator. Hold on to your seats as we dive into some of the more advanced Essbase topics.

Become a Master Essbase Administrator

Chapter 14:
Calculate with Calc Scripts

In Chapter 11, we discussed using outline consolidations and member formulas. Quite often, these tools provide all the calculation power an application will need. However, as member formulas start to reference other levels or other dimensions, they can get very complex, very quickly. In Sample.Basic, the Budget member has no formula. Let's say you're in charge of setting goals for the remainder of the year. We don't want our goals to be reasonable or obtainable (else everyone would reach them), so we want to set every "Budget" member to be exactly fifty percent greater than the "Actual" number from last year. The problem is that this calculation would be very complex, and probably not a good thing to store directly in the outline as it may change frequently, so we'll need to override the default calculation. Calc scripts to the rescue..

WHAT IS A CALC SCRIPT?

At this point, you're probably asking yourself "What the heck is a calc script?" If you're not, then you're skipping the headings that introduce each section. A calc script is short for "calculation script" and it allows you to override the standard outline calculations and take complete control of how your database derives its numbers. While most of the time calc scripts are run at regular intervals to do simple things like aggregate subsets of your database, they can also be run sporadically such as at the start of budgeting season when you want to run your allocation processes with each what-if iteration.

A calc script is really just a sequential series of commands, equations, and formulas. It is stored in a standard text file with a .CSC extension, so you can even open them in Notepad if you want to. Here's the calc script that will set all of your budget values to 50% above your actuals:

```
/* Creates Initial Budget */
SET UPDATECALC OFF;

CLEARDATA Budget;
Budget = Actual * 1.5;
CALC ALL;
```

You might have noticed that this calc script actually does a few things beyond just creating the budget, but we'll get to those in due time.

There are a lot of reasons to use a calc script. If you're not happy with the order that Essbase uses to calculate the members and dimensions, a calc script can easily override the default order. If you don't want to calculate the entire database, a calc script can be written to only calculate the current month. If you want to clear data or copy data from one place to another, calc scripts can do the job. Want to create formulas that aren't in the outline? Calc scripts are there for you. Calc scripts will even let you perform allocations and multi-pass calculations. When one of the end-users passes you a multi-stage allocation calculation that would make most Excel gurus run home crying to their mommies, you can just tie on your cape and write an Essbase Calc Script to save the day.

CREATE A CALC SCRIPT

Normally, people edit their calc scripts in Administration Services. It is possible to create and modify calc scripts in your favorite text editor, but only nerds do this. Since I'm a nerd, I'm completely okay with that. [Other Author's Note: Edward wrote that last line. I, Tracy McMullen, am definitely not a nerd (not that there's anything wrong with that).]

There are some definite advantages to using your own text editor. Text editors tend to let you see more lines at once, allow better find and replace functionality, have better line numbering, and provide greater printing options than Administration Services' built-in Calc Script Editor. If you do create your calc script in an external editor, it is very easy to copy and paste the body into Administration Services, or you can also save your calc script as a text file in the appropriate database directory (when you do this, remember to save the file with a .CSC extension).

My First Calc Script

For now, let's pretend that you're not a nerd for a second and use Administration Services to create your first calc script.

1. Open Administration Services and drill down below the database to the section named "Calculation Scripts."
2. Right click on "Calculation Scripts" and choose *Create Calculation Script*:

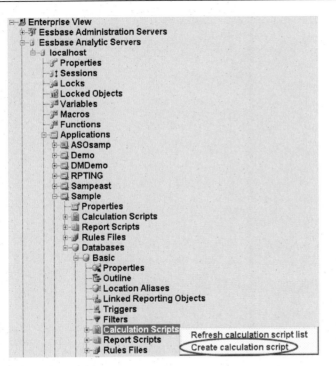

Tip!

You can also create a calc script by going to the menu and choosing *Editors >> Calculation Script Editor*.

3.   A window will appear called the "Calculation Script Editor":

This editor has three main panes:

1. Outline. This pane helps you to select members from the outline and add them automatically to the calc script being edited.

2. Functions. This pane lets you select functions and commands and add them to the calc script being edited. The check boxes above this pane determine if arguments to the functions and commands will be inserted as well.

3. Data entry. This is where you actually type your calc script. While you could live without panes one and two (though it would be a royal pain), all of the power of calc scripts is entered into pane three.

The calc editor (as we'll call it from now on) has a toolbar at the top of the screen just below the menu:

While most of the buttons are the same ones you'd see in fancy Windows applications like Notepad, the rightmost three icons are calc editor specific. The check mark icon validates the syntax of your calc script. The outline icon associates an outline with your calc script. You'll need to do this if you don't see an outline in the outline pane (pane one, remember?). The final icon (the green down arrow next to a cash register receipt) runs the calc script that's open in pane 3. We're not going to be using the toolbar for right now, but go right ahead if you'd like to. It's a free country.

Note!

If you are in Cuba, then you're not actually in a free country but rather are under the ironclad grip of a communist dictatorship. Hopefully this won't stop you from using the toolbar, though.

Simplest Calc Script

While it's small in stature, it's powerful in nature. This single line will aggregate all of the dimensional hierarchies in your outline, calculate all of the formulas attached to members, perform time balancing on time balanced members, and does it all quickly using "intelligent calculation". We'll be covering more sophisticated calc scripts throughout this chapter, but you should always remember that no matter what we create, we'll always have the power of default.

```
CALC ALL;
```

Try It!

Type "CALC ALL;" into the data entry pane. Go up to the menu and choose *Syntax >> Check Syntax* (or press *Ctrl-Y*). After you see the validation message, go up to the menu to *Options >> Execute Script* (or just press *F5*) to calculate Sample.Basic.

Calc Script Syntax

There are a few simple rules to follow when writing a calc script:

1. End every statement with a semicolon.
2. You do not talk about fight club.
3. You can break a statement onto multiple lines, but the end of the statement must have a semicolon.
4. If a member name contains spaces or starts with a number, surround it with "double quotes."

5. Start comments with /*
6. End comments with */
7. Statements must have a semicolon at the end.
8. Calc scripts are not case-sensitive.
9. Spaces between member names, commands, and functions don't matter.

There are many more rules, but these are the important ones that people tend to forget and then wonder for hours why their calc scripts aren't working. Here's a calc script that demonstrates several of those syntax rules:

```
/* Increase Opening Inventory */

"Opening Inventory" =
 "Opening InVeNtOrY" * 1.1;
```

Notice that the first line is a comment and it has the appropriate start and end characters. "Opening Inventory" has a space in the member name, so it's surrounded by double quotes. At the end of the entire statement (although not at the end of the comment), there's a semicolon. (You can tell the calc script language was written by a programmer, because only programmers end sentences with semicolons;) Finally, observe that the second instance of Opening Inventory uses wacky cases just to show you that calc scripts are indeed *not* case-sensitive (unless you have explicitly told Essbase to behave otherwise).

SIMPLE CALCULATIONS

One of the simplest calculations you can perform is to tell Essbase to do the calculation for a single member. In a production system, this is the leanest, meanest calc script you can write, and is used when you want the script to finish in the quickest possible time.

Calculate Single Members

Imagine for a moment that the "Variance" member in Sample.Basic was stored and not dynamically calculated. We've just loaded data and we want to tell Essbase to calculate the formula on "Variance" and leave the rest of the outline alone. All we have to do is spell the member name and add a semicolon:

```
Variance;
```

How do you think you'd modify the calc script to calculate both Variance and Variance %? Hopefully it's something like this:

```
Variance;
"Variance %";
```

Notice that we have to use double quotes around "Variance %" due to the space in the name.

Tip! If you want to be safe about it, put double quotes around all member names (even "Variance"). It doesn't hurt anything, and it does help you identify your member names quickly during troubleshooting exercises.

The technique of specifying a member name on a line by itself can be applied to members that do not have formulas but do have members aggregating into them. Imagine that we have just loaded data in Sample.Basic to the great state of Texas. Now we want to roll-up the Texas numbers to the top of the Market dimension:

```
South;
Market;
```

The nice thing about this script is that it doesn't bother rolling up totals that haven't changed. There's no Texas in the North (thankfully) so we know we don't need to modify the totals for North.

It's also possible to temporarily override the formula in the outline for a member. Let's return to our earlier example where we were an evil budget manager trying to set our budgets slightly higher than our actuals so no one could ever meet their numbers. To do this in a calc script, we just set up an equation with Budget on the left-side of the equal sign:

```
Budget = Actual * 1.5;
```

This script will set the budget to be 50% greater (notice that we're multiplying times 1.5) than actuals. If you're really in need of a raise, you could set the profit of your company to double what it should be:

```
Profit = Profit * 2;
```

Forgetting that the above calc script is probably illegal (thanks, Senator Sarbanes, wherever you are), it is interesting in that it puts the member "Profit" on both sides of the equation. It's also useful to understand that every time you run it Profit will double, so make sure you only run scripts like this once.

Tip!

There are better ways to increase your company's profitability than writing an illegal calc script.

Intelligent Calculation

Before we go any further, you have to learn the command to turn off intelligent calculation. Intelligent calculation allows Essbase to remember which blocks in the database need to be calculated based on new data coming in, and which haven't been impacted (and don't need calculation). Intelligent calculation is wonderful when you're running a default calc.

But (there is always a "but") intelligent calculation is the devil's work when you're running a calc script. Think about the budget calc script from earlier:

```
Budget = Actual * 1.5;
```

Do we want this calc script only to operate on so called "dirty blocks" or do we want all budgets throughout the entire system to be set 50% above actuals? If we leave intelligent calculation turned on during the running of our calc, Essbase will only calculate our new budgets for blocks that have recently been loaded with data. That's definitely not what we want, as some business units will escape with a sensible quota. We definitely can't have that!

The good news is that you don't have to turn off intelligent calculation for the entire database: you can just tell Essbase to ignore it during the calc script with this command:

```
SET UPDATECALC Off;
```

If you want to turn Intelligent Calc on again later in the script (maybe you want a "CALC ALL" command at the end of your script to calculate just the dirty blocks), include the command **SET UPDATECALC ON;** and everything past that point will work "intelligently. We recommend that you include the command to turn intelligent calculation off at the top of every calc script. If there's a case where you actually want to use it, go ahead and remove the line on a case-by-case basis. Leaving it out is courting disaster (and take it from a guy who dated disaster back in high school: you don't want to be courting her).

Calculate Entire Dimensions

As we've already mentioned, there's a simple command that you can include in a calc script that tells Essbase to evaluate all your member formulas and do all of your outline aggregation. While "CALC ALL" is great and powerful, there are times when you only want to calculate specific dimensions. For instance, what would we do if we just wanted to calculate Sample.Basic's Product dimension? We have a new command for this called "CALC DIM" (short for calculate dimension):

```
CALC DIM (Product);
```

This line calculates the Product dimension doing both outline aggregation (such as rolling all the Colas up into the parent value) and member formulas, if they exist for members in that dimension. If we want to calculate multiple dimensions using this command (say, Market and Product), just separate them with commas:

```
CALC DIM (Market, Product);
```

Remember how we said that "CALC DIM" not only does aggregation but also member formulas? Well, how many member formulas are there in the Market and Product dimensions? That's right - none, so "CALC DIM" is wasting time looking for formulas that you know aren't there. For dimensions that don't have formulas, there's a faster command that only does aggregation:

```
AGG (Market, Product);
```

Note!   "AGG" can only be used on sparse dimensions. If you have a dense dimension with no formulas that you only want to aggregate, you cannot use "AGG." You must use the "CALC DIM" command.

Calculate a Subset of Data

While calculating entire dimensions makes you feel very powerful, sometimes you just want to calculate a portion of the database. For instance, let's say you just updated your budgets but you didn't touch actuals. How could you ignore the Actual member? Well it turns out that there's an optional argument to the "CALC ALL" command called "EXCEPT". You use it to calculate everything except specific dimensions (DIM) or members (MBR). If we didn't want to calculate actuals, we'd say:

```
CALC ALL EXCEPT MBR (Actual);
```

It's also possible to list multiple members. Say that we didn't want to calculate Texas and New York (no offense to either state). We'd list the members separated by commas:

```
CALC ALL EXCEPT MBR (Texas, "New York");
```

If there's an entire dimension you don't want to calculate, replace "MBR" with "DIM":

```
CALC ALL EXCEPT DIM (Measures);
```

While this method may be fun at first, it's not nearly the most powerful method for limiting a calculation to a small portion of the database. Remembering Wolverine Jugglers, Incorporated, let's say we just loaded our budgets for next year for the street peddling we do on "System 9th Ave". Now we just want to calculate our accounts dimension for that one member, ignoring the rest of the database. The "CALC ALL EXCEPT..." method from above is really used to do the majority of a database and not just a smidgen, so we need a new command: "FIX" and its sister command "ENDFIX".

If we just want to calculate "System 9th Ave", we put this in double quotes after the "FIX" as such:

```
FIX ("System 9th Ave")
     CALC DIM (Account);
ENDFIX
```

While the indentation is not necessary, it helps make it easier to see which commands the FIX affects.

Tip!

"FIX" and "ENDFIX" are called sandwich commands because one command is like the top layer of bread and the other as the bottom with lots of things thrown in between. For instance, we could choose to calculate a few specific accounts:

```
FIX ("System 9th Ave")
      Op_Income;
      Margin;
ENDFIX
```

It's also possible to give list multiple members in a FIX as long as you separate them with commas:

```
FIX ("Essbase 7th Street", "System 9th Ave")
      Op_Income;
      Margin;
ENDFIX
```

Let's say you only loaded budgets to next year (which for our purposes, we will call "NY") for both the customers above. Here's one way to accomplish that by nesting one "FIX" within another:

```
FIX ("Essbase 7th Street", "System 9th Ave")
      FIX (NY)
            Op_Income;
            Margin;
      ENDFIX
ENDFIX
```

Note! Each "FIX" must conclude with an "ENDFIX". It is not necessary to end a "FIX" or "ENDFIX" statement with a semicolon, but it doesn't hurt anything to use one either.

While this is a valid method, two "FIX"es are not necessary. You can list members from multiple dimensions within one "FIX" command, and this is the traditional way to do it:

```
FIX ("Essbase 7th Street", "System 9th Ave", NY)
     Op_Income;
     Margin;
ENDFIX
```

Tip! Using "FIX" commands on sparse dimensions will speed up the performance of your calculations, because it limits the number of blocks pulled into memory to just what's listed in the "FIX" statement.

Point to Another Member

While you're inside a "FIX" command, blocks outside are ignored. What if you want to refer to values from blocks that aren't being retrieved into memory? Surely there must be a way, you cry out of quiet desperation. Stop your incessant bawling, because there is indeed a way. It's called the cross-dimensional operator. Its job is to point to another member in the database and it looks like this:

```
->
```

Note! There is no "cross-dimensional operator" symbol on your keyboard. You type this in by pressing dash followed by a greater than symbol.

If we wanted to set net revenue for the Hyperion User Conference equal to net revenue for the Oracle User Conference, we could write a calc script that looks like this:

```
FIX ("Hyperion User Conference")
     Net_Rev = Net_Rev->"Oracle User Conference";
ENDFIX
```

What exactly is this doing? On the right-side of the equation, we told Essbase to get the value from net revenue for the Oracle User Conference. The left-side of the equation told it to put the result in net revenue, but which net revenue? Well as you see from the "FIX", we told Essbase to only calculate the Hyperion User Conference, so it will put the value into net revenue for the Hyperion User Conference.

Whenever possible, try to avoid cross-dimensional operators. They're unseemly and slow. For instance, if we had to add another account, we would have to include it within the "FIX":

```
FIX ("Hyperion User Conference")
 Net_Rev = Net_Rev->"Oracle User Conference";
 Op_Expense = Op_Expense->"Oracle User Conference";
ENDFIX
```

We could remove the need for the cross-dimensional operator (called "cross-dim" for short) by pivoting the customer and account dimensions. That is, we'll put the account dimension in the "FIX" and the customer dimension inside the "FIX":

```
FIX (Net_Rev, Op_Expense)
  "Hyperion User Conference" =
      "Oracle User Conference";
ENDFIX
```

This is much easier to read, and more flexible as well. It's obvious now that we're focusing on two specific accounts and setting one conference to be equal to another.

Tip!

If you find yourself repeating a cross-dim to the same member, it might be possible to pivot a dimension as above to remove the need for the cross-dim.

It is also possible to string cross-dims together to point to more and more specific intersections in the database:

```
FIX ("Hyperion User Conference", CY)
 Net_Rev = Net_Rev->NY->"Oracle User Conference";
ENDFIX
```

Net_Rev->NY->"Oracle User Conference" is called a "member combination. This is how the on-line documentation refers to the intersections of members via cross-dimensional operators.

Clear Data

Have you ever had one of those days when everything was going wrong and you just wanted to wipe out the entire day and start over? Fortunately, it's much easier to do this in Essbase than it is in reality. If we wanted to clear all of the data in our cube, we'd need the following little calc script:

```
SET UpdateCalc Off;
CLEARBLOCK All;
```

The first line (as no doubt you'll recall from a few pages ago) tells Essbase to operate on all blocks in the database and not just the dirty blocks. The second line tells Essbase to clear all the blocks in the database.

Try It! Go ahead and create the calc script above and run it against Sample.Basic (assuming you know how to reload the data afterwards).

This script will run extremely quickly, and when it's finished, it will certainly appear that your database is empty, but if you look closely, it's not. Look out on your server's hard drive and you'll see that the .PAG file still exists. The reason that "CLEARBLOCK" runs like a paparazzi after Angelina Jolie is that all it does is blank out the index entries: the pointers to the corresponding blocks in the page file. Since it can no longer find the blocks, they might as well be blank.

Tip! "CLEARBLOCK" will leave your database fragmented. Remember to defragment your database periodically to improve performance (see the Tune and Optimize chapter for more information on fragmentation).

A powerful way to use "CLEARBLOCK" is within a "FIX" statement. We want to blank out our Sample.Basic budget so that we can try again (our last attempt at the budget was horrendous, let's be honest), so we write this script:

```
FIX (Budget)
        CLEARBLOCK All;
ENDFIX
```

Remember that "CLEARBLOCK" will clear out entire blocks by removing the pointers, but in Sample.Basic, Budget is in the Scenario dimension and Scenario is a dense dimension. Since Budget is in every block in the database? Does it remove all the blocks? No, "CLEARBLOCK" is smart enough to only clear out index entries when the entire block is not being "FIX"ed on. In cases where just a portion of a block needs to be cleared, "CLEARBLOCK" will read the blocks into memory, clear out the necessary slices, and write the blocks back out to the page file. As such, "CLEARBLOCK" when used inside a "FIX" on a dense dimension is noticeable slower.

If you want to blank out a specific dense member, there's a simpler way than including a "CLEARBLOCK" inside a "FIX" on that dense member:

```
CLEARDATA Budget;
```

The "CLEARDATA" command allows you to specify a single member (in our case, budget). Do not use this on a sparse member, because the "CLEARBLOCK" command will always be faster. It is also possible to use a cross-dim operator on the right-side of a "CLEARDATA" command. If we wanted to clear out only our sales budget, we could write:

```
CLEARDATA Budget->Sales;
```

If you need to clear out multiple dense members, do not write your script like this:

```
CLEARDATA Actual;
CLEARDATA Budget;
```

This will result in multiple passes through your database since Essbase will not know to clear your data from actual and budget during a single pass. In this case, go back to using the "CLEARBLOCK" command within a "FIX":

```
FIX (Actual, Budget)
     CLEARBLOCK All;
ENDFIX
```

At various times, you'll want to make sure that all of the aggregated blocks in your database are cleared. For instance, if you're about recalculate all of the totals in your database, it's faster if Essbase doesn't have to read the old totals into memory before writing out the new ones. There is an argument you can use in place of "All" called "Upper":

```
CLEARBLOCK Upper;
```

This command will clear all of the upper-level blocks in your database. As before with the "All" argument, "CLEARBLOCK Upper" can be used within a "FIX" statement. A related argument is "NonInput":

```
CLEARBLOCK NonInput;
```

This will clear out all the blocks that haven't had data directly input to them. Assuming we're following best practices and only entering data into level-0 blocks, this command will only clear out the upper-level blocks like "CLEARBLOCK Upper".

There's one other way to clear data. You can set a member equal to #Missing:

```
Budget = #Missing;
```

While this is valid syntax (and we've even seen a few sub-par consultants use it), it's just weird. Stick to "CLEARBLOCK" or "CLEARDATA".

Copying Data

There are two common ways to copy data. The first is with a simple equation:

```
"Hyperion User Conference"="Oracle User Conference";
```

This equation copies the Oracle conference data over to the Hyperion conference data. Depending on the settings in your database, this method may or may not create blocks. The way to be sure you create all necessary blocks is by using the "DATACOPY" command. It takes two arguments: a member to copy the data from and a member to copy the data to. This command accomplishes the same thing as the line of code above, but with added comfort that there will be no block creation hijinx:

```
DATACOPY "Hyperion User Conference" TO
         "Oracle User Conference";
```

Both of these methods can be used within a FIX command. Do not use multiple "DATACOPY" commands on dense members:

```
DATACOPY Jan TO Feb;
DATACOPY Feb TO Mar;
```

In the case of Sample.Basic, this calc script will actually cause two passes through the database since Time is a dense dimension. In this case, the first method of setting one member equal to another would be better.

Tip!

To oversimplify, use the equation method on dense members and the "DATACOPY" method on sparse members.

IF and Its Other Brother, ENDIF

You learned earlier how easy it is to use the "IF...ENDIF" sandwich commands (technically, they're functions, but since they don't start with @, we like to think of them as commands) inside of a member formula. As a refresher, let's say we wanted to check and see if our number of dropped wolverines exceeded our number of juggled wolverines. If so, let's fire everybody (i.e., set headcount equal to zero). Here's what this would look like if you made it the member formula for "Headcount" in the outline:

```
IF (Avg_Wolverines_Juggled < Avg_Dropped_Wolverines)
     Headcount = 0;
ENDIF
```

Now since this is attached to the Headcount member, it's technically not necessary to specify "Headcount =" on the third line. As a matter of policy, we don't tend to include it, because if the "Headcount" member gets renamed, the member formula reference to it will *not* rename. As such, we'd write the formula like this:

```
IF (Avg_Wolverines_Juggled < Avg_Dropped_Wolverines)
     0;
ENDIF
```

Now, if you just type this into a calc script and verify it, you'll get the following message:

"Error: 1012061 The CALC command [IF] can only be used within a CALC Member Block"

First of all, note that the error message calls "IF" a command, so we were right all along about it not being a real function, on-line documentation be damned. To translate the error message into semi-English, "IF" can only be used in a member formula.

"Uh, oh," you say, "but I want to do IFs in a calc script. Is now the time for ritual suicide?"

While it may indeed be, don't do it over this, because there's a simple work-around: create a temporary member formula within your calc script that contains the needed "IF". You do this by specifying the member that you want to assign the temporary formula and then include the formula in parentheses. For example:

```
Headcount
    (
    IF (Avg_Wolverines_Juggled <
                Avg_Dropped_Wolverines)
            0;
    ENDIF
    )
```

Notice "Headcount" at the top and the parentheses surrounding the "IF...ENDIF". Voila! The calc script will now validate and run successfully.

FUNCTIONS

Everything we've done up to this point has been focused around using the calculation commands. There are also at least 135 functions that let you do most of the interesting things that Microsoft Excel functions can do (like absolute values, statistical deviations, and internal rate of return calculations) and many things that Excel functions can not (like return the parent value of the current member in a hierarchy and allocate values down across a hierarchy).

Note! These are the very same functions that you used when creating member formulas. With very few exceptions, all of the functions can be used both in member formulas and calc scripts.

To make it easier to find the functions in the on-line help, Hyperion segmented the functions into several nebulous categories. Some of the categories are easily understood (like "Boolean"). Some, like the mysterious "Miscellaneous" category, are not.

Boolean

Boolean functions return True or False (actually, they return a 1 for True and a 0 for False). Boolean functions are generally used inside an "IF" or an "ELSEIF". One of the common boolean functions is "@ISMBR" and it's used to tell if a specific member is being calculated. Let's say that we want to set budgeted sales equal to 123.45:

```
IF (@ISMBR (Budget))
    Sales = 123.45;
ENDIF
```

It's possible to put a cross-dim operator inside the "@ISMBR". All parts of the cross-dim must be true for the entire statement to be true. In this example, the current intersection being calculated must be "New York" and "Budget":

```
IF (@ISMBR (Budget->"New York"))
    Sales = 123.45;
ENDIF
```

It's even possible to list several members in an "@ISMBR" separated by commas. For instance, if we only want to set New York and California sales, our script would look like this:

```
IF (@ISMBR ("New York", California))
    Sales = 123.45;
ENDIF
```

At times, you might want to check to see if the current member is in a range of members. For instance, say you want "COGS" to be set to 500 if the month being calculated is between January and June. To do this, separate the two members (in this case "Jan" and "Jun") with a colon:

```
IF (@ISMBR (Jan:Jun))
    COGS = 500;
ENDIF
```

You might sometimes see "Jan::Jun" with a double-colon between the two members. The single-colon method returns all members from "Jan" to "Jun" that are at the same level. The double-colon method returns all the members from "Jan" to "Jun" that are at the same *generation*. Unless your outline contains ragged hierarchies, the single- and double-colon methods will return the same list. For simplicities sake, we tend to use a single colon.

There are at least fifteen other Boolean functions, some of which are actually helpful (@ISCHILD, @ISGEN, and @ISLEV, among others).

Relationship functions

Relationship functions are used to lookup values at intersections elsewhere in Essbase. Generally, the value being looked up is in the same database, but it doesn't have to be (the extremely helpful but slightly slow "@XREF" functions looks to other databases).

One of the common needs is to look at the value at a parent member. For instance, say Sample.Basic had a stored member named "Product Share" that needed to show each level-0 product's sales as a percentage of its parent's sales:

```
"Product Share" =
    Sales / @PARENTVAL (Product, Sales);
```

The first argument to the "@PARENTVAL" function is the dimension for which you want to take the value at the parent. If we had a "Market Share" member, we could calculate it like this:

```
"Market Share" =
    Sales / @PARENTVAL (Market, Sales);
```

Mathematical, Statistical, and Forecasting

Mathematical functions perform standard arithmetic type calculations such as absolute value, integer, and factorial. The "@VAR" function used in Sample.Basic to calculate variances is, for no apparent reason, a mathematical function.

While simple statistical functions like maximum and minimum are found in the Mathematical category, advanced statistical functions get their own category: Statistical.

There are also some statistical type functions that have to do with moving sums, averages, minimums, and so on. These functions are found in the Forecasting category along with "@SPLINE" which finds a curve most closely fitting a range of data and "@TREND" which predicts the future (well, kinda). If you're ever curious how "@TREND" comes up with its trend calculations, the programmers at Hyperion were kind enough to put the formulas in technical reference documentation. Here's a snippet of the "Algorithm for Triple Exponential Smoothing (TES)." Sing along if you know the melody:

@TREND

Back to main @TREND topic.

Algorithm for Triple Exponential Smoothing (TES)

$Ylist \qquad y_1, y_2, \ldots, y_K$

$Xlist \qquad x_1, x_2, \ldots, x_K$

TES with period T (if T is not given, it is assumed to be $T = 1$)

$\quad x_1, x_2, \ldots, x_K, \qquad y_1, y_2, \ldots, y_K$ are input to TES, x is forecast value.

$$a_i = (1-c)^{x_{i+1} - x_i} \qquad d_i = (1-d)^{x_{i+1} - x_i} \qquad e_i = (1-e)^{x_{i+1} - x_i}$$

Note: When *Xlist* is missing, the exponents disappear.

Default $\qquad c = .2$
$\qquad\qquad\quad d = .05$
$\qquad\qquad\quad e = .1$

Step 1,

$$S_1 = y_1$$
$$b_1 = \frac{y_2 - y_1}{x_2 - x_1}$$
$$l_1 = 1$$

We'll bet you are wishing you hadn't slept through your statistics class in college right about now.

Member Set

Member Set functions simply return lists of members. These are commonly used in "FIX" commands. Say that we wanted to focus on just aggregating products in the East region. Rather than hard-code all the members in "East," we could use a member set function called "@CHILDREN":

```
FIX (@CHILDREN (East))
     AGG (Product);
ENDFIX
```

Essentially, the "@CHILDREN(East)" portion of the "FIX" is replaced by a series of members before the calc script runs. In essence, the calculation actually performed is this (once the "@CHILDREN" is evaluated):

```
FIX ("New York":"New Hampshire")
     AGG (Product);
ENDFIX
```

Or to put it another way (not using the single-colon range indicator):

```
FIX ("New York", "Massachusetts", "Florida",
   "Connecticut", "New Hampshire")
     AGG (Product);
ENDFIX
```

A common request is to calculate all of the members from a certain member on upwards to the top of the dimension. For instance, let's say you just loaded a value to the great state of Utah (thought we were going to say "the great state of Texas," didn't you?). You want to aggregate this value up through the Market dimension, but you don't want to aggregate the entire dimension (since nothing else has changed). Use the "@ANCESTORS" function on a line by itself:

```
@ANCESTORS (Utah);
```

Remembering that member set functions essentially return lists of members, the script is exactly the same as this request:

```
Utah;
West;
Market;
```

Note! If a member set function returns any dynamic calc or dynamic calc and store members, they will not be evaluated

What if you wanted to calculate just the regions in the Market dimension? You could use the "@CHILDREN" function on a line by itself:

```
@CHILDREN (Market) ;
```

Range and Financial

Range functions (sometimes called "Financial" functions just to be contrary) operate on a range of members. The most commonly used range function is "@PRIOR" which looks to earlier members in the outline and "@NEXT" which looks to later members in the outline. Both of these functions assume that you want to look forward and backward through the dimension marked as the "Time" dimension if you do not otherwise specify a range. As such, many people think of them as time-specific, but they do not have to be.

The member "Opening Inventory" in Sample.Basic uses the "@PRIOR" function to refer to the prior month's "Ending Inventory":

```
IF (NOT @ISMBR(Jan))
        "Opening Inventory" =
                    @PRIOR ("Ending Inventory");
ENDIF;
```

The "IF (NOT ..." is used to make sure that we don't try to look back to the prior period if we are in the month of January (because Sample.Basic only contains one year of data, this wouldn't make any sense).

Allocation

Allocation functions allocate summarized higher level values down to detailed members. This is often used for top-down budgeting or targeted forecasting (when values are often loaded to parent members and then spread downward). There are only two functions. "@ALLOCATE" allocates values down a single dimension and its more impressive counterpart "@MDALLOCATE" which allocates values down multiple dimensions simultaneously.

Try It!

Look up the syntax for "@ALLOCATE" in the on-line help and create a calc script using it. Don't use any of the optional arguments for right now: there are too many to deal with right now what with everything else going on in your life and all.

While the allocation functions are powerful, they're not very efficient at complex allocations. If you find that using these functions is slow, you can generally improve performance by "rolling your own" allocations in the form of a more complicated calc script.

Date & Time

Date & Time functions change dates in the form of strings to numeric dates. This category only has one function in it at the moment, "@TODATE", which makes me wonder why they didn't just put this function in the Miscellaneous category. Somehow, we think the marketing department is involved.

Miscellaneous

Miscellaneous is the category for functions that don't have a place elsewhere. The "@TODATE" function should be here, but it's not. Instead, you get the bizarre "@CALCMODE" function which changes the way Essbase calculates a member and three string manipulation functions (@CONCATENATE, @NAME, and @SUBSTRING).

Custom-Defined

Custom-defined functions are whatever you want them to be. It is possible to write your own functions in Java, register them with Essbase using the MaxL "create function" command, and call them from a calc script as if they were part of the native language.

One of the best uses of CDFs (custom-defined functions) is for iterative type calculations (such as the common retail metric "Weeks of Supply") that would take up pages in a calc script but are just a few lines of custom Java code. Other CDFs we've seen include a better implementation of internal rate of return than the "@IRR" function that comes with Essbase and a function that checks a weather database to pull back high and low temperatures.

The most popular CDF ever exports a slice of your Essbase data to a text file or a relational database. As of the time of this writing, this CDF was available on the Hyperion Developer's Network (http://dev.hyperion.com/download/code_library/exportcdf_readme2.cfm). It is unsupported software (AKA "shareware"), but it eventually got so popular that Hyperion included the equivalent functionality in the System 9.3 version of Essbase Analytics.

WHERE DO WE GO FROM HERE?

Learning everything there is to know about calc scripts would take several years, we're fairly certain. We are considering writing a sequel to this book that focuses entirely on calc scripts.

We are sure we could fill at least 400 pages with non-stop, wall-to-wall, hot, steamy, calc action. We are also sure that it would sell no more than 100 copies world-wide including the fifty copies we bought just to prove to our families that we had more than just one book in us.

Rather than drag this chapter on any further, we'll point you in the right place for further information: the Essbase Technical Reference. From within Administration Services, click on Help>>Information Map. When this comes up, click on Technical Reference to be taken to a bounty of detailed, look-up information:

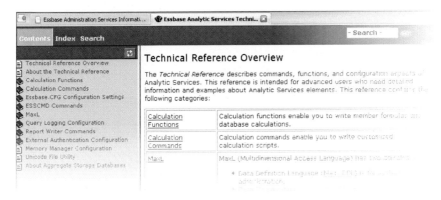

The "Calculation Functions" section contains details on all of the @Functions. The "Calculation Commands" section is where you go to find information on all of the commands that can be used in a calc script that don't start with an @ symbol. Several of the calculation functions contain examples showing you how to use them. While they're not in depth, they're plentiful, so maybe that makes up for it.

If you'd like to pre-reserve an advance copy of "Look Smarter than You Are with Calc Scripts: Essbase Goes Hardcore," please e-mail info@interrel.com. If we get 100 advance orders, we'll start writing. Don't hold your breath.

Chapter 15:
Automate with MaxL

MaxL is the scripting language for Essbase, and is used by system administrators to automate various tasks and functions. It is installed with every instance of the Essbase server, on all operating systems. These are some of the more common actions that MaxL is used for:

- Loading a database
- Building a dimension
- Adding a user
- Altering a substitution variable

Having a good knowledge of MaxL is absolutely essential to the smooth running of your Essbase environment. Developers can also automate repetitive tasks in order to speed up testing cycles, a trick that can save much stress when under tight deadlines.

Here is a sample MaxL script that will connect to the local Essbase server, unload the Sample application, then delete it.

```
LOGIN admin password ON localhost;
ALTER SYSTEM UNLOAD APPLICATION Sample;
DROP APPLICATION Sample;
EXIT;
```

EXECUTE MAXL

MaxL can be run in two ways: interactive and batch. Both methods use the essmsh executable (*ESS*base *MaxL SH*ell) at the command prompt. There is a visual editor for MaxL scripts in the Administration Services console, but this is used for development only and is not normally used in production.

To run MaxL interactively, simply type **essmsh** at the command line and the MaxL interface will then be ready to accept your commands:

To run MaxL in batch mode, add the name of a script file as an argument to the command. MaxL will then read and interpret each line in succession until it reaches an EXIT command or the end of the file:

There are also MaxL interfaces for Perl and Java, but their usage is not covered in this book. More details of this can be found in the DBA Guide and Technical Reference publications.

SECURE MAXL

In Essbase 9.3, Hyperion added the ability to secure a MaxL script using public/private key pair encryption. In prior versions, the password would either be stored as clear text in the script or passed in as a variable from the command shell, which poses a security risk.

To create a key pair, run the MaxL shell with this argument: `essmsh -gk`

Then, to encrypt a script using this key pair, run: `essmsh -E [scriptname] [public key]` Note that this process creates a new secured script with the same name and a ".`mxls`" extension. To run this script you will need the corresponding private key: `essmsh -D [scriptname] [private key]`

If you try to run this script without the key you will see an error message, so don't lose the private key!

BASIC MAXL SYNTAX RULES

MaxL is neither case-sensitive nor space-sensitive, meaning you are free to format your scripts any way you see fit. The only general restrictions are that the file can only contain ASCII text, and every command must be terminated with a semicolon. Other than that, you can insert tabs, spaces, and new lines as you see fit to make the code easier to read.

Capitalizing the MaxL keywords only will make it much easier to identify which words are your variables and which are MaxL commands.

Tip!

Application and Database names are case-sensitive on UNIX hosts, even in MaxL scripts.

Note!

However, there is an important difference between single and double quotes in MaxL. Single quotes tell the engine to translate the text they enclose literally, while double quotes allow for variable translation. Consider the case where we want to output the system environment variable ARBORPATH. Here are two different MaxL statements that attempt to do this:

```
ECHO 'ARBORPATH is $ARBORPATH'

ECHO "ARBORPATH is $ARBORPATH"
```

The first statement with single quotes will output literally **ARBORPATH is $ARBORPATH**, while the second will evaluate the variable first and output the desired result of **ARBORPATH is c:\hyperion\essbase**.

If you want to output a single quote, you need to enclose the entire statement in double quotes:

```
echo "Essbase admins who don't use MaxL aren't
     spending their time wisely";
```

Backslashes are considered special characters in MaxL, and need to be doubled up when specifying a Windows file location:

```
'c:\\hyperion\\essbase\\app'
```

LOGIN

The login command is used to connect to an Essbase server. The IDENTIFIED BY syntax is completely optional and was probably only included for script readability.

```
LOGIN [username] IDENTIFIED BY [password] ON
      [hostname]

LOGIN [username] [password] ON [hostname]
```

Tip!   To run MaxL interactively and to easily login to the machine local to your session, type **essmsh -l [username] [password]** at the command line.

REDIRECT OUTPUT

Most of the time, you will schedule MaxL jobs to run in the middle of the night as part of an automated process. Of course, you will want to see everything that happened when you arrive at the office in the morning.

Redirecting the output of the script is usually the first command that you will issue in a script. The syntax for this is as follows:

```
SPOOL ON TO [File Name];
```

Tip!

There is no easy way to create a unique log file identifier in MaxL, but you can easily do this in most operating system command shells and pass a unique value in as a runtime variable (see the next session).

USE VARIABLES

There are three types of variables that you can use inside your MaxL scripts.

1. Environment variables from the operating system. If you want to reference a variable set in the operating system shell, you can reference it directly by name and prefixed with a dollar sign (e.g. **$ARBORPATH**)

2. Positional variables passed in on the command line. You can also add parameters to essmsh that will be translated to variables inside the script. For example, consider the script myscript.mxl that contains these commands:

```
ECHO "The third variable is $3.";
ECHO "The second variable is $2.";
ECHO "The first variable is $1.";
```

When you execute this script using this syntax:

```
essmsh myscript.mxl ten twenty thirty
```

The output will be:

```
The third variable is thirty.
The second variable is twenty.
The first variable is ten.
```

3. Temporary variables that you set inside the MaxL script. You may also want to set variables inside your MaxL scripts. To do this, use the following syntax:

```
SET myvariable = 'ten';
ECHO $myvariable;
```

MAXL ACTIONS

It can be overwhelming for first-time users to look at the large list of MaxL commands. However, everything becomes much simpler when you understand that there are only ten core actions.

The following table summarizes what each of these core actions does.

Alter	Change the state of an object.
Create	Create a new instance of an object.
Display	Show information about an object.
Drop	Delete an instance of an object.
Execute	Run a calculation or aggregation process.
Export	Output data or LRO's.
Grant	Assign security to users or groups.
Import	Load data, dimensions, or LRO's.
Query	Get information about an application or database.
Refresh	Reload partitioning information or custom Java function definitions.

SAMPLE MAXL STATEMENTS

The following sections will illustrate some of the most frequently used MaxL actions, and provide commentary on the nuances of the syntax.

Update an outline from a text file

The following statement will import dimensions from a text file (named products) using the rules file (named prod_bld) existing in the database directory. Note that the error file is being written to a common directory but the file name contains both the database name and the dimension being built for easy reference.

```
IMPORT DATABASE Sample.Basic DIMENSIONS
 FROM SERVER TEXT DATA_FILE 'products'
 USING SERVER RULES_FILE 'prod_bld'
 ON ERROR WRITE TO
        'c:\\hyperion\\MaxL_logs\\build.sample_basic.p
        roducts.err';
```

Load a database from a SQL source

This statement will load data from a SQL database. You don't have to specify the ODBC data source name as that is contained within the load rule itself (named sql_load).

```
IMPORT DATABASE Sample.Basic DATA
 CONNECT AS dbadmin IDENTIFIED BY dbpasswd
 USING SERVER RULES_FILE 'sql_load'
 ON ERROR WRITE TO
        'c:\\hyperion\\MaxL_logs\\load.sample_basic.er
        r';
```

Run a Calc Script

Of course, MaxL can run a calc script that you've already saved (in this example, the calc script named "Allocate" is executed). There are two ways to do this (both of these commands have the exact same result, it's your choice which you prefer to use):

```
EXECUTE CALCULATION 'Sample.Basic.Allocate';

EXECUTE CALCULATION 'Allocate' ON Sample.Basic;
```

A nice capability that is often overlooked is the ability to send custom calc commands directly from MaxL, which is incredibly useful when you want to test different settings or commands using variable substitution.

```
EXECUTE CALCULATION
 "SET UPDATECALCOFF;
  CALC ALL;"
ON Sample.Basic;
```

Create a user

When creating users, you most often use the OR REPLACE syntax to overwrite any existing users. This is important because no changes will be accepted by Essbase if there is a "User already exists" error thrown by the MaxL command. This example shows how to add a user authenticated externally against an LDAP server.

```
CREATE OR REPLACE USER 'Roger Clemens'
 TYPE EXTERNAL WITH PROTOCOL 'LDAP'
 IDENTIFIED BY 'ou=Finance, dc=MyCorp,
       dc=com@ldapserver2:389';
```

Run an MDX Query

MDX queries are interesting in that they do not have an action of their own. Rather, you execute the entire MDX statement as an action itself.

```
SPOOL ON TO 'mdx_output.txt';
SELECT
 {Products.Generation(2).Members} ON ROWS,
 {Time.Level(0).Members} ON COLUMNS
FROM Sample.Basic;
SPOOL OFF;
```

ERROR HANDLING

Error handling in MaxL is a two-stage process. The first involves redirecting the script after the error occurs so no more statements are executed. In this example, we are testing for a login failure and if not successful then there is no point in executing the load and calculate commands so we divert the MaxL script immediately to the "no_login" error handling section.

```
LOGIN admin password ON server01;
IFERROR 'no_login';

ALTER SYSTEM LOAD APPLICATION 'Sample';
EXECUTE CALCULATION DEFAULT ON 'Sample.Basic';
EXIT;

DEFINE LABEL 'no_login';
EXIT;
```

The second stage takes place in the operating system command-line environment that called **essmsh**. The **essmsh** process will return a 0 (zero) if everything was successful, but will return a non-zero number if an error was encountered. The operating system script will then be responsible for further actions.

Chapter 16:
A True Essbase Ghost Story

Just when you thought you couldn't keep your eyes open a second longer (don't worry, MaxL does that to all of us), we bring you a story that will keep you awake at night, peaking out from under the covers and looking for the ghosts of Essbase. This story is 100% true. Disbelieve if you dare.

As told by a client who shall remain nameless (with a bit of dramatization added for the reader's entertainment)...

It was a dark and stormy night. I was working late, all alone in the dimly lit office. We'd closed out the GL just that morning and I was responsible for updating our Essbase financial reporting application. I'd run our monthly process of building the dimensions and loading and calculating the database. But something wasn't right. The hairs on the back of my neck tingled with the sensation of doom. I opened my check worksheet and held my breath as I hit Retrieve. Time froze. The numbers weren't tying.

I don't understand, I told myself, trying to ignore the tremble in my voice. Please, please, I begged as if that would help the situation. It didn't and I knew I had to do something.

Trying to find some inkling of courage, I zoomed in on the numbers, again and again until I couldn't believe what I was seeing. I screamed in terror. Some of the data was double counted in my Organization dimension. How could that happen?

Closing my eyes, not standing to look anymore, I reached for the phone. I fumbled the numbers twice before getting it right.

"Tracy, what's happening? What's happening to my numbers?" I whispered, hoping the consultant could make things right again. "Help, please help."

"Calm down," Tracy reassured. "You have to calm down and explain to me exactly what happened."

Knowing that I wasn't alone anymore helped a bit. My eyes darted around before resting on my Monthly load checklist. I run the dimension build process to update the Organization dimension, run the data load process from GL, and then run the Actuals calculation script.

"I think I know what's happening," Tracy said. "Did you have any reorganizations this period?"

"How did you know?" I asked, shocked because I hadn't mentioned that fact. The IT department had broken up the Infrastructure department into two departments: Networking and

Hardware. That was where my data issue was occurring. I still had a value for the Infrastructure member when the cost centers rolling up to Infrastructure should have been remapped to the two new departments. In fact, the cost centers had been remapped. I'd checked. So how was there still data in the Infrastructure member?

Here is my Check Worksheet. The red cells should be blank but they still have a data value, which is doubling the expense amounts:

	A	B	C	D	E	F	G	H
		Product	Actual					
		Jan	Feb	Mar	Apr	May	Jun	Jul
		Expense	Expense	Expense	Expense	Expense	Expense	Expense
	Infrastructure	100	100	100	100	100	100	
	Networking	50	50	50	50	50	50	50
	Hardware	50	50	50	50	50	50	50
	Applications	250	250	250	250	250	250	250
	Custom Development	100	100	100	100	100	100	100
	IT	550	550	550	550	550	550	450
	Support & Admin Services	1000	1000	1000	1000	1000	1000	1000
	Total Company	4000	4000	4000	4000	4000	4000	4000

"Ghost data," Tracy said.

I shuddered. "A ghost?"

"Yes, here's what happened. You first ran your dimension build process that moved all cost centers from the Infrastructure department to the two new departments. This left the Infrastructure member as a level zero member with data still stored in that member. Then you ran your load and calc process, which aggregated the Org dimension, including the amount still stored in the Infrastructure member. This is what we call ghost data."

"How do I get rid of ghost data?" I asked, picturing a large contraption similar to what the Ghostbusters used in the movie.

"Simple. You need to update your process to clear upper level members before you run the dimension build process. Picture how this would work. You clear upper level members, which would clear the Infrastructure department. You can clear upper level data manually in Administration Services or via a calc script using the ClearBlock command. Then you run the dimension build which would remove the cost centers from the Infrastructure department and move them to the new departments. But that's OK because any data in the Infrastructure member has been cleared. You load and calc as always. The end result – no ghost data."

So the moral of the story is your overall Essbase load and calc processes (in most cases) should follow this order:

1. Clear data for upper level members.
2. Update dimensions.
3. Load data.
4. Calculate.

Chapter 17:
Essbase Under the Covers

To become an all knowing, all seeing Essbase administrator, you have to understand some of the more complex aspects of Essbase. So let's pull back the covers and take a look.

ESSBASE AGENT

First, let's review the Essbase Agent, otherwise known as essbase.exe (on Windows) or ESSBASE (on UNIX). The Essbase Agent starts and stops all applications, manages security, and in controls the flow of communications. It is THE CRITICAL piece of Essbase. It can be started in the foreground as active operating window but you must stay logged in to keep the server up. The recommended method is to start the Essbase Agent in the background. In the "A Day in the Life of an Essbase Administrator" section, we reviewed commands to communicate with the Essbase Agent.

ESSBASE SERVER

The Essbase Server is the component that actually does all the heavy data work. An esssvr.exe (Windows) or ESSSVR (UNIX) process is started for each Essbase Application that is created. This process handles all database activity, and this design wisely isolates other Applications from any evil-doing that goes on in a rogue Application (you know, the ones that hang out by the bike racks after the books are closed).

ESSBASE DIRECTORY STRUCTURE

Next we will tackle the Essbase directory structure. Here are the folders and files created when you install the program. Essbase demands a system variable called arborpath be present, which surprises us that Hyperion's marketing department (who must be awfully un-busy with some of the other silly changes they've requested) have missed changing this name after the Arbor merger nearly ten years ago. Anyway, you would refer to this environment variable as %ARBORPATH% in Windows and $ARBORPATH in UNIX, but we're just going to assume you know which one and refer to it generically as "arborpath".

arborpath\bin stores Essbase executables, the Essbase.cfg configuration file, the Essbase.sec security definition file, and the Essbase.bak backup security file.

arborpath\app stores server-based applications (more on this shortly).

arborpath\client stores any client based files and applications.

arborpath\docs stores online documentation.

arborpath\locale contains the character-set files necessary for multi-language use.

Need To Know – Essbase Executables

Helpful
Info

Stored in *arborpath*\bin
- Essbase.exe – Essbase server agent process
- Esssvr.exe – application process
- Essmsh.exe – MaxL shell
- Esscmd.exe – Esscmd command line interface

Stored in *eas*\Server\bin
- Starteas.exe – start the Administration Server executable
- Admincon.exe – Administration Services Console application

The *arborpath*\app directory contains all of the application files. An application will contain databases. A database will contain one outline file. Objects like report scripts, calc scripts, and rules files can be stored at the application or database level.

The official definitions for application and database are as follows: An application is the management structure containing one or more Essbase Analytic Services databases and related files. A database is the repository of data that contains a multi-dimensional storage array. Each database consists of a storage structure definition (outline), data, security, and optional calculation scripts, report scripts, and rules files.

Let's take a look at the directory structure for Sample.Basic:

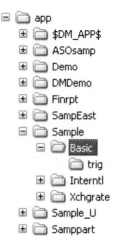

Tip!

You can store rules files, calc scripts, and report scripts at the application OR database level. If you have a calc script that will be run against one or more databases, store this script at the application level once instead of being replicated at the database level.

ESSBASE.CFG

The Essbase.cfg file is the main configuration file for Essbase, and it is simply a text file stored in the arborpath\bin directory. Administrators may add or change parameters and values in this file to customize Essbase functionality. Most of these settings apply to the entire Essbase Server. Essbase reads the configuration file at startup of the Essbase Agent and every time an Application is loaded. Be aware of the potential requirement to restart the system or an application when you are making changes to this file.

In this file you can define settings that control TCP/IP ports and connections, define how detailed you would like your log files, specify cache settings for performance improvements, define query governors for the server or specific application, and much more highly technical gobbledygook. Here is a sample Essbase.cfg file:

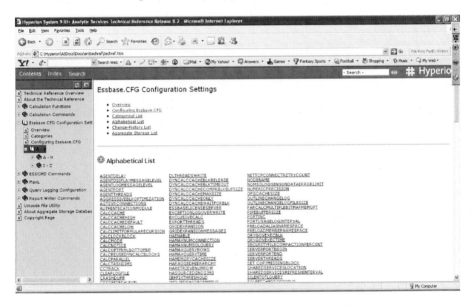

```
essbase.cfg - Notepad
File  Edit  Format  View  Help
; The following entry specifies the full path to JVM.DLL
; JvmModuleLocation  C:\Hyperion\common\JRE\Sun\1.4.2\bin\client\jvm.dll
;This statement loads the essldap.dll as a valid authentication module
;AuthenticationModule LDAP essldap.dll x;
EssbaseLicenseServer C:\Install
AnalyticServerId 1
UPDATECALC FALSE
CALCCACHEHIGH  150000000
CALCCACHEDEFAULT 50000000
CALCCACHELOW  20000000
CALCNOTICEHIGH 20
CALCNOTICEDEFAULT 10
CALCNOTICELOW 5|
```

For a full listing of the Essbase.cfg settings, see the Technical Reference provided by Hyperion:

To update the Essbase.cfg settings,
1. Edit the file in text format with any text editor, such as Windows Notepad.
2. Enter each setting on a separate line in the file. You do not need to end each line with a semicolon.
3. Make sure the file is named essbase.cfg,
4. Save the file in the arborpath \ bin directory.
5. Restart the Essbase Server or the Essbase Application after changing the configuration file.

Find the Essbase.cfg file on your server and take a look at the settings defined.

Try It!

ESSBASE.SEC

The Essbase.sec stores information about users, groups, passwords for native security, and privileges on applications and databases. It also stores many application and database properties. This isn't a file you can open and read but it is critical to your Essbase server. It lives next door to essbase.exe in the arborpath\bin neighborhood.

Each time that you successfully start the Essbase Server, a backup copy of the security file is created (named essbase.bak). You can restore from the last successful backup by copying essbase.bak to essbase.sec. If you have a corrupt application, you often times will need to recover from the security file backup as well as recreate the application from scratch.

Find the Essbase.sec file on your server and take a look at the security settings assigned. WAIT! This was a trick "Try It!" *Do not* open the Essbase.sec. You don't ever open up this file and read it. To view security, go to the Security section in Administration Services.

Try It!

CALCULATE THE BLOCK SIZE

We've already learned the basics about the Essbase block structure. Blocks are composed of dense members. In the case below, Measures, Time and Scenario are dense dimensions. The dense members, like Jan at Profit at Actual, make up the cells within the block.

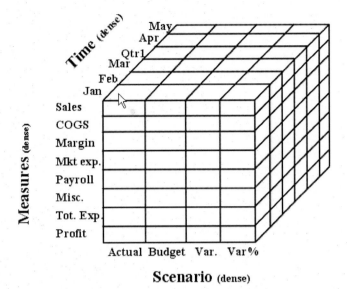

Scenario (dense)

A unique block is created for each intersection of the sparse members. Product and Market are sparse dimensions in the example below. A block is created for Cola at New York, for Cola at Florida, for Cola at East, and so forth.

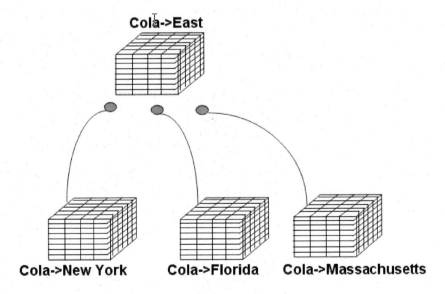

So what else is there to know? And why do you care? Oh, if only we could go back to the innocence of a new Essbase administrator. Everything seemed so simple – dimensions, hierarchies, and spreadsheets.

For some reporting and analysis databases, you may not need to worry about this. But we can imagine you will be building larger database with thousands and thousands of members with complex calculation and reporting requirements. So why do we need to dig deeper into the Essbase structure? Understanding these components helps us more effectively tune and optimize our Essbase databases. Let's start digging.

First, we will learn how to calculate block size. Data block size is determined by the amount of data in a particular combination of dense dimensions. Data block size is $8n$ bytes, where n is the number of cells that exist for that combination of dense dimensions. Here is an example:

Measures (Dense): 40 stored members
Time (Dense): 17 stored members
Scenario (Dense): 2 stored members

Block size = 40 * 17 * 2 * 8 = 10880 bytes or 11 KB

Note! Use the number of stored members when calculating block size; not the total number of members.

Despite what the Essbase Database Administrator's Guide says, we recommend a block size of about 8 KB. Larger block sizes will hurt parallel calculations (which is what most of your calculations will be these days). Too small block sizes may result in an increased index file. size. This forces Essbase to write and retrieve the index from disk, slowing calculations When in doubt, error on the side of smaller. That is, 1 KB is better than 40 KB. Unless you're using 64-bit Essbase (in which case 1+ MB block sizes are not abnormal), avoid blocks larger than 40 KB and strongly avoid blocks larger than 100 KB.

Tip! As with anything Essbase, these guidelines are not definitive and are just a starting point. Hence, the term "guideline". We have implemented applications that violated the block size guideline and still realized fast performance.

Let's calculate the block size for our wolverine juggling application. We have three dense dimensions right now: Account,

Period, and Scenario. The period dimension has 12 stored members (the upper level members are dynamically calculated so we will exclude those from the block size calculation):

```
Period Time <4> (Dynamic Calc)
    Q1 (+) <3> (Dynamic Calc)
        Jan (+)
        Feb (+)
        Mar (+)
    Q2 (+) <3> (Dynamic Calc)
        Apr (+)
        May (+)
        Jun (+)
    Q3 (+) <3> (Dynamic Calc)
        Jul (+)
        Aug (+)
        Sep (+)
    Q4 (+) <3> (Dynamic Calc)
        Oct (+)
        Nov (+)
        Dec (+)
```

The account dimension has eight stored members:

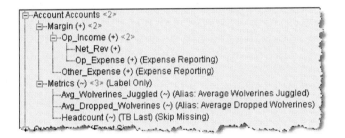

```
Account Accounts <2>
    Margin (+) <2>
        Op_Income (+) <2>
            Net_Rev (+)
            Op_Expense (+) (Expense Reporting)
        Other_Expense (+) (Expense Reporting)
    Metrics (~) <3> (Label Only)
        Avg_Wolverines_Juggled (~) (Alias: Average Wolverines Juggled)
        Avg_Dropped_Wolverines (~) (Alias: Average Dropped Wolverines)
        Headcount (~) (TB Last) (Skip Missing)
```

The scenario dimension has three stored dimensions (Variance is dynamically calculated):

```
Scenario <3>
    Actual (~)
    Budget (~)
    Variance (~)
```

So the block size for the wolverine juggling application is 12*8*3*8 = 2304 bytes or 2 KB.

Try It! Calculate the block size for the juggling wolverine application if we changed the Scenario dimension from dense to sparse.

Oh, we forgot to mention that Essbase also calculates the block size for you. Select the database and right click. Select *Edit Properties*. Select the Statistics tab:

So why did we teach you how to calculate block size? One, it is important to understand the concept of what members make up a block. Getting the block size to a reasonable size is important in tuning. You can reduce block size by making more members dynamic and changing a dense dimension to sparse. Two, you may want to use this calculation when you are performing an initial design to figure out your starting point dense and sparse dimensions.

CALCULATE THE NUMBER OF BLOCKS

So now we know the size of the data blocks. But how many blocks could we possibly have? A block is created for each unique intersection of stored sparse members. So to calculate the total possible blocks, multiply the number for stored members for each sparse dimension. Here is an example:

Product (Sparse): 19 stored members
Market (Sparse): 26 stored members

Number of Possible Blocks = 19*26 = 494

This time we will mention up front that Essbase also calculates the total possible blocks for you. Select the database and right click. Select *Edit Properties*. Select the Statistics tab again:

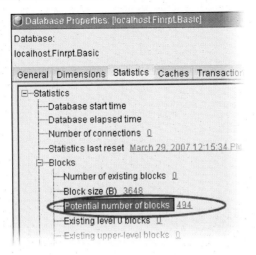

When you see this number for a production database, you may get really scared. This number will probably be really big, sometimes into the quadrillions. But remember, we've tagged these dimensions sparse for a reason. The likelihood that data exists for every single combination is very, very rare. So we recommend you understand this concept but don't worry about it any further (don't you just love it when the teacher teaches you something that you won't ever really use?). In certain cases, really large potential block counts (in excess of 100 trillion) can cause inefficient calcs, so watch out if you see this occurring.

The more helpful statistic is the number of existing blocks. Make sure you have loaded and calculated the database before you check this statistic. Go back to the Statistics tab under Database Properties:

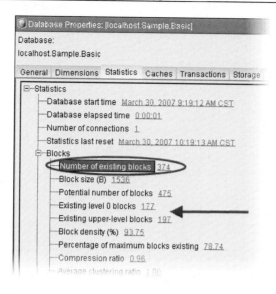

While you are there, note that Essbase also tracks the number of existing level-zero blocks and upper level blocks.

INDEX AND PAGE FILES

The index file is a file that contains pointers to all of the different blocks in the database. The index file is named ess*n*.ind and is stored in your database directory (n starts with 00001 and increments by 1 every time the file size reaches 2 GB). Essbase uses this file to locate the blocks that are requested during Essbase operations.

Index of sparse dimensions

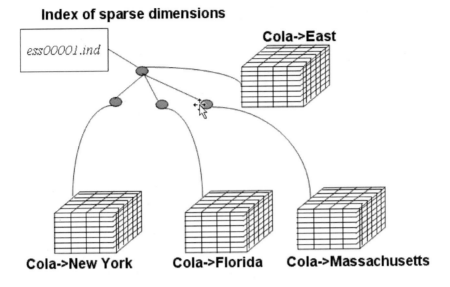

Data is stored in page files, named ess*n*.pag and stored in the database directory (also starting with 00001 and incrementing every 2 GB). These files are stored in the database directory. Essbase uses both the index and page files when performing operations on data blocks.

Try It!
Find the index and page files for the juggling wolverine application. Let's open the page files and take a look at the data. WAIT! We caught you again. This was another trick "Try It!" Do not open the page or index files. Ever. Leave these files alone always (unless you are backing them up). You cannot view data via the page files or a list of sparse blocks in the index file. If you open these files, not only will you see quite a bit of mumbo jumbo, you will probably corrupt your application and database. Don't say we didn't warn you.

Memory (index and data caches) can be set aside to help performance during operations. The index cache stores a portion or all of the index in memory for quicker access. The data cache stores a portion of the data blocks in memory for quicker access. We'll show you how to define these memory caches in the tuning and optimization chapter.

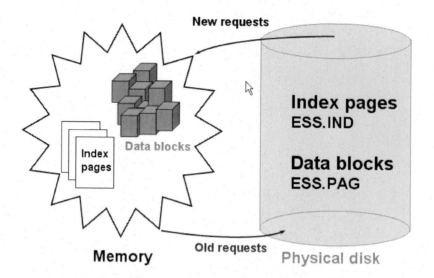

Did you know that interRel Consulting provides free concierge service for every paying client? Just kidding. We wanted to make sure you were still awake and paying attention through this valuable but dry and slightly boring section (OK, really boring section).

RESTRUCTURING

Restructuring of your Essbase database takes place after the outline changes, like when you add new, edit, and delete members and dimensions. Any and every change forces Essbase to restructure the database, so think of it as "re-saving" the database. This can be a time consuming process depending on the type of restructure and database size.

A full restructure, the most time consuming type of restructure, will take place when an outline is updated with the moving, deletion, or addition of a member from a dense dimension. This will reorganize every data block in the page file and regenerate the index. A re-calculation will also be required.

A sparse restructure is a much faster type of restructure, and takes place when you move, delete, or add a member from a sparse dimension. This type of restructure regenerates the index file but does not restructure the data blocks.

An outline restructure is the last type of restructure and will take place when you make a change that impacts the outline only, like changing an alias or member formula. This restructure will not regenerate the index file or restructure the data blocks, so is very quick indeed.

Note!   Each action you perform on an Essbase outline will cause some type of restructure. For a full list of the actions and what type of restructure will occur, see the Essbase Database Administrator's Guide and search for a table called "How Actions Affect Databases and Restructuring".

If your restructuring times are taking too long and impacting your users, consider the following tuning tips:

- If you change a dimension frequently, make it sparse.
- Use incremental restructuring to control when Essbase performs a required database restructuring.

INCREMENTAL RESTRUCTURING

One way to optimize your Essbase application is to enable incremental restructuring. This option will help with performance if you make frequent changes to your outline. Essbase will defer restructuring if possible, not restructuring either the index or affected blocks until the time that the block is accessed.

There are a few actions that will cause restructuring even if you have turned on incremental restructuring:

- Add or delete a non-attribute dimension.
- Delete a stored member of a sparse dimension.
- Change a dimension from sparse to dense or dense to sparse.

Note!   You cannot use incremental restructuring if you use LROs in your database.

To turn on incremental restructuring for a database, all databases in an application, or all databases in all application, update the Essbase.cfg file with the INCRESTRUC setting.

```
INCRESTRUC Sample Basic TRUE
```

RESTRUCTURE DATA OPTIONS WHEN SAVING AN OUTLINE

Once your application is up and running, sooner or later you will need to update an outline for a database that contains data. When you save an outline with data attached, you will be prompted with the following restructuring options: "All data", "Level zero data", "Input data" or "Discard all data". In most cases (if you've added, moved, or deleted members or changed storage properties), you will need to recalculate the database, so we recommend choosing input or level 0 data to restructure. This allows you to restructure a smaller data set which is much faster than the entire data set. If you've just made outline changes like aliases or change that doesn't require a recalculation, you could select a restructure of "All Data".

Restructure Database Options	☒
⊙ **All data**	
○ **L**evel 0 data	
○ **I**nput data	
○ **D**iscard all data	
▨ Warn if restructuring affects Hybrid Analysis	
OK Cancel Help	

Try It!

We've just checked the block size for our juggling wolverine application and it is too big (larger than the 8 KB guideline). Change the Scenario dimension from dense to sparse. What type of restructuring will occur? Ding, ding, ding – a full restructure. Choose the option to restructure level zero data. Then rerun the default calc. Next go check out the block size, number of potential blocks, and number of existing blocks. How did these numbers change?

Chapter 18:
Tune and Optimize

There is so much to be said about tuning Essbase we could write another full book (Look Smarter Than You Are with Essbase: Tuning Faster than the Speed of Light). For an introduction, this chapter will succinctly list different tuning and optimization steps that you can take for your Essbase applications.

Disclaimer: **There isn't simply one right answer when it comes to tuning.** Some of the tuning guidelines can contradict other tuning guidelines. Optimizing can have different perspectives: are you tuning for calculations or retrievals or both? In some databases, these tuning tips will have significant impact and in other databases, the tuning tips won't. Make sure you test, test, test. Did we say that tuning wasn't an exact science?

TUNE THE INDEX CACHE

The index cache is a reserved set of memory that is used to store all or a portion of the index file for quick access. You want to try and place as much of the index file into memory as possible to help with performance.

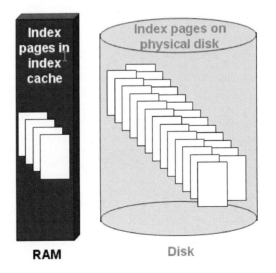

Here is a guideline for setting the index cache:

Set the index cache equal to the combined the size of all ess*n*.ind files, if possible. If you can't do that, then size the index cache as large as possible. Do not set this cache size higher than the total index size, as no performance improvement will be realized and you'll be consuming memory that other processes might need to use. It is possible that the index can be too large: Essbase will spend more time looking in the index cache than it would use by giving up and reading from the hard drive. In other words, if your index is 1,750 GB, don't set your index cache to 1,750 GB.

Here's an example: the index size for Sample.Basic is 8024 KB. We have enough memory on the server, so we will increase the index cache to 8024.

To set the index cache,
1. Select the database.
2. Right click and select *Edit Properties*.
3. Select the Caches tab.
4. Enter the new index cache value:

Database Properties: [localhost.Sample.Basic]

Database:	Status:
localhost.Sample.Basic	Loaded

General Dimensions Statistics **Caches** Transactions Storage Currency Modifications

- Caches
  - ☐ Cache memory locking
  - Cache sizes
    - Index cache setting (KB) `8024`
    - Index cache current value (KB) 1024
    - Data file cache setting (KB) 32768
    - Data file cache current value (KB) 0
    - Data cache setting (KB) 3072
    - Data cache current value (KB) 0
  - Index page setting (KB) 8
  - Index page current value (KB) 8

Apply   Refresh   Close   Help

---

5. Click *Apply*.

Note! Be aware. In some places, like in Caches, Essbase will reference KB (KiloBytes) for size. In other places, Essbase will reference B (bytes).

TUNE THE DATA CACHE

The data cache is the memory set aside to hold data blocks. You'll want to place as many blocks in memory as possible, but with the caveat that too much places a management burden on the system and can hurt overall performance.

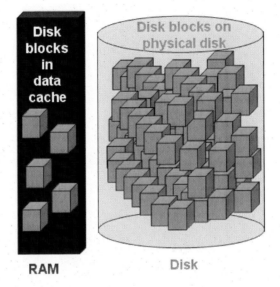

A guideline for setting the data cache is to set the data cache to 0.125 times the combined size of all ess*n*.pag files with a minimum value of about 307,200 KB. Consider increasing this value even further if you have a high number of concurrent users and they're complaining about retrieval times during peak times. Another time to further increase the Data Cache is when you have calculation scripts that contain functions that operate across sparse ranges and the functions require all members of a range to be in memory, for example, when using @RANK and @RANGE.

Here's an example of the recommended initial setting: the page size for your database is 3 GB. We have more than enough memory on the server, so we will increase the data cache to .125 * 3072000KB or 384,000 KB.

To set the data cache,
1. Select the database.
2. Right click and select *Edit Properties*.
3. Select the Caches tab.
4. Enter the new data cache value:

Database Properties: [localhost.Sample.Basic]

Database: Status:
localhost.Sample.Basic   Loaded

General Dimensions Statistics **Caches** Transactions Storage Currency Modifications

- Caches
  - ☐ Cache memory locking
  - Cache sizes
    - Index cache setting (KB) 8024
    - Index cache current value (KB) 1024
    - Data file cache setting (KB) 0
    - Data file cache current value (KB) 0
    - Data cache setting (KB) | 256000
    - Data cache current value (KB) 2047
  - Index page setting (KB) 8
  - Index page current value (KB) 8

Apply   Refresh   Close   Help

5. Click *Apply*.

The priority for cache tuning is as follows:
1. Index Cache
2. Data File Cache (if using Direct I/O)
3. Data Cache

Try It!

Tune the index and data caches for the wolverine juggling application.

Note!

The new cache settings will not take effect until the database is restarted.

Cache hit ratios will tell you how well your caches are being utilized. The ratio will tell you the percentage of time that a requested piece of information is available in the cache. As a general rule, the higher the ratio, the better. The goal for the index cache ratio should be 1. The goal for the data cache ratio should be 1, but values as low as 0.3 are acceptable. Why so low for data cache ratio? Your page files are a lot bigger than the index file. The chances that you can fit all of the page files or data into memory is pretty slim to impossible.

To view the cache ratios, right click on the database and select *Edit Properties*. Select the Statistics tab to view hit ratios:

TUNE THE CALCULATOR CACHE

Warning – this topic is confusing. We'll give you the background information related to calculator cache but when all is said and done, use this cache when the database has at least two sparse dimensions, and either you calculate at least one, full sparse dimension OR you specify the SET CACHE ALL command in a calculation script. Be prepared to read this section at least two or three times for full comprehension.

The best size for the calculator cache depends on the number and density of the sparse dimensions in your outline. First let's review a few terms:

The bitmap is a highly efficient mechanism that is used to very quickly tell the Essbase Calculation Engine whether a block exists or not at a given location. As the engine will not have to perform this lookup by reading the index file (which is relatively slow), and large Essbase databases can have a massive number of potential blocks, this little time saving for each potential block location can save a very large amount of time overall.

The bitmap dimensions will be the sparse dimensions from the database outline that Essbase fits into the bitmap until the bitmap is full. Each member combination of the sparse dimensions placed in the bitmap occupies (wait for it) 1 bit of memory. There must be enough space in the bitmap for every member combination of a sparse dimension for it to be placed in the bitmap, so we will need to make sure we size the cache to be large enough for what we want to load into the bitmap.

The anchoring dimensions are the remaining one or more sparse dimensions in the database outline that do not fit into the bitmap.

The calculator cache controls the size of the bitmap; therefore controlling the number of dimensions that can fit into the bitmap.

In case you found that section too simple, here are some equations:

Calculator cache = Bitmap size in bytes * Number of bitmaps

Bitmap size in bytes = Max ((member combinations on the bitmap dimensions/8), 4)

Number of bitmaps = Maximum number of dependent parents in the anchoring dimension + 2 constant bitmaps

Minimum bitmap size is 4 bytes

There are a few different ways to define the calculator cache. The default calculator cache size is set in the essbase.cfg. You can also set the size of the calculator cache within a calculation script, at which time the setting is used only for the duration of that script.

This is definitely one of those settings that you will want to test to get the maximum performance from your calc scripts, but be prepared to spend a lot of time tweaking the settings to get it just right.

DEFINE COMPRESSION METHOD

Attention readers: this section is for the IT geeks in the audience (OK, maybe this entire chapter is for the IT geeks). When Essbase stores blocks to disk, it can compress the blocks using one of three different algorithms to save space. When a compressed block is requested, Essbase will uncompress the block before sending the data into the main engine for further processing. Luckily this is all happening behind the scenes, so you can just make your choice and Essbase will handle all these details for you.

No compression is an option, but we've never seen anyone use it in production.

zLib compression is good for very sparse data.

Index value pair is good for large blocks with sparse data though you don't directly assign this compression type. Use index value pair when your blocks are very large (8-100 bytes is the recommended block size range, so large means closer to 100).

Bitmap is the default and is good for non-repeating data. If bitmap compression is chosen, then Essbase can choose between bitmap and index value pair compression types for the best fit.

RLE or run length encoding compression type is good for blocks with many zeroes or repeating values. If RLE compression is chosen, then Essbase can choose between RLE, bitmap, and index value pair compression types for the best fit.

To set compression,
1. Select the database.
2. Right click and select *Edit Properties*.
3. Select the Storage tab.
4. Select the desired compression type:

5. Click *Apply*.

Dimension order within your outline will make a difference with respect to optimizing compression. If you think of a block on disk like a spreadsheet, the first dense dimension determines the columns in the page file. Compression then works from left to right, top to bottom. Historically, people said that Accounts should be the first then Time the second dense dimension:

	A	B	C	D	E	F	
1		Budget					
2		Sales	COGS	Margin	Exp	Profit	
3	Jan	100	50	50	30	20	
4	Feb	100	50	50	30	20	
5	Mar	100	50	50	30	20	
6	Apr	120	50	70	30	40	
7	May	120	50	70	30	40	
8	Jun	120	50	70	30	40	
9							

That said, we almost *always* recommend using RLE compression under Essbase 7.x and later. When using RLE compression, you should switch the order of dimensions, listing Time first, then Accounts, so that Essbase can take advantage of the high probability of values repeating in successive periods:

	A	B	C	D	E	F	G	
1		Budget						
2		Jan	Feb	Mar	Apr	May	Jun	
3	Sales	100	100	100	120	120	120	
4	COGS	50	50	50	50	50	50	
5	Margin	50	50	50	70	70	70	
6	Exp	30	30	30	30	30	30	
7	Profit	20	20	20	40	40	40	
8								

QUICK APPLICATION DESIGN TIPS

Minimize the number of dimensions

The general rule for the number of dimensions in a block storage database is 7-10 dimensions. Make every one of them count! You will want to avoid dimensions that do not offer descriptive data points. This will help reduce complexity and size of database. Remember that adding a dimension increases the size and complexity of a database *exponentially*, not arithmetically.

Avoid Repetition in dimensions

Repeating members indicates a need to split dimensions, thereby reducing redundancy. In the example below, we repeat FTE, Average Hourly Rate (AHR), and Expense dollars for every payroll account. A better design would be to split the metrics from the Accounts dimension.

Before: 1 Dimension (Payroll):

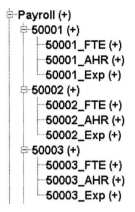

After: 2 Dimensions (Payroll and Metric):

Although this rule might seem to contradict the first tip in this section about minimizing the number of dimensions, this one is really about making sure you have the *right* number of dimensions given a specified analytical requirement. Repeating members can become awkward for end-users and causes a potential maintenance nightmare for administrators.

Avoid interdimensional irrelevance

This occurs when many members of a dimension are irrelevant across other dimensions. For example, Product and Customer dimensions will probably not be needed in a Human Resources headcount analysis database. Another example would be an Asset Category dimension placed in a sales analysis application.

The important point here is not to try to meet everyone's requirements into a single database. Split databases into meaningful analytical domains with common dimensions wherever possible.

DIMENSION ORDER WITHIN THE OUTLINE

Here is another tuning tip related to the order of dimensions within an outline. Dimension ordering within outlines is critical to your overall Essbase performance. You will want to test different iterations of dimension orders to determine the optimal structure. Historically, outlines were ordered from largest dense to smallest dense to smallest sparse to largest sparse (sometimes called the "hourglass" format). This works well when parallel calculation is not utilized. Since Essbase 7.x, though, everyone is using parallel calculation, so an improved method for ordering the dimensions was created.

First a few definitions:

Dense dimensions are the dimensions that define the internal structure of the data block. They should reside at the top of the outline.

Aggregating Sparse dimensions are dimensions that will be calculated to create new parent values. These dimensions should reside directly below the last Dense dimension in the outline. Placing these dimensions as the first Sparse dimensions positions them to be the first dimensions included in the calculator cache. This gives them an ideal location within the database for optimized calculation performance.

Non-Aggregating Sparse dimensions are dimensions that organize the data into logical slices. Examples include Scenario, Year or Version. It is not crucial for these dimensions to be included in the calculator cache because their members are typically isolated in FIX statements.

With this in mind, try the following guidelines to create an optimal outline order (sometimes called a "dressform" or an "hourglass on a stick"):

1. Largest Dense Dimensions
2. Smallest Dense Dimensions
3. Smallest Aggregating Sparse Dimensions
4. Largest Aggregating Sparse Dimensions
5. Non-aggregating Sparse Dimensions

Example – An Employee Analysis Database:

Dimension	Type-Stored Member Count	Density After Calc	Density After Load	Data Points Created
Time Periods	D – 21	85%	85%	-
Metrics (Hrs, AHR, $)	D – 14	22%	22%	-
Accounts	D – 94	3 %	2%	-
Scenarios	AS – 9	22%	11%	199
Job Code	AS – 1,524	.56%	.23%	853
Organization	AS – 2,304	.34%	.09%	783
Versions	NAS – 7	19%	19%	-
Years	NAS – 7	14%	14%	-

D=Dense, AS=Aggregating Sparse, NAS=Non-Aggregating Sparse

Outlines can be ordered based on dimension stored member count or on dimension density. Ordering by stored member count is the easy option but may not be as accurate as ordering by dimension density. In the example above, the optimized outline should follow this order (assuming we order the outline based on dimension density):

Original Dimension Order (Typical Hourglass)	Optimized Dimension Order (Modified Hourglass)
Accounts (D)	Time Periods (D)
Time Periods (D)	Metrics (D)
Metrics (D)	Accounts (D)
Years	Job Code (AS)

Versions	Organization (AS)
Scenarios	Years (NAS)
Job Code	Versions (NAS)
Organization	Scenarios (NAS)
Employee Status (Attr Dim)	Employee Status (Attr Dim)
Fund Group (Attr Dim)	Fund Group (Attr Dim)

To figure out the density of a dimension, set that dimension to dense and set all other dimensions to sparse. Load and calculate the single dense dimension. Check the block density value in Administration Services. Right click on the database and select *Edit Properties*. Select the Statistics tab and scroll down to find the block density:

Tip!

Order the dimensions in the juggling wolverine application per the guidelines above.

Try It!

OTHER OUTLINE TIPS

Here are a few other quick tips related to outlines. Avoid large flat sparse dimensions like an Employee dimension with 10,000 employees rolling up to a total. Adding additional levels into the hierarchy will speed up retrievals and dynamic calculations. If you want to optimize the outline for fast retrievals, place the most queried sparse dimensions as the first sparse dimension in the outline.

OPTIMIZE DATA LOAD RULES

Make sure your source data file follows a reverse order of the outline: Non-aggregating sparse dimensions, aggregating sparse dimensions, and finally the dense dimensions (assuming your outline follows the dressform model).

Outline Order	Data File Order and Sort
Time Periods (D)	Scenarios (NAS)
FTE Metrics (D)	Versions (NAS)
Accounts (D)	Years (NAS)
Job Code (AS)	Organization (AS)
Organization (AS)	Job Code (AS)
Years (NAS)	Accounts (D)
Versions (NAS)	FTE Metrics (D)
Scenarios (NAS)	Time Periods (D)
Employee Status (Attr Dim)	
Fund Group (Attr Dim)	

Tip!

If you ever forget the order for an optimal data load file, do a columnar export. Look at the order of the dimensions in the file (and the dense dimension across the columns). Match your input file to the order of the dimensions in the export file.

Other tuning tips for faster data loads include using dense dimension members for data column headers and avoid using the single "data field". For example, an optimized data file with columns for each period and each account will load much quicker than a file with only one data value per line and the periods and accounts repeating across the rows.

Avoid unnecessary columns in the source data file. For example, your data file has columns for period, account, product, sales manager, product description, and product introduction date. Unless your rules file updates the product dimension and loads data, take out the extraneous columns like sales manager, product description, and product introduction date. For large data loads, every little bit counts.

Copy data load files directly to the Essbase server. It is faster to load from the server than the client where the network can sometimes become a bottleneck.

And lastly, pre-aggregate records before loading. Here is a data file where the Jan records will have to be added together during the load process:

```
01/01/2007, Jan, California,Caffeine Free Cola, Sales, 145
01/02/2007, Jan, California,Caffeine Free Cola, Sales, 123
01/03/2007, Jan, California,Caffeine Free Cola, Sales, 132
01/04/2007, Jan, California,Caffeine Free Cola, Sales, 145
01/05/2007, Jan, California,Caffeine Free Cola, Sales, 102
01/06/2007, Jan, California,Caffeine Free Cola, Sales, 116|
```

Here is an optimized data file with records pre-aggregated by month. This is a very simple task for any relational database.

```
Jan, California, Caffeine Free Cola, Sales, 762
Feb, California, Caffeine Free Cola, Sales, 775
Mar, California, Caffeine Free Cola, Sales, 862
Apr, California, Caffeine Free Cola, Sales, 700|
```

Review the load file that we created for the wolverine juggling application. Is this rules file optimized per the guidelines above? If not, then optimize.

Try It!

OPTIMIZE CALCULATIONS

We get a lot of calls that ask "Why does my calc script take 5 hours?" or "How can I get my calc time down?" Changing a number of the database and outline settings can significantly impact your calculation time. These settings are discussed in other sections of the book, but here are a few more tips.

Calculate only those dimensions requiring calculation. For example, do you need to rollup Scenario (Actual + Budget)? If all of the upper level members in your Accounts dimension are dynamic, do you need to calculate Accounts? Nope. By utilizing a lean and mean "CALC DIM" or "AGG" with only the dimensions that need it, you'll shave valuable time from your calc scripts.

"AGG" and "CALC DIM" are not the same. "AGG" is faster for straight aggregation of sparse dimensions with no member formulas so use this when you can. There are some cases where a sparse dimension with 7+ levels may CALC DIM faster than it AGGs, but this is rare.

You cannot "AGG" dense dimensions. Your dense dimensions should be dynamic, so you should not be using CALC DIM.

Note!

Always use "Fix" on Sparse dimensions and use "If" on Dense dimensions if you're going to be doing different logic on different members from the same dimension. If you need to do a bunch of logic against a set of members of a dimension (dense or sparse) and you don't need to do *different* logic against different members of that dimension, always use a FIX.

Simplify the calculation if possible by using unary calcs instead of member formulas, and member formulas instead of logic within a calc script. Take advantage of built-in Essbase functionality like Dynamic Time Series whenever possible.

OPTIMIZE RETRIEVALS

You *can* speed up data retrievals by increasing the value of two retrieval-specific buffer settings. These buffers hold extracted row data cells before they are evaluated or sorted. If the buffer is too small, retrieval times can increase with the constant emptying and re-filling of the buffer. If the buffer is too large, retrieval times can increase when too much memory is used when concurrent users perform queries. The default buffer is set to 10KB for 32-bit platforms and 20 KB for 64-bit. As a rule, don't exceed 100KB for either buffer.

To set the retrieval buffers,

1. Right click on the Database and select *Edit Properties*.

2. Go to the General tab and set the retrieval buffers:

FRAGMENTATION

Fragmentation can be a potentially crippling side-effect of frequently updated databases that use one of the compression techniques mentioned earlier in this chapter. Let's assume that we have a very simple block with only eight cells:

100	#Missing	#Missing	#Missing
#Missing	#Missing	#Missing	#Missing

Any one of the compression methods would work well on this, but for the sake of example let's assume Run-Length Encoding is used and is able to compress the data storage component to 32 bytes (8 Bytes for the 100 and 24 Bytes to compress all the #Missing values together). Then, a user writes some budget data to this block:

100	150	200	#Missing
#Missing	#Missing	#Missing	#Missing

This block will now require 48 Bytes to store (8 Bytes for each number, and 24 Bytes for the #Missing values). Fragmentation happens because Essbase can't fit 48 Bytes back into the original 32 Byte location and it is written to the end of the file. The original block still remains in the file, but there is no corresponding pointer in the index file so it is lost forever but still taking up space. Actually, it's not quite forever. Essbase tracks empty space in the database directory in a .esm file.

Now that you understand fragmentation, an alarm should be going off for all budgeting application administrators – Ding, Ding! Budgeting not only involves frequent updates, but also calc scripts that expand block size. Fragmentation also runs rampant when data load rules aren't sorted properly and blocks are written to the .pag file, then updated later in the load and re-written to a new block location.

To eliminate fragmentation, you can export the data from the database to a file, clear all data from the database and reload from the export file (see the Backup and Recovery section in "A Day in the Life of an Administrator" chapter). This workaround (and various other unseemly workarounds like adding "dummy members" to dense dimensions) was the only method to defragment an Essbase cube until recently. Newer versions of Essbase MaxL support a command called "alter database *[database name]* force restructure" which removes all fragmentation from the database.

Defrag the wolverine juggling application by exporting the data to a file, clear all data, and reload the exported data file. What happened to the size of the database on disk?

Try It!

COMMIT ACCESS

In all of our years of Essbase implementations, we've very rarely changed the default Commit settings for Essbase. Still, if you want to be a *master* Essbase administrator you need to be aware of this concept. It is something you can tune to help with performance in certain cases.

Commit access in Hyperion Essbase tells the engine how and when to save the data to the physical disk. This concept will be familiar if you have worked in-depth with relational databases. When you run an update statement against a SQL database, you must run a commit after the fact to ensure changes are saved to the database. Commit access in Essbase works similarly.

When you use uncommitted access, Essbase writes the data blocks to disk when the commit level is reached. The default commit level is set to 3000 blocks. So let's say you are performing a data load, once 3000 blocks have been loaded (triggered by the arrival of the 3001st block), they will commit to disk. Essbase will then continue with the load, committing again once 3000 more blocks are loaded. So Essbase is going back and forth writing to disk (also called I/O or input/output) which could impact performance. By increasing the Commit level, you will be sending more data fewer times, and by decreasing this value you will be sending less data more times.

Committing by rows is for environments where there is a risk that the data load process will be interrupted mid-stream and the administrator will want to continue the load from a logical starting point. For example, if the Commit setting is equal to 1000 rows, Essbase will save the blocks to disk at this interval. If the load fails on the $3,462^{nd}$ record, there will be a record of 3,000 rows successfully saved into the Essbase database and the administrator can restart the load from record 3,001. Yes, this will reload the records from 3,001 to 3,461 redundantly, but better that than losing data.

You can also set the commit blocks to zero. With this setting, Essbase will only write to disk at the completion of the entire transaction (in our example, this is at the end of the data load). This can dramatically improve performance, BUT (that was a big ass "but") this can significantly fragment the page file (see section on Fragmentation). Only do this if you're running calculations infrequently as part of a periodic batch updating process.

To change the Commit setting,
1. Select the database.
2. Right click and select *Edit Properties*.
3. Select the Transactions tab.
4. Select either Committed or Uncommitted access.
5. If you chose Uncommitted access, next define the synchronization point:
   a. Commit blocks OR

b. Commit rows

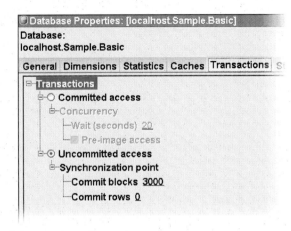

6. Click *Apply*.

Congratulations! If you've made it this far, you are in the home stretch. We are in the last two miles of the Essbase marathon. You are in some degree of pain, your feet are killing you, you are dehydrated, and you just want to fall down and collapse. Grab an energy bar, some Gatorade, and keep going. You are almost there. You can do eet!

Chapter 19:
Introduction to ASO

Coming soon (if we have enough demand from you)... A complete book called "Look Smarter Than You Are with Aggregate Storage: Essbase Super-sized". Unfortunately we won't cover aggregate storage databases in great detail in this book but we will give you enough of a basic introduction to get you started.

First, everything we've discussed up until this point has been for block storage option Essbase databases (BSO). You now know and understand all there is to know about Essbase BSO databases. Block storage option databases allow us to create complex business models, including write back capabilities for users. BSO databases utilize things like member formulas, blocks, dense and sparse dimensions, and page and index files. Unfortunately the block storage architecture that lets us create complex business models starts to have performance issues as dimensionality and outline sizes grow. No matter how powerful computers have become in the past fifteen years since Essbase was created, you just can't have it all.

Aggregate storage option databases were created specifically to deal with requirements for very large sparse data sets with a high number of dimensions and potentially millions of members (any one of these requirements would make a BSO database hide under the bed and whimper for its mommy). ASO utilizes a new kind of storage mechanism that allows improved calculation times from ten to one hundred times faster than BSO databases – the calculations just aren't as complex. ASO can also store up to 2^{52} dimensional combinations. If you aren't that great at math, just know this is a really, really big number. New types of Essbase databases are now possible (imagine background music coming in as you read. It's the theme from Aladdin, "A Whole New World"). This includes Customer analysis on potentially millions of customers, logistics analysis where we can analyze near real-time updates of product shipments, and market basket analysis where we can analyze what products are purchased along with other products.

The beauty of all of this is that front-end tools like the Excel Add-In, SmartView, and Web Analysis/Analyzer really don't care if the database is BSO or ASO (even MaxL sees only minor differences between the two). They both seem like multidimensional databases that have Zoom In and Zoom Out and

Keep Only and Remove Only and Pivot and all that nice stuff. There are some differences, of course, but for the most part the database type is pretty much transparent to the end-user.

Let's start diving into the ASO deep end by taking a look at the ASOSamp.Sample outline:

⊟ **Outline: Sample (Active Alias Table: Default)**
  ⊞ **Measures Accounts** <6> (Label Only)
  ⊞ **Years Dynamic** <4> (Label Only)
  ⊞ **Time Time Multiple Hierarchies Enabled** <3> (Label Only)
  ⊞ **Transaction Type Stored** <3>
  ⊞ **Payment Type Stored** <4>
  ⊞ **Promotions Stored** <5>
  ⊞ **Age Stored** <3>
  ⊞ **Income Level Stored** <6>
  ⊞ **Products Multiple Hierarchies Enabled** <2> (Label Only)
  ⊞ **Stores Stored** <2> {Square Footage, Store Manager}
  ⊞ **Geography Stored** <6> {Area Code}
  ⊞ **Store Manager Attribute** [Type: Text] <200>
  ⊞ **Square Footage Attribute** [Type: Numeric] <7>
  ⊞ **Area Code Attribute** [Type: Text] <9>

Yes, you are seeing correctly. No blurry vision. We have an outline that has 13 stored dimensions. Note you can also have attribute dimensions in ASO databases, and they act just like they do in the BSO world.

Tip!

You can easily spot an ASO database in the Administration Services Console by the red star beside the application name:

⊟ 📇 **ASOsamp**

You may be saying "Yes, yes, I'm sold. ASO is so awesome that I'm wondering why we even need BSO databases anymore?" The answer, dear reader, lies just below...

HOW DOES ASO DIFFER FROM BSO?

First, a quick disclaimer: this chapter was written mainly from knowledge gained with the Essbase 7x versions. The hard working Hyperion developers have constantly enhanced the ASO engine in System 9 so this has been a rapidly moving target (see the System 9 chapter for more details). We will denote these System 9 differences where appropriate.

With that said, let's jump into some of the core differences between ASO and BSO that will remain indefinitely. Remember all of your hard work in learning dense and sparse? Well, throw that knowledge out the window when you are working with ASO databases, as there is no concept of dense and sparse. There is neither two-pass logic, nor built-in time-balance functionality (Although this changes in System 9.3. In System 9.3 you have time functionality coming out the whazzoo). Member formulas are not supported in stored hierarchies and you are restricted to the non-consolidation (~) operator and addition (+) operator in shared hierarchies (there are more enhancements related to this in System 9). You are limited to one database per ASO application. ASO does not utilize procedural calc scripts and all ASO formulas are written in MDX syntax. There is still an "Accounts" dimension in ASO but alas this "Accounts" dimension is totally different than the "Accounts" dimension in BSO.

There are also differences in the way ASO behaves when data is loaded or when the outline is restructured. You can only load data to level-zero members. The database must restructure after any members in a standard dimension are added, deleted, or moved. All data is cleared when this happens (which is really, really annoying, but also partially addressed in System 9). In fact, most actions on an ASO outline will either cause a loss of data and or a restructure. To be on the safe side, plan any changes to the outline very carefully. One last difference (and it's a biggie): ASO is read-only. You cannot write to ASO databases, but there is a workaround using transparent partitions and pointing to an attached BSO database for those duties.

Wow, that was a lot to process in such a short space of time (and that was just a summary of the main points!)

Use BSO for applications that require complex calculations and write back capabilities.

Tip!   Use ASO for applications that require a large number of dimensions and members that simply "roll up" (i.e. minimal complex calculations are required).

The Essbase Database Administrator's Guide has a handy set of tables that compare the BSO vs. ASO features. Look for the "Comparison of Aggregate Storage and Block Storage" chapter:

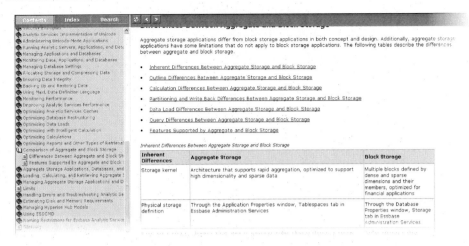

CREATE AN ASO APPLICATION

The Old Fashioned Way

There are three ways to build an ASO application. The first way we can build an ASO database is using the steps for which you should be familiar.

To create an ASO application and database in Administration Services,

1. Select *File >> New*.
2. Choose Aggregate Storage Application:

3. Select the Analytic Server and specify a new application name:

Create Application

Analytic **S**erver:

localhost

Application name:

ASOjuggl

OK   Cancel   Help

4. Click *OK*. You now have an application with no databases within it. This is completely useless, so don't stop now.
5. Right click on the application you just created and select *Create Database*:

Applications

ASOjugg

Prope   Start

Repo   Stop

Rules   Copy...

Datak   Rename...

ASOsan   Delete

Prope   **Create database...**

Repo

Rules   View log

6. Your server and application should already be selected, so type in a new database name:

Create Database

Analytic **S**erver:

localhost

Application:

ASOjuggl

Database name:

ASOjuggl

Database type:

Normal   Currency

OK   Cancel   Help

7. Click *OK*.

That's it. The same steps as the creating the BSO application and database. From there you can open the outline and begin adding members manually if you would like, just like BSO outlines.

ASO outlines have two types of hierarchies: stored and dynamic. A dimension can contain one or both types of hierarchies (if you enable multiple hierarchies for the dimension). Other properties that you can set for dimensions and members include dimension type, data storage (store, never share, label only), member solve order, and alias. This is just skimming the top of dimension and member properties in ASO. Remember we are just introducing the concept, not trying to give you the detailed steps.

While you can manually add members to the outline using the visual editor, this isn't really a good idea for any real-life databases. Luckily, you create dimension build rules just like you did for BSO databases.

> Unlike in block storage; ASO does not allow you to preview outline changes. If you are unsure of the result of your build rule, make a backup of your outline before running the new build rule.
>
> **Tip!**

Next, to load data, use load rules just as you do for BSO databases. What comes next? Calculating, right? For ASO databases, after data values are loaded into the level 0 cells of an outline, *the database requires no separate calculation step.* From any point in the database, users can retrieve and view values that are aggregated for only the current retrieval. ASO databases are smaller than block storage databases, enabling quick retrieval of data. For even faster retrieval, pre-calculate data values and store the pre-calculated results in aggregations.

To retrieve data from an ASO database, retrieve and analyze just as you would from a BSO database. That's it.

Use the ASO Outline Conversion Wizard

You can also create an ASO application using the aggregate storage outline conversion wizard. The advantage of the wizard is that you have a starting point outline since the wizard uses an existing BSO database to convert to an ASO database. The disadvantage to using the wizard is that the existing BSO outline was not designed with ASO in mind. Therefore reengineering of the dimensions and hierarchies will still need to take place, but in many cases this is less work than creating an ASO model from scratch. In the following section we will explore how to use the wizard.

To use the wizard in the Administration Services console, select on *Wizards >> Aggregate Storage Outline Conversion*:

Select the BSO outline to convert to ASO. Don't worry, the wizard does not modify the BSO outline in any way.

Click *Next*. In the next step, Essbase will determine and validate what sections of the outline can be converted to ASO. This is the point at which features not supported by ASO would be modified. You can either have the wizard manage the modifications automatically, or you can do them manually using the interactive interface:

In the last step specify where to place your new ASO outline. Select "Create Aggregate Storage Application" to create a brand new application or save over an existing ASO database on the Essbase Server. You can also save the outline to the file system:

The Automated Way

The final way we can create an ASO application is by using the "Create Application", "Create Database", and "Create Outline" commands using MaxL. Typically this method would be used when you are running the MaxL command as part of a batch job.

MDX INTRODUCTION

So now that we have an ASO outline, what's the next step in the conversion? We are not able to use calculations as we know them in BSO, but we can use MDX to create some very powerful member calculations. Always keep some basic rules in mind prior when using MDX. The first and most important rule to keep in mind is that all MDX calculations in ASO are dynamic. This means that if your outline has a dimension or two with a million plus members, it's probably not a good idea to apply an MDX query that works on level-0 members.

Here are some examples of MDX member formulas:

```
AvgUnits/Transaction =   [Units]/[Transactions]
Variance =[Curr Year]-[Prev Year]
Variance % = ([Curr Year]-[Prev Year])/[Prev
      Year]*100
% of Total =
                  Transactions/(Transactions,Time,
                  [Transaction Type],[Payment Type],
                  Promotions,Age,[Income Level],
                  Products,Stores,Geography)
```

You may notice a few immediate differences between your calc script syntax and MDX syntax – the use of brackets around member names (vs. double quotes) and the lack of semicolons.

Besides member calculations, you can also create MDX queries that you save and later run. To create MDX queries you need to open the MDX Script Editor located under *File>>Editor*.

Documentation on Query format can be found in the Technical Reference Guide under MDX.

Note!

ASO TRANSPARENT PARTITIONING

Remember that one sticky issue about not being able to write to an ASO database. One way to work around this issue is to create a BSO database (which allows write back) and set up a transparent partition to the ASO database. We haven't defined partitioning so let's give you a quick definition. A partition is a mechanism in Essbase that allows data sharing between cubes. Using a transparent partition from an aggregate storage database to a block storage database allows us to leverage the power of both models (large number of dimensions and members for analysis in ASO and write back and calculations for BSO) and for the most part ignore the weaknesses at the same time. An Aggregate Storage Partitioning wizard is provided in Administration Services to create the transparent partition. For example, you have an ASO database with detailed customer sales data. You wanted to model complex budgeting and forecasting scenarios, so you partition the sales data at a high level to the block storage cube. Using write-back enabled members you can now compare your actual data to budget or forecast. To use the wizard, select *Wizards>>Aggregate Storage Partition*.

There's so much more that we want to cover, and so much you need to know about ASO. Due to space and time limitations, we'll have to conclude our introduction at this point. More will come in a later Look Smarter installment, "Essbase Super-sized", we promise.

Note!

One last note... ASO in System 9 is called "Enterprise Analytics".

Chapter 20:
Other Essbase Features

As we drew up the outline for this book, we began with a list of fairly simple items. From an end user perspective, we wanted to show you how to use both the Essbase Excel Spreadsheet Add-In and the Smart View Add-In. From an administrator perspective, we wanted to show you how to create, optimize, and manage the application. While we didn't want to overwhelm you, we still wanted to make you knowledgeable and able to dig in immediately. But Essbase has *so many* features and functions that it is almost impossible to include in one book without overwhelming you (in addition, the book would probably weigh about 100 pounds). There are still many topics that we can't cover in detail so in this section, we'll give you a brief overview of those additional topics.

INTRODUCTION TO UNICODE APPLICATIONS

Do you need to increase the length of your aliases? Do you need to roll out an application in a foreign language? Do you feel like you're stuck in a never-ending infomercial? Essbase fully supports Unicode applications for these reasons. Unicode applications use UTF-8 encoding form to interpret and store character text, providing support for multiple character sets. Let's take a look at the Sample_U.Basic application.

We can see that Sample_U has a different alias table for each foreign language plus an additional alias table for long names:

```
⊟ Alias tables
    ├── Default <Default table>
    ├── Long Names
    ├── ChineseNames
    ├── JapaneseNames
    ├── RussianNames
    └── GermanNames
```

Notice, if we change the active Alias table in the Outline editor to German names, we can see the German aliases:

To set the active alias table, open the outline editor. Select the Properties tab. Under the "Alias tables" section, right click on the desired alias table and select "Set as active".

Note!

```
⊟ Outline: Basic (Active Alias Table: GermanNames)
  ⊞ Year (Alias: Jahr)
  ⊞ Measures ⮕Alias: Umsätze)
  ⊞ Product (Alias: Produkt)
  ⊟ Market (Alias: Markt)
     ⊞ East (+) (Alias: Ost)
     ⊞ West (+)
     ⊞ South (+) (Alias: Süd)
     ⊞ Central (+) (Alias: Mitte)
  ⊞ Scenario (Alias: Szenario)
  ⊞ Caffeinated (Alias: Koffeinhaltig)
  ⊞ Ounces (Alias: Unzen)
  ⊞ Pkg Type (Alias: Art der Verpackung)
  ⊞ Population (Alias: Einwohner)
  ⊞ Intro Date (Alias: Datum der Einführung)
```

To set up a unicode application,

1. Setup a computer for unicode support by doing one of:
   - Install a font that supports UTF-8 encoding, or
   - Install a unicode editor
2. Set the Essbase Server to Unicode Mode via Administration Services or MaxL (use Server Properties).
3. Check the Unicode box when creating a new unicode-mode application.
4. You can also migrate non-unicode applications to unicode applications (but NOT the other way around).

It's important to understand that unicode is supported for Block Storage option databases only. Partitions cannot connect non-unicode mode databases to unicode mode databases and if you do partition unicode databases, all databases in the partition must use the same encoding.

REPORT SCRIPTS

Essbase comes with a report script engine that you can use to create reports. Do we recommend this? No. Hyperion delivers much, much better reporting solutions using the Add-Ins and tools like Web Analysis/Analyzer and Financial Reporting/Reports. Still report scripts can be helpful when extracting subsets of data from Essbase for online backups or feeding into other systems.

The report script editor is the text editor where you will create a report script. There are two types of commands in report scripts: extraction and formatting. The basic layout of a report script will contain a page, row, and column definition (sound familiar?).

```
<Page
<Row
<Column
```

Here is what a report script will look like in the report script editor:

Here is an example of a report script that extracts a subset of data in a loadable format:

```
<COLUMN("Fiscal Year")
Sep Oct Nov Dec Jan Feb Mar Apr May Jun Jul Aug
<ROW("Market", "Scenario", "Accounts")
{TabDelimit}
{Decimal 2}
{NoIndentGen}
{SUPMISSINGROWS}
{SUPZEROROWS}
{RowRepeat}
{SupBrackets}
<Link (<DESCENDANTS("East") AND <LEV(Market,0) )
"Actual" "Budget"
<Link (<DESCENDANTS("Margin") AND <LEV("Accounts",0)
     )
!
```

Note!   // denotes a comment in report scripts.

Tip!   System 9.3 introduces a new calc script command that will allow you to extract subsets of data from an Essbase database. We recommend you take a look at this new command as a possible replacement for your data export report scripts.

WIZARDS, WIZARDS, WIZARDS

No, this section isn't part of the last Harry Potter installment (although we wish we had their special effects budget). Essbase comes with several wizards to assist you in various tasks, and Hyperion is always adding more. Try it - select *Wizards* from the Administration Services menu. The wizards are so easy to use we will let you get to know these magical creatures on your own:

WIZARDS WINDOW HELP

Migration
Aggregate Storage Outline Conversion
Aggregate Storage Partition
User Setup
Data Mining Wizard

The User Setup wizard will walk you through the process of creating Administration Services users. The wizard will help map Administrative Services users to Essbase users.

The Migration wizard will walk you through the process of migrating (copying) applications and databases across Essbase Servers with no server downtime. You can copy from any platform to any platform (Window to Unix and back again). Migrations can be run in the background, freeing up Administration Services for other activities.

The remaining wizards are discussed in their own relative sections.

DATA MINING

Data mining is the process of searching through large amounts of data to find hidden relationships and patterns. Data mining results can be descriptive (provide information about existing data). For example, people who bought root beer in July also bought ice cream in July. The results can be predictive (forecast future trends.) For example, forecast next year's root beer sales based on this year's.

 Data mining is not supported for ASO databases.
Note!

There are six data mining algorithms provided for creating new data mining models: simple regression, multilinear regression, clustering, association rules, decision tree, and neural net. Luckily, Essbase provides a wizard to assist in the creation of data mining models.

TRIGGERS

Triggers allow users to monitor data changes in Essbase. If data meets a trigger's rules, Essbase can send an e-mail or log the information in a file. An example of this would be to send an e-mail to the department manager if the wolverine juggling revenue in the Western region fell below the revenue for the same month in the previous year. Triggers are evaluated during the following system events: data load, calculation and lock and send from the Spreadsheet Add-In.

MDX

MDX is the Data Manipulation Language for Essbase. MDX provides the ability to perform advanced data extraction (an alternative to using Essbase report scripts). MDX queries with statements that typically include the verb SELECT (like SQL). It is also the only mechanism for defining member calculations in ASO. MDX is a joint specification of the XML for Analysis founding members: http://www.xmla.org. The MaxL Shell (essmsh) or MDX Editor in Administration Services executes MDX queries.

ESSCMD

We haven't mentioned ESSCMD in this book on purpose. Don't use ESSCMD (this is the old way of scripting in Essbase). Use MaxL for all Essbase scripting needs.

HYPERION BUSINESS RULES

Business Rules was once a standalone product, but is now an integrated component of Administration Services. You can use Business Rules to run simple or complex calculations on Essbase databases, just like calc scripts. So why use Business rules over calc scripts? Business rules provides a graphical tool that guides users through the creation, maintenance, customization, documentation, and execution of calculations. Although you don't need to know specific calc script syntax to create a business rule, you will need to understand the Essbase dimensional design at least at an intermediate level. Also, watch out for performance as these graphical rules aren't always the most efficient.

The other big difference with Business Rules is the ability to prompt users for values when running a business rule. Say you wanted users to be able re-calculate their department budget after submitting data. You can create a single business rule with a prompt that will allow users to select which department to calculate (versus 50 different calc scripts for 50 different departments). Thank us later for time we just saved you in development and maintenance of calc scripts.

Two other incredibly valuable features include the ability to launch Business rules from a web interface and the ability to use macros and sequences to reduce maintenance of logic.

OPTIONAL ESSBASE COMPONENTS

There are a number of optional Essbase components that you may want to consider adding to your environment:

- SQL Interface provides the ability to load data directly from a relational table to Essbase using ODBC connectivity.
- Spreadsheet Toolkit provides the ability to create custom functions and applications in the Spreadsheet Add-In.
- Partitioning provides the ability to share dimensions and data between Essbase databases along with linking ("drill-to") capabilities.
- Application Programming Interface (API) provides the ability to develop custom applications on top of the Essbase platform.
- Visual Explorer provides a highly visual query and analysis interface for large data sets.

While it may have been a bit painful (and not the least bit boring), you've now developed a highly sought after skill that will aid you in creating well designed, finely tuned Essbase applications.

Chapter 21:
System 9 Mythbusters

So. You're running an older version of Hyperion and you hear about this new System 9. Hmmm. Should you implement it? Because you've heard that System 9 has some big benefits. But wait. Could that actually be *true*? Sounds like a job for interRel MythBusters!

It's a tough job separating truth from urban legend, but the interRel MythBusters are here to serve and investigate. In this section, your Hyperion Certified authors will take on System 9 myths and help you better understand the new System 9.

Myth #1: Hyperion System 9 as we know it today (November 1, 2007) will not significantly change over the next few years.

Did you just feel the earth shake below your feet? Oracle has acquired Hyperion. This is huge news in the world of BPM (or as Oracle calls it, EPM - Enterprise Performance Management). There will be many, many changes coming in the next years with the Oracle-Hyperion acquisition (some of the name changes have already started). So with that said, certain sections in this System 9 chapter may not be applicable in the future. We're sure that Hyperion/Oracle is now trying to figure out how Data Management Services will work, how Oracle reporting tools will work with Hyperion reporting tools, and thousands of other integration points. What about the core Essbase product, the one for which you are a *master* administrator? Oracle has publicly said that the Essbase product is one of the major reasons for the acquisition, and will not change. That means that 99% of this book will still apply in the new Oracle world. Stay tuned... we'll let you know when we know more.

Myth #1: Hyperion System 9 as we know it today (November 1, 2007) will not significantly change over the next few years. - **BUSTED**

Myth #2: Hyperion System 9 will revolutionize business performance management.

In the fall of 2005, Hyperion introduced System 9. This was a pretty big deal and pretty darn confusing to everyone, across the board. Let's break down what System 9 is, exactly.

Hyperion describes System 9 as "the most comprehensive performance management solution, and the first to integrate financial management applications with a business intelligence platform." Which is true... Another way to describe System 9 would be "the same great products you already know and love with some cool new features and plenty of tools that help them work together."

Here is a handy picture that Hyperion gave us to illustrate System 9.3:

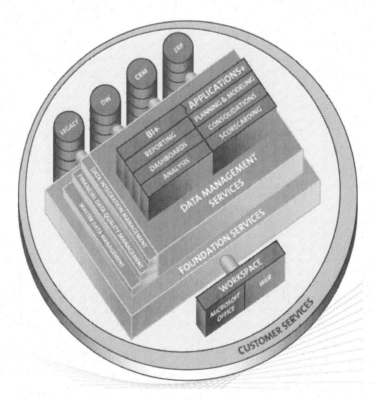

Hyperion System 9 introduces two supporting layers for all Hyperion products: Foundation Services and Data Management Services. This is part of the "...plenty of tools that help them work together."

Foundation Services includes Shared Services which provides a central place to manage all Hyperion security (this is also called User Provisioning). In early versions of System 9, Foundation Services included eLicensing to manage licenses for all

Hyperion products. Beginning in System 9.3.1, there is not an eLicensing Server component. With System 9, you get a single installation and configuration interface and process (which sounds nice and simple, but trust us, the System 9 install process can be pretty complex). Foundation Services also includes the core services (or underlying "plumbing") for session management, authentication and authorization, repository services, and logging that all other Hyperion components leverage.

Data Management Services (DMS) is a new a layer introduced in System 9.3. DMS includes the following three components:

Data Integration Management (DIM) is a graphical tool that accesses, integrates, transforms, and moves data and metadata between Hyperion System 9 applications and/or other systems such as SAP, PeopleSoft, Siebel, and Oracle. It includes bidirectional Hyperion adapters. To understand DIM, think "ETL".

Financial Data Quality Management (FDM) is a graphical tool that automates the collection, mapping, verification and movement of data. FDM provides validation and check points for all collection and mapping steps and extensive reporting for audit, log, and process management information. Sounds a lot like DIM, right? DIM is typically used by IT. FDM is typically used by business users.

Data Relationship Management or DRM (the artist formerly known as Master Data Management or MDM) is a tool that allows business users to manage master data (i.e. their dimensions and hierarchies). DRM provides audit controls and accountability and allows synchronization of master data across all systems (even outside of Hyperion).

Hyperion has combined Essbase with the reporting and analysis tools into a grouping called BI+. At the same time, the packaged applications (Financial Management, Planning, Strategic Finance, and Performance Scorecard) belong to Applications+.

At the front of it all is a common web-based user interface called "Workspace." This is complemented nicely by the SmartView suite, which includes access to all Hyperion products from all Office products (want to run an HFM report in PowerPoint? No problem!).

In summary, one foundation layer for all Hyperion products, one data management services layer for all Hyperion products, one reporting and analysis layer for all Hyperion products, one set of reporting and analysis tools to access both relational and multi-dimensional databases, one web interface to get to all Hyperion products, and access to all Hyperion products from all Microsoft applications. Yes, Hyperion System 9 revolutionizes business performance management.

Myth #2: Hyperion System 9 will revolutionize business performance management. - **CONFIRMED**

Myth #3: Hyperion System 9 is introducing a new set up BI products.

In fact, we discover that Hyperion has not introduced new BI products; they've just renamed them.

Intelligence	⟹	Interactive Reporting
SQR	⟹	Production Reporting
Reports	⟹	Financial Reporting
Analyzer	⟹	Web Analysis

One other note of the Essbase names: Somewhere along the way Hyperion started to call Essbase "Analytic Services". When System 9 was introduced, Hyperion called Essbase Block Storage Option (BSO) databases "Essbase Analytics" and Essbase Aggregate Storage Option (ASO) databases "Enterprise Analytics". With the Oracle acquisition, we're back to plain old "Essbase" (thank you Oracle for realizing that the name Essbase has some brand equity!) Depending on your version you may see Essbase Administration Services (EAS) or Analytic Administrative Services (AAS) for managing your Essbase environment. The Essbase server could also be referred to as the Analytic Server.

Myth #3: Hyperion System 9 is introducing a new set up BI products. – **BUSTED**

Myth #4: You can manage security for all Hyperion products in one interface.

User provisioning is one of the big new features available in System 9. You will manage security for all Hyperion products in the Shared Services User Management Console. You can enable single sign on to all Hyperion System 9 products and utilize external authentication to LDAP, MSAD, or NTLM. Other cool features include role based security, security reporting and copy security functionality:

In the User Management Console, you can:

- Create a user once for all Hyperion System 9 products.
- Assign user to groups.
- Assign user to roles (one set of common roles across modules).
- Assign application access for users.
- Copy security across applications.
- Run security reports.

Tip! Understanding the new System 9 roles is one of the challenges you will face. We strongly recommend that you review the "hyp_security_guide.pdf".

Myth #4: You can manage security for all Hyperion products in one interface. – **CONFIRMED**

Myth #5: You can access Financial Reporting (Reports), Web Analysis (Analyzer), and Interactive Reporting (Intelligence)

documents from one Workspace along with my Planning and Financial Management applications.

System 9 delivers a new Workspace as the main client user front end. It is a single thin client environment bringing BI+ and Applications+ modules together in one tool. Yes, you read correctly - one front end tool for all BPM applications:

Most companies today have a multitude of BI tools, requiring a number of training courses, requiring end users to learn many tools. With System 9, your end users will have to learn the one interface. They will still need to learn the specifics of each application but the look and feel is the same across all Hyperion products. This will help reduce training costs while increasing user acceptance and productivity. From a design perspective, Hyperion has modeled this interface to look like Windows with friendly menu selections and icons.

Myth #5: You can access Financial Reporting (Reports), Web Analysis (Analyzer), and Interactive Reporting (Intelligence) documents from on Workspace along with my Planning and Financial Management applications. – **CONFIRMED**

Myth #6: System 9 Analytic Services (Essbase) doesn't really have any new helpful features.

For those of you still on Essbase 6x (yes, we know there are still some of you out there), here is a recap of the extremely beneficial Essbase 7x enhancements.

- Business Rules is now part of Administration Services.
- Wizards, wizards, wizards are introduced in Administration Services.
- Enhanced log viewing capabilities are available for administrators.
- Start and Stop the Essbase Server from the Administration Services Console.
- User friendly script editors for MDX, MaxL, Calc Scripts, and Report Scripts are available with Essbase tree navigation, color coded scripting, and quick access to functions and commands.
- Auto-Completion in Script Editors speed up script generation.
- Rules File Printing allows for one view of the rules file definition (vs. searching in 5-6 different locations within the rules file).
- MetaData Security adds security to the dimensions and members.
- Unicode Support enables longer names and additional character support.
- Triggers and data mining are introduced.
- All of the EssCMD commands are now available in MaxL.
- Essbase 7.1 introduced Aggregate Storage Option databases.

For those of you on Essbase 7x, let's make the case for why you need to get to System 9. Here are some of the new System 9 features for Essbase.

- Essbase will support for outlines with duplicate member names.
- Essbase provides advanced relational access with the ability to specify any non-accounts dimension as advanced relational access enabled and the ability to tag members up to generation 2 as hybrid analysis enabled.
- This is a big one – Essbase has extended the substitution variable support. You can use substitution variables in outline formulas, security filters, areas and mapping definitions for partitions, and MDX statements. You can also use substitution variables in rules file specifications for

dimension/member names in the data load header and in field specification and for data load columns DSN definitions associated with using the SQL interface.

- In System 9.3, you can export subsets of data to a text file or relational database via calc scripts. So if you want to extract current year budget for the west region, you can easily do this in a simple calc script.

- A new "non-consolidating" data storage tag is introduced ^. The ^ indicates 'do not aggregate this member for any dimension. Price is a good example as price should not be aggregated by any dimension. This is different than the ~ data storage tag which will not rollup to the parent and within its dimension but the member will rollup across the other dimensions.

- You're now familiar with how FIX / ENDFIX works in Essbase, right? Focusing on a specific section of data in Essbase. Essbase 9.3 introduces the ability to exclude sections of data. Two new commands are "EXCLUDE" and "ENDEXCLUDE" that you use in a calc script similar to how you use "FIX" and "ENDFIX". Everything will be calculated via the enclosed logic *except* the data blocks defined in the "EXCLUDE" statement. Here's an example where we calculate Accounts and Market for all regions except the South and West regions.

```
EXCLUDE (South, West)
     Calc Dim (Accounts, Market):
ENDEXCLUDE
```

- You can now encrypt passwords in MaxL. This is helpful if you don't want to display the god-like supervisor password in a MaxL text file stored on the server.

- A new "run as" feature allows supervisors to login in as another user. This is helpful when debugging someone's security access.

- Other general enhancements include broader 64 bit platform support and a new feature called reference cubes. Reference cubes allow you to improve the performance of XREF calculations by creating small cubes in memory.

System 9 Enterprise Analytics (ASO) enhancements include:

- Improved restructuring (in most cases, you can now change a database outline and restructure without clearing data from the database).
- Exporting level zero data from an ASO database is possible.
- Several kernel improvements were implemented, providing enhanced support for deep, ragged hierarchies and improved database compression (sometimes up to 3X).
- A new tool can help choose the accounts dimension by estimating what the database size will be depending on which dimension is tagged accounts.
- Enterprise Analytics also supports duplicate names in outlines and extended Substitution Variable support (discussed earlier).
- A big enhancement in System 9.3 is the new feature, automated Time Dimensions.
- Other improvements in 9.3 include the ability to understand time as a continuum, the ability to cross-tab report on time, and the ability to load data based on time stamp.

Myth #6: System 9 Analytic Services (Essbase) doesn't really have any new helpful features. - **BUSTED**

And with that last myth busted, you've reached the end of the road on this journey through Essbase. There are still a few helpful sections in the appendix so we encourage you read through that information. But we officially grant you *master* Essbase administrator (sniff, sniff...we are a bit teary-eyed. Our junior administrator is all grown up now.). So get out there, start diving into Essbase and apply everything that you've just learned. While we hope this book will be invaluable to all Essbase users and administrators, there is nothing like hands-on practice with the tool itself. Go out and look smarter than you are with Essbase.

Appendix

A NOTE ON VERSIONS

This book is based on Essbase 7x. If you are on Essbase 6x, the Essbase fundamental concepts will apply and most of the Essbase Add-In chapters will be the same. Content on Administration Services and specific steps will not apply for Application Manager (which is the maintenance tool for Essbase 6x).

If you're on Hyperion System 9, 98% of the content in this book will apply to you. The main difference in System 9 and Essbase 7x is the security maintenance process. In System 9, you will utilize the Shared Services User Provisioning to create users and groups and in Essbase 7x, you utilize the Administration Services console for managing security.

Note!

Technically, you could still use Essbase security in Hyperion System 9 if you use Essbase and the Essbase Add-In only. If you use any of the BI+ modules, you are required to "externalize" your Essbase users and utilize Shared Services.

A NOTE ON THIS BOOK

Our objective is to teach you Hyperion Essbase. We've tried to be as detailed as possible but if we described every single click or button, you'd be 100 years old before you were ready to use Essbase (and at that point, Hyperion would probably not even be an independent company but rather bought by some totally awesome firm like Oracle and Hyperion's CEO would be replaced with a really great guy like Larry Ellison, who if he's looking for an heir apparent should contact me at eroske@interrel.com). So we don't mention the fairly obvious tasks and buttons. For example, if there is a Close button, we probably skipped defining what this button does. Cancel means Cancel (don't save anything that you just did). Nothing tricky there.

NAVIGATING HYPERION'S DOCUMENTATION

Hyperion Documentation Definition Matrix

Have you ever tried to find the answer to a question in the Hyperion documentation? The documentation itself is a thing of beauty (okay, at least let's agree that it can be helpful) but it took me several hours to find the right PDF user guide. We've done the hard part for you, mapping the Hyperion PDF documentation guide names into something a bit more helpful.

Hyperion Zip File	PDF File Name	What the PDF File name should be
Eas71600_install_doc.zip	Eas_new_features.pdf	Essbase Administration Services New Features
	Eas_install.pdf	Essbase Administration Services Installation
	Eas_install_checklist.pdf	Essbase Administration Services Installation Checklist
	Xauth.pdf	Hyperion External Authentication Configuration Guide
Haxxx_product_doc_en.zip	Ha_admin	Hyperion Analyzer Administrador Guide
	Ha_html_users.pdf	Hyperion Analyzer HTML User Guide
	Ha_java_users.pdf	Hyperion Analyzer Java User Guide
	Hsv_user.pdf	Hyperion Smart View User Guide
Hrxxxx_product_doc_en	HRUsers.pdf	Hyperion Reports User Guide
	HRADmin.pdf	Hyperion Reports Administrador Guide
	Hsv_user.pdf	Hyperion Smart View User Guide
Hbi93000_product_doc.zip	Hs_user.pdf	Hyperion System 9 BI+ End User Guide (Covers most aspects of workspace and the BI+ features available within Workspace)
	Hs_admin.pdf	Hyperion System 9 BI+ End Administrator Guide (Covers most administrative aspects of workspace and the BI+

Hyperion Zip File	PDF File Name	What the PDF File name should be
		features)
	Hs_developer.pdf	Hyperion System 9 BI+ Developer's Guide (for customization and development)
	Hs_migration.pdf	Hyperion System 9 BI+ Migration Guide (how to migrate from pre-system 9 reporting modules to System 9; e.g. migrate from Hyperion Reports to Financial Reporting)
	Hs_alcm_util.pdf	Hyperion Artifact Life Cycle Management Utility Guide (how to migrate objects from development to test to production using the Artifact Life Cycle utility)
	Hsv_user.pdf	Hyperion Smart View End User Guide
	Fr_user.pdf	Financial Reporting User Guide (develop Financial Reporting reports, books, and batches)
	Ir_developer-volx.pdf	Interactive Reporting Administration and Developer Guides
	Ir_user.pdf	Interactive Reporting User Guide
	Pit_setup.pdf	Portal Integration Toolkit Guide
	Pr_developer-volx.pdf	Production Reporting Administration and Developer Guides
	Wa_user.pdf	Web Analysis Administrator and User Guide
Aas_93000_product_doc.zip	Aas_93000_readme.pdf	Analytic Administration Services Readme

Hyperion Zip File	PDF File Name	What the PDF File name should be
	Aas_dev.pdf	Analytic Administration Services Developer's Guide (For custom application development)
	Hbradmin.pdf	Hyperion Business Rules Administrator Guide
	Hbrweb.pdf	Hyperion Business Rules End User / Web Launcher Guide
Aps_93010_ins tall_doc.zip	Aps_install.pdf	Analytic Provider Services Installation Documentation (in System 9, Hyperion has combined Smart View Provider and High Availability Services into one new provider called 'Analytic Provider Services'
	Aps_new_features .pdf	Analytic Provider Services New Features
	Sv_new_features	Smart View New Features
	Sv_user.pdf	Smart View User Guide
Hls_93000_inst all_doc.zip	Hss_93000_read me.pdf	Hyperion Shared Services Readme
	Hss_windows_ins tall.pdf	Hyperion Shared Services Installation Documentation
	LicensingEndUse rGuide.pdf	Hyperion License Server End User Guide
Hss_93010_ins tall_doc.zip	Hss_YYY_install. pdf	Hyperion Shared Services Installation Documentation
	Hyp_security_gui de.pdf	Hyperion Shared Services Security Guide

Essbase Database Administrator Guide

Where is the Essbase Database Administrator's guide? This documentation will come with a documentation installer. The installed documentation application is pretty cool, including both an html and PDF version of the DBA Guide. Definitely install the Essbase documentation. Here is a quick tour.

You'll begin at the Information Map (note there are different Information Maps for different Hyperion products):

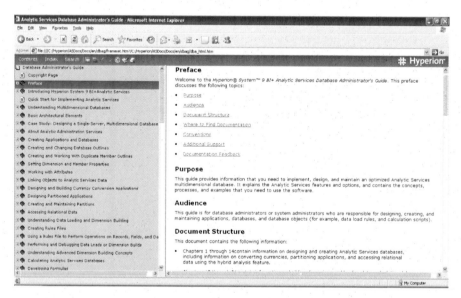

The database administrator's guide (second to this book, of course) is your best friend:

The really cool feature about the DBA Guide is that you can search for topics. In this example, we'd like to find some more information on backups. We select the Search option at the top of the html version of the guide. Type in the word(s) to search:

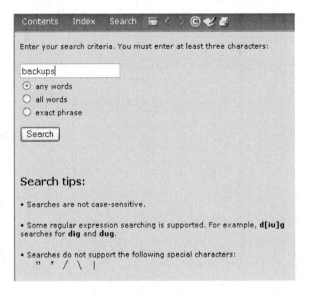

The results look like the following:

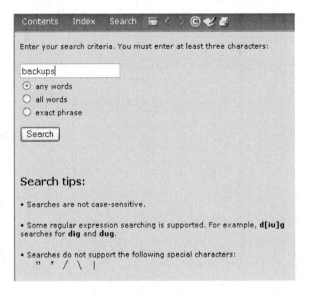

The Technical Reference

The Technical Reference documentation is a life saver when developing calc scripts, MaxL script or updating your Essbase.cfg file. This document has the complete listing of available functions with examples of the syntax and how it used:

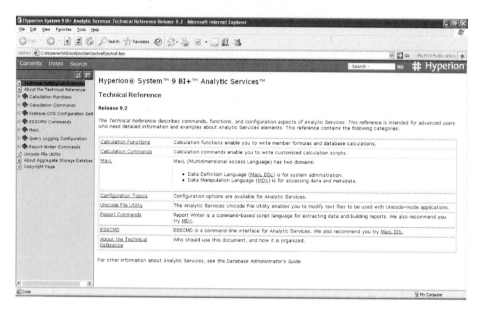

If you would like to use a certain calculation command, you can look for an example in the Technical Reference Calculation Commands section:

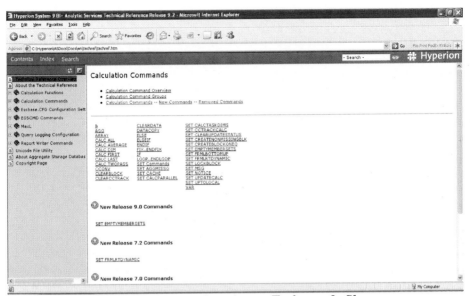

If you need to define settings in my Essbase.cfg file, you can find a complete list of Essbase configuration settings.:

If you need to develop a MaxL script to export data from the database (or any other Essbase action), you can find the syntax to do so in the MaxL settings section:

Ever wonder what are the new features available in a new Hyperion version? Yes, of course. You want to know 'what does this new version mean to me and my end users'. You can find most of this information in the readme files provided in the installation zip files. Hyperion's readme documents provide helpful information on new features, bug fixes, and known issues.

INSTALLING THE ESSBASE ADD-IN

While this is not a book on installation of the Essbase server (for that, reference those 400+ pages of installation documentation or realize the unique value of money well spent by hiring a qualified consultant from interRel), it is possible that the client software is not installed on your machine. Go ahead and launch Excel on your computer.

Since it happens frequently, let's assume that the worst possible thing has occurred, and that when you start up Excel, you don't see the Essbase Add-In. There are two clues that this "worst possible thing" has occurred. First clue: you don't see the Hyperion marketing window pop-up as Excel is starting. Since we don't want you to mistake the marketing window for, say, something informative, here's what it looks like:

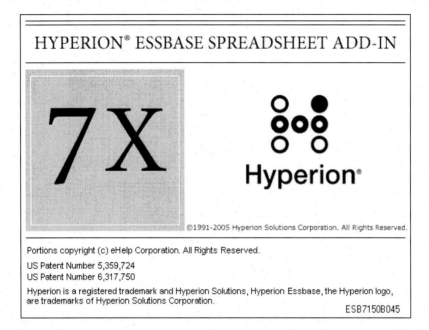

If you see this window appear as Excel is starting, everything should be fine. If you're like me, though, you were probably paying no attention whatsoever as Excel was loading. Time for clue two: once Excel starts, you don't see the *Essbase* menu. Here's what it should look like once Excel is finished opening:

See the *Essbase* menu option between *Window* and *Help*? That means that everything is most likely working. If your Excel menu goes directly from *Window* to *Help*, you should try installing (reinstalling?) the Essbase Add-In.

To begin with, you need to obtain the installation file. It's a huge single file (40+ Mb). Generally, the Essbase Administrator at your company will download this file from Hyperion's download site and place it on some network drive. While the documentation mentions that you might be able to find a CD-ROM with this file on it, we haven't seen one in five years. It's best to have somebody with proper access go download it.

The installation file won't be called anything helpful like "Essbase Excel Add-In." It will instead refer to a Windows Client for Essbase. The file will also probably include the version you're installing as well as the language you're using. For instance, the file we are using is called "esb7150_client_windows_en.exe" since the version of Essbase we are using is 7.1.5.0 and we're using English (that's where the 'en' comes from towards the end). If your file is called something like "Format_Your_Hard_Drive.exe" then your Essbase Administrator is playing a cruel joke on you. Key his car.

Assuming that you have the right file, log into your PC as the administrator and shut down all the other applications since you'll be rebooting your machine at the end of the installation. Double-click the file and you should see:

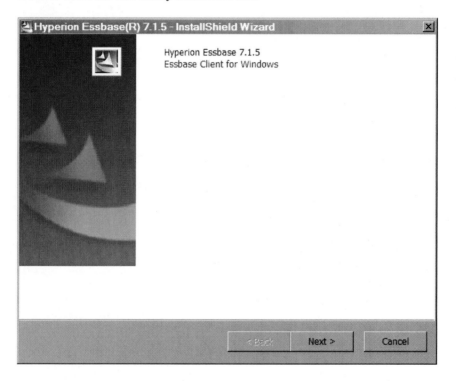

Click *Next* to get to the first really hard question.

Where do you want to save the files used for installation? Accept the default by clicking the *Next* button. It's worth pointing out that you'd probably be all right if you clicked on the defaults for the remainder of the installation program. Assuming you want to understand what each window does, though, continue reading.

A couple of windows will fly by showing you that the installation program is extracting some installation files and that "InstallShield" is preparing to do some hard work. Don't get bored and give up, because eventually you'll see a window asking you for your language.

Assuming that you speak English or you'd be reading a different book right now, leave the language on English and click *OK*.

This window is completely useless unless you were about to violate some international treaties (see the text after "WARNING:"). If you're not a nasty treaty violator, click *Next*.

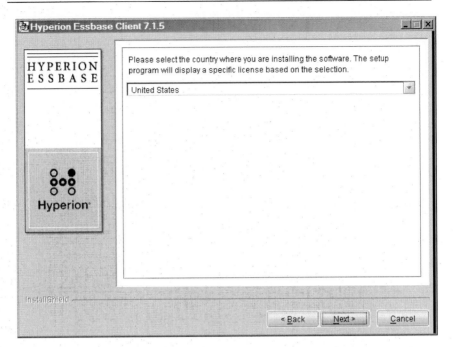

Select your current country from the drop-down box and click *Next.* If your country isn't listed, then you're probably violating one of those international treaties right now. Do not proceed until you are within the borders of a country in the drop-down box.

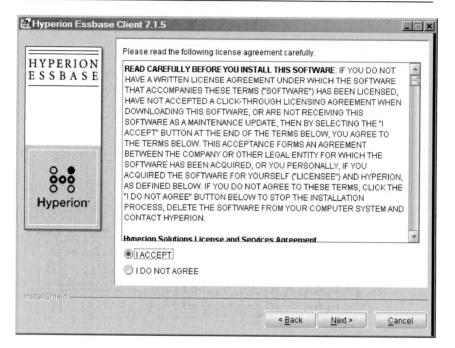

Read the license agreement extremely carefully (your life just may depend on it), click *I Accept* and then click *Next*. If you've previously installed the Essbase Client (as the installation program likes to call it), you'll get a warning window:

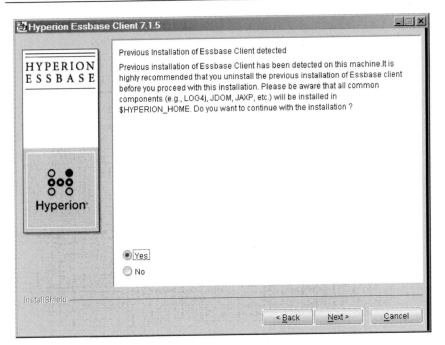

Click *Yes* and then click *Next*.

Note!   It's highly recommended that you uninstall your older version of Essbase before installing or reinstalling the newer version.

If you clicked *Yes* or if you've never installed Essbase on this machine, you'll see a window asking you where you want to install the Essbase files.

The default location is the "C:\Hyperion\Essbase\" directory. Why doesn't Hyperion default to putting the files in the "Program Files" directory? Because many years ago, various Hyperion products (Essbase included) didn't like to see spaces in the path where the executable was stored (a hold-over to the old MS-DOS days of 8 character filenames with no spaces). While everything should work these days if Essbase is put into a directory with spaces, various people are still skittish. Make them happy by not putting a space in your path name, and clicking on *Next*.

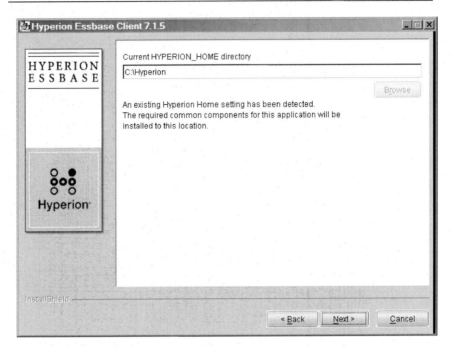

If you've installed Essbase before on this machine, you'll see a window asking you if you want to use the current "HYPERION_HOME" directory. Since it's good when all the Hyperion products share files (to reduce the amount of hard drive Hyperion takes up), go ahead and click on *Next*.

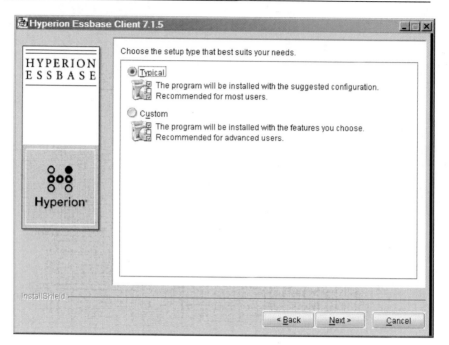

In general, you want to choose the *Typical* installation. If you want to blaze your own trail, click on *Custom* and you'll see three products that you can install:

If you had chosen *Custom*, the products that would be installed are "Runtime Client" and "Excel Spreadsheet Add-In" (finally, they call it the same thing we've been calling it). The Runtime Client is used if you want to install a program that requires some of the Essbase libraries but does not require the Essbase Add-In. An example would be the Hyperion Reports 7.2 Designer.

The Excel Spreadsheet Add-In is what we want (because we want to see *Essbase* show up between Window and Help). The Essbase API should be selected if you've purchased a custom-built Essbase program (or someone at your company has built one) that will be run on this computer.

For our purposes, select *Runtime* and *Excel* and then click *Next*.

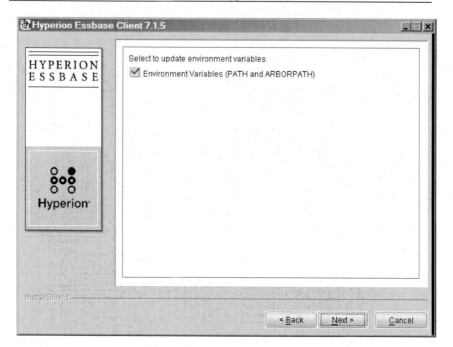

There are two environment variables that Essbase needs to run. One is the PATH variable. When you install Essbase, it adds the directory that contains the Essbase support files to the PATH variable.

The other variable is ARBORPATH. Yes, this is a hold-over from before Hyperion and Arbor merged back in 1998. Rumor has it that they're going to do away with this variable as soon as someone finds all the spots in the code that use it. Until then, the ARBORPATH variable points to the directory you chose to install Essbase (C:\Hyperion\Essbase if you chose the default). Since you want to make sure that these variables are up-to-date, leave the checkbox checked and then click *Next*.

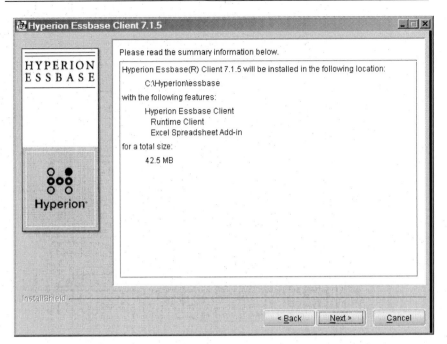

You'll see a confirmation window that shows you what you're about to install. Click *Next* and the files will begin to install.

When the progress bar reaches 100%, don't assume that it's complete. A few more steps will need to occur. Wait until you see this window:

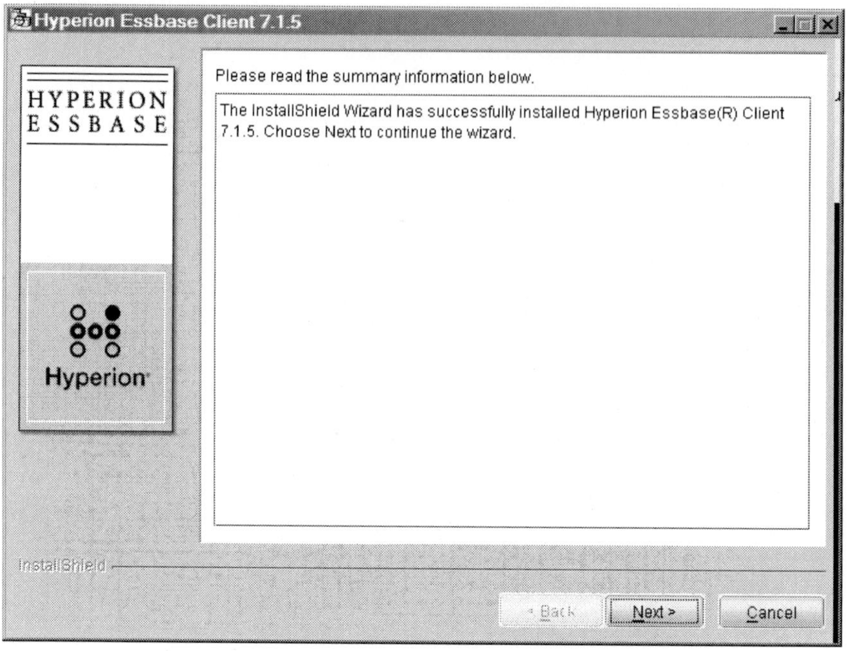

Click *Next* and you'll be asked to restart your computer.

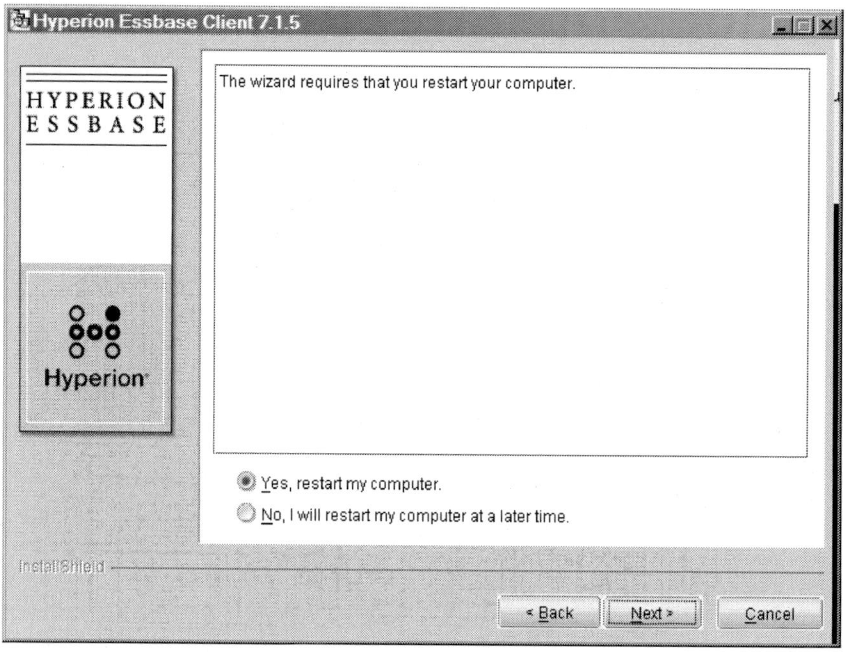

Make sure all of your other programs are shut down and then click *Next* to restart your computer. Once you've restarted your computer, start Excel and verify that you can see the *Essbase* menu:

ESSBASE ADD-IN ERRORS

Let's assume that you've installed the Essbase Add-In (see page 4) but that it still isn't there.

Error Loading the Add-In

The most common error that will occur is when Excel doesn't understand how to read the Add-In. If this is the case, you'll see the following error when Excel starts up:

Once you click on *OK*, you'll be shown a screen of Sanskrit:

What Excel just did was to show you the raw text (control codes and all) of the Essbase Add-In itself. Immediately go to *File >> Close* to remove this monstrosity from your screen.

The reason that this normally occurs is that you didn't reboot your PC after the install program finished. If you haven't done that yet, go ahead and do it now.

If you now start Excel and you still see this error, the problem is probably with your environment variables (remember PATH and ARBORPATH from page 446). The best thing to do is to verify that they're set correctly. We'll show you the steps for Windows XP (your steps should be similar).

Go to your *Start* menu and click on *Control Panel*. Click on *Performance and Maintenance*. Click on *System*. What we're going to do is considered very advanced, so click on the *Advanced* tab.

Click on *Environment Variables*. The variables you're concerned with are under the System Variables section.

ARBORPATH should be one of the first variables you see and it should be pointing to the directory where Essbase is installed (for instance, C:\Hyperion\Essbase). If it isn't there, click on New and add it. If it's wrong, click on Edit and correct it.

Scroll down the list until you get to HYPERION_HOME. Make sure it's set to the parent directory of ARBORPATH (for instance, C:\Hyperion). Continue scrolling down until you get to

PATH (or 'Path' since case doesn't matter). The first part of the PATH variable should look like either "%ARBORPATH%\Bin;" or "C:\Hyperion\Essbase\Bin;". If it doesn't, go ahead and click on *Edit* and add "%ARBORPATH%\Bin;" to the beginning of the PATH variable like so:

Click on *OK* and close all the windows you just opened. To make sure that the variables are set correctly at start-up, go ahead and restart your machine. Open Excel and you should now see the *Essbase* menu.

Add-In is Missing

The next most common problem with the Add-In is when the Add-In is missing even though you've completed the installation and you're not getting any errors. The most common cause for this is that the Add-In was installed under a different user ID than you're currently logged in as.

To correct the problem, we need to tell Excel where the Essbase Add-In is located. From within Excel, click on *Tools >> Add-Ins*. On the box that appears, you might see a few Hyperion Add-Ins.

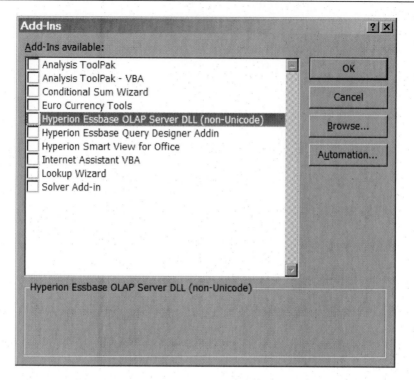

If one of these is the Essbase Add-In (it might say "Hyperion Essbase OLAP Server DLL" since none of the developers at Hyperion can remember what the Add-In is called), just click the box next to it and click *OK*. If the *Essbase* menu then appears, read no further.

If you don't see the box for Essbase, click *Browse*. The file you wanted is called ESSEXCLN.XLL and it's stored in the "Bin" directory under wherever you installed Essbase. If you chose the defaults, this file is probably in C:\Hyperion\Essbase\Bin. Click on the ESSEXCLN.XLL file and then click *OK*.

If you see a message that says the Add-In already exists in this location, click on *Yes* to replace it:

Click on *OK* until you've closed all the windows you've opened, and the Essbase Add-In should finally appear.

The End. Really? Yes, go forth, Essbase *master* users and *master* administrators. Find the meaning of life, show us the way to world peace, and revolutionize your business with Hyperion Essbase.

INDEX

NO WOLVERINES WERE HARMED DURING THE MAKING OF THIS BOOK.